The Arizona Project

THE ARIZONA PROJECT

*How a Team of Investigative Reporters
Got Revenge on Deadline*

by
Michael F. Wendland

SHEED ANDREWS AND McMEEL, INC.
Subsidiary of Universal Press Syndicate
Kansas City

Library of Congress Cataloging in Publication Data

Wendland, Michael F
    The Arizona Project.

    1. Reporters and reporting—Arizona. 2. Bolles, Don.
3. Organized crime—Arizona. 4. Crime and the press—
Arizona. I. Title.
PN4897.A724W4   070.4'3   77-16383
ISBN 0-8362-0728-9

TO JENNIFER

Who May Not Always Follow
But Taught Me How to Lead

Contents

Acknowledgments

In March and early April, 1977, newspapers across the country printed a series of investigative reports based on an unprecedented group effort in journalism, the banding together of some thirty-six reporters and editors from almost as many different news agencies for a single story. That the story was actually concerned with a number of areas made no difference. In the end, twenty-three major articles, most of them with accompanying sidebars, were produced. The incident that prompted this unique gathering was the June 1976 assassination by bombing of Phoenix newspaper reporter Don Bolles. And the purpose of the joint media response was twofold. First, the team attempted to pay tribute to a slain colleague by finishing what he had started, by getting to the heart of the political corruption and organized crime in Arizona that had made Bolles's killers believe that murder was a logical response to a reporter's work. Second, by clearly demonstrating the solidarity of the American press, the team effort would reemphasize the old underworld adage: "You don't kill a reporter because it brings too much heat." Like any major news story, the newspaper series that resulted from the Arizona project has been controversial.

I am a reporter for the Detroit News. From the beginning of the project on October 4, 1976, to February 1, 1977, when the active reporting ended, I was a part of the team of journalists working in Arizona. While only a handful of us were able to spend full time on the project, the others stayed as long as they could, usually a minimum of two weeks. Several members devoted vacation time to the project and paid their own way.

I decided to write this book upon my return to Detroit, after the project was completed. For what I saw and was a part of in Arizona was the Free Press of America at its finest. The thirty-five other journalists and the fifteen researchers, volunteers, and secretarial workers who assisted the team were as diverse as the nation. Six were from the Arizona media, the others from all parts of the country. They were young and old, from news agencies large and small, liberal and conservative. And at all times they worked together smoothly and professionally, putting in sixteen-hour days, seven days a week. When we left Arizona, we left still friends.

This book would not have been possible without the help and encouragement of a great many people. In writing it, I have relied on personal notes, observations, and conversations during my stay in Arizona. In addition, my fellow team members have been most cooperative in helping me fill in the holes. Many of them have kindly given me access to their personal diaries, notes, memoranda, tape recordings, and files.

To the entire team, particularly project leaders Bob Greene and Dick Cady, I express my respect and admiration. Deserving of special acknowledgment for the assistance he has provided me with this book is Ron Koziol, who is not only a hell of a reporter but the best friend anyone could ask for. Others whose friendship, time, energy, advice, and sympathy helped me greatly include Nina Bondarook, George Weisz, John Rawlinson, Alex Drehsler, Harry Jones, Dave Offer, Dick Levitan, Dave Overton, Tom Renner, and Ross Becker.

Special thanks, for assigning me to the Arizona team and offering me editorial guidance and support, to the Detroit News and particularly Martin Hayden, Burt Stoddard, Ben Burns, Bill Lutz, and Bob Lubeck.

To Jim Andrews, my publisher, and Philip Nobile, my patient editor, go my sincere appreciation and thanks for their guidance, criticism, and support.

Finally, to my wife, Jennifer, who supervised three demanding children alone for four months and then struggled with my terrible handwriting in typing this manuscript, I express my love and gratitude and promise that there won't be another Arizona project.

At least not for a while, anyway.

Cast of Characters

THE IRE TEAM

LOWELL BERGMAN, free-lance reporter, Berkeley, California

DON DEVEREUX and STEVE GOLDIN, free-lance reporters, Santa Fe, New Mexico

ALEX DREHSLER and JOHN RAWLINSON, *Arizona Daily Star*, Tucson

JACK DRISCOLL, *Boston Globe*

ROBERT GREENE, TOM RENNER and TONY ANSOLIA, *Newsday*, Long Island, New York

BILL HUME, *Albuquerque Journal*

SUSAN IRBY, *Gulfport* (Mississippi) *Daily Herald*

HARRY JONES and DICK JOHNSON, *Kansas City Star*

RON KOZIOL, *Chicago Tribune*

LARRY KRAFTOWITZ, Jack Anderson Associates, Washington, D. C.

DOUG KRAMER, *Elyria* (Ohio) *Chronicle*

DICK LEVITAN, WEEI Radio, Boston

DICK LYNEIS, *Riverside* (California) *Press-Enterprise*

JACK McFARREN, Reno (Nevada) Newspapers, Inc.

BILL MONTELBANO, *Miami Herald*

DAN NOYES, *Urban Policy Institute*, Los Angeles

DAVID OFFER, *Milwaukee Journal*

DAVE OVERTON, KGUN-TV, Tucson

MYRTA PULLIAM and DICK CADY, *Indianapolis Star*

ED ROONEY and PHIL O'CONNOR, *Chicago Daily News*

MIKE SATCHELL, *Washington Star*

RAY SCHRICK, *Wenatchee* (Washington) *World*

BOB TEUSCHER, *St. Louis Globe-Democrat*

NORM UDEVITZ, *Denver Post*

JERRY UHRHAMMER, *Eugene* (Oregon) *Register-Guard*

BOB WEAVER, *San Jose* (California) *Mercury*

GEORGE WEISZ and ROSS BECKER, investigative researchers, Tucson

MICHAEL WENDLAND, *Detroit News*

STEVE WICK and DAVID FREED, *Colorado Springs Sun*

JACK WIMER, *Tulsa Tribune*

JOHN WINTERS, *Arizona Republic*, Phoenix

OTHER CHARACTERS

JOHN ADAMSON, the confessed killer of Don Bolles

LOUIS "FAT LOUIE" AMUSO, Phoenix underworld character

HERBERT APPLEGATE, restaurateur, Phoenix

BRUCE BABBITT, attorney general, Arizona

MOISE BERGER, former county attorney, Maricopa County, Arizona

WILLIE BIOFF, a.k.a. William Nelson, convicted pimp and labor racketeer; major contributor to Barry Goldwater's initial Senate campaign

DON BOLLES, *Arizona Republic*

JOSEPH "JOE BANANAS" BONANNO, Tucson Mafia boss

RAUL CASTRO, governor, Arizona

WALTER CRAIG, chief U.S. District Judge, Phoenix, former president, American Bar Association

MOE DALITZ, Las Vegas gambling czar

PAUL DEAN, *Arizona Republic*

EDWARD "ACEY" DUCI, Phoenix nightclub proprietor and underworld figure

JACK DUGGAN, Phoenix gambler

MAX DUNLAP, building contractor, Lake Havasu City, Arizona

BOB EARLY, *Arizona Republic*

BARRY GOLDWATER, senior U.S. Senator, Arizona

ROBERT W. GOLDWATER, banking, investments, citrus, Phoenix

GUS GREENBAUM, Phoenix-Las Vegas gambler and underworld figure, friend of Barry Goldwater's

DONALD HARRIS, interim county attorney, Maricopa County, Arizona

JACK HAYS, justice, Arizona Supreme Court

CHUCK KELLY, *Arizona Republic*

PAUL LAPRADE, Superior Court Judge, Maricopa County, Arizona

PETER "HORSEFACE" LICAVOLI (PETER LICAVOLI, SR.), longtime hoodlum, former boss of Detroit Purple Gang, Tucson Mafia figure

HERBERT LIEB, night club owner, Phoenix

KEMPER MARLEY, rancher, owner of liquor distributorship, Tucson

JOSEPH F. MARTORI, restaurants, citrus, investments, Phoenix

JOSEPH MONTOYA, U.S. Senator, New Mexico

HARRY ROSENZWEIG, jewelry store owner, investments, Phoenix

ANTHONY SERRA, convicted Arizona land swindler

BENJAMIN "BUGSY" SIEGEL, Las Vegas racketeer

SAM STEIGER, U.S. Representative, Third District, Arizona

J. FRED TALLEY, real estate commissioner, Arizona

NED WARREN, SR., the czar of the Arizona land fraud racket

DEL WEBB, real estate developer, Phoenix

1 | The Death of a Reporter

June 2, 1976—Max M. Klass, a forty-nine-year-old attorney, sat in his second-floor office in the Mahoney Building. A Democratic candidate for Congress from Arizona's Third District in the coming fall election, Klass had spent most of the morning going over campaign material with his staff. At 11:35, he was trying to catch up on legal work before his wife drove into town for their weekly luncheon date. Klass was dictating a routine auto accident claim into his desktop recording machine when it happened: "I've received reports from the doctors, which I enclose under cover of this letter. The property claim is in the amount of $1,205.25, together with $400 for each of the two girls for a total amount of $2,005.25. Paragraph. If we are unable to resolve this rather simple matter, I suspect that the next stage would be for me to file a—"

The sound of the blast stopped Klass short. He shut off the machine and spun around in his chair, wondering whether the floor-to-ceiling window behind his desk had broken. It had sounded like a sonic boom, but it was much too loud. It had actually jarred him from his seat. Klass stood up and pulled open the heavy draperies.

Directly below his window, he saw someone crouched low beside a late-model pickup truck. The man was looking toward the Clarendon House. Klass followed his gaze, spotting a thick plume of white smoke reaching skyward from the south side of the hotel.

"Quick, Shirley, call the fire department. There's been an explosion at the Clarendon," he shouted to his secretary, bursting out of his office.

Klass ran outside, stopping at the back door of his office building for another look.

"Help—Help me," a thin, high-pitched voice wailed from the direction of the hotel.

Klass strained his ears. Again he heard it, realizing that the explosion had come from a car, not the Clarendon.

"Help me—Help—"

He trotted toward the sound, almost tripping several times over hubcaps, tires, and chunks of metal torn loose by the blast from dozens of cars in the parking lot. Other people from nearby offices raced across the pavement from all directions, only to suddenly turn around on seeing the bombed car, their faces ashen, their eyes terrified.

The first thing Klass noticed was the blood—thick and bright— dripping into a widening pool beneath the car. His stomach reeled. A man sprawled half out of the driver's side, his torso face down on the asphalt, his legs draped at a grotesque angle across the seat and onto the floor of the car. The injured man was conscious, though obviously in deep shock. His glazed eyes darted frantically back and forth and his shoulders heaved, as if he was trying to push himself upright.

Lonnie Reed, a young refrigerator serviceman who had been installing an air conditioner nearby, stood over the bleeding driver of the bombed car.

"Take it easy, fella, a doctor will be here in a minute," soothed Reed, who had once worked as a hospital orderly.

Bending over, he took off his belt and looped it around the driver's right leg, attempting to fashion a tourniquet to halt the gushing blood. Incredulously, he looked up at Klass.

"Oh my God! There's nothing left to get a hold on."

Klass had no belt. He looked desperately up to the second-floor balcony of the Clarendon. The explosion had blown out every window on the south side of the hotel and a dozen or so guests stood amidst the broken glass outside their rooms.

"Somebody, please," Klass shouted, "throw down some towels." For a moment, the hotel guests just stared back. "Please, quick, some towels. Throw down some towels."

Someone did and Klass had started to put the towel on the bleeding leg of Don Bolles when there was a tug on his shirtsleeve.

The reporter had managed to twist around and raise himself up on an elbow. He was tightly clutching Klass's shirt and staring intensely into the attorney's eyes.

"Adamson," he said through clenched teeth, his face contorted in shock and pain. "Adamson."

Klass was sure of the name. Bolles pronounced it clearly. But the rest of the message was not so distinguishable—either "Adamson sent me" or "Adamson set me."

With that, Bolles fell back, lapsing into unconsciousness. Sirens suddenly filled the air as an ambulance and two fire trucks screamed into the Clarendon parking lot. Klass and Reed stepped aside. A softball-sized chunk of what was unmistakably human flesh, lying ten feet from the twisted wreckage, caught the attorney's eye. He swallowed a wave of nausea and looked away, the smell of blood and smoke engulfing him.

Once more, briefly, as paramedics from the Phoenix Fire Department worked over him, Don Bolles regained consciousness.

"They finally got me," he said. "Emprise—the Mafia—John Adamson—Find him."

Klass couldn't take it anymore. As the experts began administering an IV and labored to stop the bleeding, Klass wheeled around and ran back to his office. As he neared the back entrance, his wife pulled her car into a parking spot not far from his own car. In a voice tight with emotion, the attorney tried to tell her of the injured man.

It was Mrs. Klass who discovered the white overalls lying in a heap next to the trash container at the rear of Klass's office building. She thought they belonged to a painter. Somehow, she hadn't understood Klass's description of the bombing and thought the ambulance was for a painter who had accidentally fallen from the Mahoney Building. The attorney again explained what had happened. Then he remembered the pickup truck he had seen parked below his window immediately after the explosion. Could the man he saw crouched next to the truck have anything to do with the bombing? He walked over to the trash container and examined the overalls. They looked almost new, with just a trace of grease in one spot. With them was a white sheet that also looked new.

Klass found a police officer and told him of the pickup truck and the overalls. After filling out a witness report, he rejoined his wife. He no longer felt like lunch.

"Who was it, Max?" his wife asked of the injured man.

"I don't know, some bum I guess. Probably someone who just got out of jail."

Don Bolles was in excellent spirits on the morning of June 2. It was his wedding anniversary. And it was Wednesday, downhill to the weekend. That morning he had a routine hearing at the Capitol. And once he drove over to the Clarendon House to talk with this Adamson fellow, the day would pass quickly. There would be a good lunch at the Phoenix Press Club with friends. Back at the office, it wouldn't take long to rough out his notes from the hearing into story form for the Thursday editions. If he was lucky, he'd be home by four. That would give him some time with the kids before he and Rosalie went out to celebrate the eighth year of their marriage with dinner and a movie.

A tall, bespectacled man who wore his fair hair in an out-of-style pompadour, Bolles looked forward to seeing the movie *All the President's Men*. Despite the fine reviews, he wondered whether Hollywood had oversimplified his profession just as it did with police shows.

Don Bolles didn't particularly like the term "investigative reporter," even though that job description fit his work for the past decade. Since reporters have nothing to report without first investigating, he felt the adjective was redundant and hoped that 1976's sudden infatuation with "investigative reporters," evidenced by the Watergate film and a host of shallow television shows, wouldn't cheapen the public image of his profession. For he was proud of his job.

Considering the Eastern dominance of the media, he hadn't done too badly. While his newspaper, the *Arizona Republic*, was almost unknown nationally, Bolles was not. Just the week before, he had been invited to fly to the Midwest to speak to an important group of reporters and editors. Bolles was miffed when the *Republic* refused to pay his expenses, but the invitation pleased him immensely. While the general public did not know his name, his peers did. His style was not great; nobody confused his prose with H. L. Mencken's. But he could dig. He knew his craft.

Don Bolles was born to newspapering. His father was an editor for the Associated Press and he grew up hearing newspaper stories. In 1953, after serving with the army in Korea, he followed his father and landed a job with AP, learning the business in the East and the South as a sports reporter and rewrite man. In 1962, he came to Phoenix from New Jersey and joined the staff of the *Republic*, a conservative newspaper owned by the Pulliam family. It didn't take Bolles long to become the star of the paper. Less than a year on the job, he exposed the Arizona Department of Public Safety—the state's highway patrol—which maintained a secret slush fund used to entertain state legislators. Next, he focused in on the Arizona State Tax and Corporation Commissions, writing page one banner stories of bribery and kickbacks that eventually led to indictments against two tax commissioners and to a Pulitzer Prize nomination. In 1967, he turned his attention to land fraud, Arizona's number one industry, uncovering a swindle involving more than a thousand people across the nation.

Bolles was the first to link an ex-con named Ned Warren, Sr., to the state's billion-dollar land swindle, documenting how Warren, in secret associations with some of Arizona's most prominent businessmen, had scammed millions of dollars from Easterners who thought they were buying a retirement home rather than a chunk of barren desert.

By 1970, Bolles was enmeshed in the tangled world of the Emprise Corporation, a many-tentacled sports concession firm based in Buffalo which was closely linked to organized crime in a number of states. Bolles's reporting stopped the firm from taking over horse and dog racing in Arizona after Bolles discovered, and wrote stories about, the taps Emprise had placed on his telephone in an effort to learn his sources. Bolles became such an expert on Emprise that he was flown to Washington, D.C., to testify on the firm before a Senate investigating committee. His Emprise work introduced him to the ways by which organized crime takes over legitimate businesses. Months of careful record checking gave Bolles a list of nearly 200 known Mafia members or associates who had recently settled in Arizona. With another *Republic* reporter, he wrote a series called "The Newcomers" which named the mobsters and their new business associations in Arizona.

All of this Don Bolles shared with reporters across the country. In a craft crowded with huge egos and ruled by fierce competition, Don Bolles's generosity was rare. When checking into a mobster from Chicago or Detroit or New York, Bolles was quick to get on the telephone and urge colleagues from those cities to join him. He did not hog glory. He felt too strongly about what he was doing.

But paranoia got to him in the end. He tired of attaching a piece of Scotch tape to the hood of his car to make sure that no one tampered with his engine, a routine practice when working on particularly sensitive stories. He became frustrated with the pious platitudes of politicians who vowed action on his stories but never did a thing. He began drinking too much and told his friends that the only things he believed in anymore were "God and children." He blamed his malaise on a policy of "official gutlessness in town," and said he had had his fill of muckraking because "no one cares." His first marriage broke up. He was a burnt-out case.

The business does that to good reporters. It's nothing new. After a while, it just isn't worth it. The twenty-four-hour-a-day pressure; the worry of million-dollar libel suits; the late-night anonymous telephone threats; the anger that comes when no one cares; indifferent, timid editors; the difficulty in making a twenty-thousand-dollar-a-year salary support two families—all this eventually overwhelmed Don Bolles. He had done his part. So, in September of 1975, as he entered middle age, Don Bolles asked to be taken off the investigative beat.

His life began to come together again. Transferred to the legislative bureau in the state capital, he adjusted to the beat of a new drum, working a basic ten-to-six day. The job finally took a back seat to his wife and seven children. Six-year-old Diane, who was born deaf, was his and Rosalie's. Four of the kids came from his first marriage and two were Rosalie's by a previous marriage. He started playing tennis and jogging, trimming his six-foot–two-inch frame into the muscled leanness of his youth. Friends said he was happier than he had been in a long time. In early 1976, he turned over his extensive files on the Mafia and organized crime to John Winters, another *Republic* staffer.

Bolles came up with a couple of pretty good pieces on the legislative beat. Most notably, he forced the resignation of millionaire rancher Kemper Marley from the state racing commission. When Arizona Governor Raul Castro nominated Marley for the position in March, Bolles searched the records and found that Marley had been Castro's largest single campaign contributor in 1974. Bolles pressed further, discovering that back in the forties Marley had been charged, though later acquitted, of grand theft while serving as a highway commissioner. Marley had allegedly taken a truck engine owned by the state. A few years later, Marley was appointed a member of the Arizona State Fair Commission, where, Bolles learned, he had been accused of financial mismanagement and flagrant nepotism.

Eight days after the seventy-year-old Marley took his racing commission seat in 1976, the controversy unleashed by Bolles's stories prompted the legislature to force Marley's resignation.

But that was March. It had been mostly routine stories ever since. And Bolles, while generally happy with his more relaxed job, was just a trifle bored.

That's probably why he jumped so fast at the call from John Adamson.

Actually, the first call came Thursday morning, May 27, from Dick Ryan, a court stenographer whom Bolles had met several years before while covering trials in the Maricopa County courthouse. During the last week of May, Ryan telephoned Bolles to say that he knew a man named John Adamson, who claimed to have information linking Arizona Congressman Sam Steiger and the Emprise Corporation to land fraud. Ryan said he didn't know Adamson well, but that Adamson had asked him to get in touch with Bolles and pass on the news tip. This sketchy information was intriguing. Rumors abounded that Arizona congressmen and senators were mixed up in the land fraud industry. But Emprise, whose organized crime associations were involved mostly with sports concessions, didn't make sense. Neither did a connection between Steiger and Emprise. During his investigation of Emprise, Bolles had received strong support from Steiger, who actively fought against the moves by Emprise to infiltrate the state's racing industry. The congressman had often spoon-fed Bolles major news tips on the Emprise scandal. Still, Bolles listened to Ryan. The reporter had learned long ago never to dismiss a tip just because it didn't make sense. He told Ryan that, sure, he'd be interested in talking to this Adamson fellow.

Adamson himself called Bolles shortly afterwards. He repeated the information relayed by Ryan, adding two more prominent political names: Arizona Senator and 1964 Republican presidential candidate Barry Goldwater, and wealthy Phoenix jeweler and former state GOP boss Harry Rosenzweig. Adamson refused to be more specific over the telephone. A meeting was set up for The Island restaurant at four-thirty that afternoon.

Adamson was a tall, swarthy man, a chunky two-hundred-pounder, who wore dark prescription sunglasses and claimed to have documentation of the charges. The two talked for about fifteen minutes. Bolles tried to zero in on just what Adamson had but got nowhere. All Adamson would say was that he could prove the land fraud connections and that he had an informant, from San Diego, to whom he would introduce the reporter and who had further proof. The meeting broke up with Adamson promising to turn over the informant and the documentation. Bolles told him to call when he had it, then left for home. His daughter was graduating from the eighth grade that night, he explained to the brooding Adamson.

On Tuesday, June 1, Adamson telephoned Bolles to say that he had the proof and that the San Diego informant was also willing to meet Bolles. Another meeting was arranged, this one for the next morning at a downtown hotel. On the desktop calendar at his office in the Capitol press room Bolles wrote: "John Adamson . . . Lobby at 11:25 . . . Clarendon House . . . 4th and Clarendon."

The morning of June 2 was routine, except that it was his anniversary. Rosalie was glowing when Bolles, wearing white shoes and a new blue leisure suit, kissed her goodbye at nine o'clock that morning. Earlier, just after breakfast, she had given him a new billfold as a present. She, too, was looking forward to the movie.

At the Capitol, Bolles covered a dull legislative hearing on a proposed automobile emissions control bill. He left the office about eleven-fifteen, telling his boss, Capitol Bureau Chief Bernie Wynn, that he was going to meet a news source downtown and then planned to go over to the Phoenix Press Club to attend a luncheon of the journalism society, Sigma Delta Chi. Bolles was to chair a meeting of the Ethics Committee at the SDX meeting. Afterwards, he said, he would return to the press room and write his story on the auto emissions bill. Bolles told Wynn he hoped to get home early that afternoon since it was his wedding anniversary.

The reporter arrived about eleven twenty-five, parked the white 1976 Datsun he had purchased the month before at the southern end of the building in the second row of the parking lot, and entered the hotel lobby. He waited about ten minutes and then heard his name being paged by the desk clerk. Bolles took the call from the house phone. It was Adamson explaining that the meeting was off because the informant from San Diego had chickened out. Bolles didn't really care. What the hell, the information had been less than specific right from the start. It was no big deal. Just another wild-goose chase. Every reporter is used to such inconveniences. Bolles thanked Adamson for calling, gave him directions to his office in the state Capitol, and told him to phone if the informant changed his mind.

Nodding to the desk clerk, Bolles left the hotel for his car in the parking lot. He had just enough time to make the luncheon.

Max Klass didn't learn who the victim really was for several hours. And when he did, he would feel like crying. He had guessed to his wife that the bleeding man in the bombed car was a bum. Later Klass found out it was Bolles. Max Klass and Don Bolles were friends. When Klass had first become active in local politics, running for mayor in Glendale, a position he held for ten years, Bolles wrote several news stories about him. Later, as Bolles did crime reporting, they often ran into each other in the superior court building where Klass was representing clients. Klass hoped Bolles had recognized him when he tried to help that morning. He wanted Bolles to know he cared.

It was a busy morning in the city room of the *Republic*. The Phoenix Police Department was expected to go on strike shortly after noon, and a half-dozen reporters had just finished a meeting with city editor Bob Early, a burly native of the Midwest whose father, Robert P. Early, was managing editor of the *Indianapolis Star*, another Pulliam-owned paper. Early assigned the reporters to cover various angles of the planned police strike and sat down at his desk. Jim Dooley, the *Republic's* picture editor, walked over to tell him what he had just heard over the police monitor.

"Something about a bombing," Dooley said. "Over at the Clarendon House."

Early didn't waste any time. Only eight months before, a hoodlum named Louis Bombacino had been blown to bits when a plastic explosive detonated beneath the rear axle of his Lincoln Continental in Tempe, the normally quiet suburban Phoenix city that is the home of Arizona State University. Bombacino, 52, had been living there with his wife and teenaged son under an assumed name provided by the FBI after his 1968 testimony helped send a half-dozen high-level Chicago mobsters to the penitentiary. The blast that killed Bombacino was so strong that it hurled portions of his car a quarter of a mile away.

Early had the city desk contact Jack West, the reporter at police headquarters covering the planned strike. He was told to go immediately to the Clarendon House. Similarly, Roy Cosway, a photographer, was dispatched from the *Republic* office. West called in on his arrival, passing on the license number of the small white import that had been blown apart in the explosion.

"But listen to this," he said, almost as a footnote. "The cops think the guy was a reporter."

The city desk called the Arizona Department of Motor Vehicles, asking for a license-plate check on the bombed car. The department would call back.

Reporters began clustering around the city desk almost the minute Dooley relayed the message he heard over the police radio. When another West call firmed up the rumor that the victim of the blast had been a reporter—a press parking sticker was on the windshield of the bombed car—they broke into a babble of confused conversation.

"Where's Sitter? Where's Sitter?" someone shouted.

Al Sitter had taken Don Bolles's place as the paper's top investigative reporter. In recent months, he had been hammering hard at land fraud, organized crime, and the political and business connections that make both possible. Sitter drove a white Toyota.

But almost at that moment, Sitter walked into the city room. "You're not dead," Early shouted, clapping him on the back. Then the phone rang and Early, as he answered it, remembered that Don Bolles also drove a white import. It was DMV. The registration on the car was to Don Bolles.

Early hung up the telephone and slammed the desk. "Jesus Christ!" he shouted. The reporters looked up. Again he slammed the desk. "Jesus Christ!" Then he told them who had been in the car.

Obscenities filled the newsroom. Wastebaskets were kicked. Reporter Paul Dean, one of Bolles's closest friends and best man at Don and Rosalie's wedding, flung his pen at the wall.

"What the hell was he working on?" asked Early. No one knew.

The outburst didn't last long. Within five minutes, twenty reporters and photographers were working on the story, tracing Bolles's last activities, going through his notes in the press room of the state Capitol and at his desk in the city room, standing by the hospital, interviewing witnesses in the parking lot of the Clarendon House, and trying to figure out just who would want Don Bolles dead and why.

Someone from the *Republic* called Rosalie Bolles at home, told her that Don had been hurt, was on his way to St. Joseph's Hospital and to sit tight, that she'd be picked up by a staffer and taken to the hospital. Rosalie Bolles waited twenty minutes. Then, thinking that her husband had been injured in an automobile accident, she couldn't wait any longer. Using the second car that Don had bought a few years before, she drove herself to the hospital. She identified herself in the emergency room to a nurse and was ushered to a waiting room. Five minutes later, she was told only that her husband was hurt and was being rushed into surgery, that his injuries were serious. A jumble of thoughts ran through her mind. It was their anniversary. There would be no quiet dinner and movie. Forty-five minutes after her arrival at the hospital, she learned that a bomb had gone off beneath her husband.

Bolles had lost more than twenty pints of blood in the Clarendon parking lot. He was in surgery for almost six hours. His legs had suffered the most extensive damage. The right one was beyond hope and was amputated above the knee. The left leg was not much better, though doctors decided to wait and hope that it could be saved. The loss of blood and the severity of the injuries had driven him into deep shock. Massive internal injuries were suspected.

It didn't take long for reporters from the *Republic*, joined by newspeople from their afternoon sister paper, the *Phoenix Gazette*, to come up with a suspect: John Harvey Adamson.

Reporters take notes. They have to. And Don Bolles, besides twice fingering Adamson as he lay suffering in his bombed Datsun outside the hotel, left adequate documentation on exactly whom he thought he was meeting at the Clarendon. He had also talked to other reporters about the man. Good news sources seldom fall so easily off a tree and land in a reporter's lap. Yet Adamson, professing to have detailed information about some of the state's most powerful political leaders, had done just that. Bolles sensed a sham from the start. He told Bernie Wynn and other reporters after his initial in-person meeting with Adamson the week before that he saw the makings of a political smear. The 1976 elections were just beginning to heat up. It was too coincidental that Adamson, whom Bolles had never even heard of before, would suddenly call him up with information of fraud and political chicanery unless there was an ulterior motive. Bolles had been off the investigative beat for more than seven months. Why was Adamson calling him now? Still, one never could rule out godsends. Maybe Adamson was a fraud, trying to string the reporter along, to get him to make a few telephone calls and thereby start the winds of political gossip. But maybe he really had something, too. Bolles had to find out. The second meeting would tell him.

Within an hour after the bombing, as Don Bolles was just entering surgery at St. Joseph's, John Adamson was the subject of a statewide police APB. By midafternoon, reporters for the *Republic* had a full description of him.

He was a classic sleaze. At thirty-two, Adamson was a heavy vodka drinker and user of Valium. The closest he had come to business success was a brief period when he ran an auto tow-away firm specializing in hauling off cars that were illegally parked and then charging the owner fifty dollars to get them back. He was a braggart and name-dropper who rubbed elbows with minor-league lawyers and real estate people who hung out in a string of look-alike cocktail lounges off Central Avenue. Of late, he claimed to be a breeder of racing dogs. In bars like the Ivanhoe, the Phone Booth, and Smuggler's Inn, Adamson was the guy to see if you wanted a good deal on turquoise jewelry, "hot" Mexican silver, or a new leisure suit. Just don't ask for a sales receipt.

The police knew him as a suspected fence, burglar, and arsonist who wasn't above performing some strong-arm stuff for a gambler in need of collecting from a reluctant loser. He was wanted even before the Bolles bombing, on a year-old warrant charging him with defrauding an innkeeper by leaving a Scottsdale motel without paying his bill. It was a minor charge, really. But at least it was a charge that would allow him to be held until something stronger came up.

As it turned out, he wasn't held long. Adamson turned himself in on the old warrant the day after the bombing, posted $100 bond, and, within an hour, was drinking vodka in the Ivanhoe, loudly bragging that he had nothing to worry about.

Republic reporters followed Adamson to the lounge and reported in detail how he sent his white shoes out to be cleaned and made and received several telephone calls. He left briefly to go next door to a manicurist and have his nails done. When Adamson left the bar, a half-dozen reporters in three cars tried to tail him. Adamson, wildly turning corners and careening through shopping-center parking lots, shook his pursuers—nearly causing a "Keystone Cops"-like smashup in the process.

Over the next week, reporters began tracing Adamson's movements, especially during the twenty-four hours following the bombing. What they found made screaming headlines each day. The evening of the bombing, Adamson fled the city on a specially chartered airplane to Lake Havasu City, a resort community on the Colorado River in the northwest corner of the state. The airplane had been chartered by Neal Roberts, a forty-five-year-old prominent Phoenix attorney.

Roberts was also a dog breeder, a raiser of springer spaniels. That's how he said he got to know Adamson, whom he described to reporters as "a colorful . . . Damon Runyon-type character" who was really a "gentleman" and a " . . . humorous, pleasant guy." Roberts was vague about why he had paid for Adamson's brief flight but said his friend was in fear of his life. He also said he had been with Adamson the morning of the bombing, that Adamson had seemed nonchalant and happy before leaving at about ten-fifteen. Roberts intimated that he had a lot more to say but was not at liberty to go into any details at the present. But then he drew still another person into the picture: Max Dunlap, a well-known contractor and land developer from Lake Havasu City.

Dunlap, according to Roberts, was also an Adamson buddy. And shortly after Roberts arranged the flight for a suddenly fearful Adamson, Dunlap visited Roberts's office with a request—to set up a $25,000 defense fund. Roberts said Dunlap was silent as to his reason for getting involved, saying only that he "owed Adamson." Several days before the bombing, Dunlap had telephoned him, related Roberts, saying what a great guy Adamson was and how, should he ever find himself in trouble, the two of them should come to his aid. At the time Roberts had thought Dunlap was being overly sentimental. But then, the day after the bombing, there was Max Dunlap again, this time setting up a John Adamson defense fund—when so far, Adamson's only legal problem was an outstanding misdemeanor charge.

Roberts, lean and silver-haired, bearing a strong resemblance to Texas's John Connally, stopped talking to reporters then.

But the newspaper stories on Roberts's statement and Dunlap's involvement soon connected Kemper Marley to the Bolles bombing. For Marley, the aging millionaire rancher and political kingmaker who, because of Don Bolles's stories, had been forced to resign from the state racing commission three months before, was almost a father figure to the forty-seven-year-old Dunlap.

Roberts fueled the fire even more. In a statement to police in which he fearfully sought immunity in the Bolles case in exchange for his cooperation, Roberts hinted that the Bolles killing may have been Marley's idea of "frontier justice," aimed at getting even for the damage done his pride by Bolles's reporting and his subsequent resignation from the racing agency. The *Republic* got hold of the statement and promptly bannered it.

On June 8, doctors amputated Don Bolles's remaining leg and his right arm in a frantic effort to halt the raging infection that coursed through the reporter's body. Four days later later he died. Bolles's doctor, William Dozer, said, "He put up the most courageous, heroic fight I have ever seen any person put up for his life."

Almost immediately, Adamson was arrested. He was drinking in the Ivanhoe when the police came for him. This time, the charge was murder.

At his preliminary hearing, the evidence was overwhelming. In his apartment police had found an instructional book on bomb making called *The Anarchist's Cook Book,* wire, tape, and magnets of the type used to fasten six sticks of dynamite on the undercarriage of Don Bolles's Datsun. Testifying against Adamson was his sometimes mistress, Gail Owens, who told how she had gone to San Diego with

Adamson shortly before the bombing and witnessed him purchasing a radio-control transmitting device. The dynamite beneath Bolles's car had been detonated by such a unit. Next, Robert Lettiere, Adamson's dog-breeding business partner and a convicted felon, testified that he had accompanied Adamson to a Datsun dealership in nearby Scottsdale where Adamson inspected the underside of a car similar to Bolles's. Adamson had also driven through the parking lot at the *Arizona Republic* to get an idea where Bolles parked his car, said Lettiere. Finally, Lettiere revealed that Adamson had bragged after the bombing about how well he had done in planting the dynamite and how he wasn't worried about his future because he had strong support from politically powerful people. Lettiere also mentioned that Adamson told him that if he ever bombed another car, he'd make sure it wasn't a Datsun, because Bolles had survived the initial blast. "That was a hell of a charge I built under that car. I can't understand how the man lived."

Adamson was bound over to stand trial in Maricopa County Superior Court on a charge of first-degree murder. There was no bond.

Beyond reasonable doubt John Harvey Adamson was Bolles's assassin. But he had not acted on his own. Someone had hired him. The question was who? And, perhaps even more important, why?

Numerous other questions emerged as the reporters from the *Republic* began delving deeper into the case. Was Bolles killed as a direct result of his investigations? Was his death meant to serve as an example to the media, to discourage reporters from sticking their noses into the mob's affairs? Don Bolles had made a lot of enemies. Yet, with only a few long-ago exceptions, the mob had avoided retaliation against reporters. And Don Bolles hadn't been working on anything particularly sensational for months. Or had he?

Bolles kept a file for future stories in his desk at the Capitol press room. In his neat, precise handwriting, he left a note in the top of the file indicating that Senator Barry Goldwater and Congressman Sam Steiger had written letters used to tout a virtually worthless land development. Bolles had jotted down that the letters had supposedly been written at the direct request of Ned Warren, Sr., the so-called godfather of Arizona's land fraud industry, who then used the letters to convince buyers—mostly U.S. servicemen stationed in the Far East—that the land was a good investment. Goldwater, known for his arch-conservative politics and outspoken defense of a strong military, was a retired brigadier general in the U.S. Air Force. His endorsement of the Warren project would be a powerful sales tool.

Both Goldwater's and Steiger's names had been mentioned by Adamson in luring Bolles to his death.

Paul Dean, Bolles's best friend at the paper, was convinced the bombing was a direct result of an ongoing Bolles investigation. "I think Don got hit because he was a phone call or a couple of interviews away from blowing the lid off this state," he said a few weeks after the bombing. "Don was the kind of reporter who didn't give up. He's the kind of reporter who could put such a story together. And the other side knew it."

As June wore on and the stifling heat of the desert began to engulf the city, the reporter friends of Don Bolles felt the same depression and frustration that had caused him to drop out of the fight. There was so much that needed to be done. While Adamson was in jail and the police were narrowing in on his coconspirators, the *Republic* staffers assigned to keeping the Bolles story on page one knew they were only tackling a part of the problem. His death—by a bomb at high noon in the very heart of the city—was obviously meant to accomplish much more than just an end to the snooping of a nosy reporter.

Bolles was killed by people who considered murder a logical reaction to troublesome inquiries.

That was what was so chilling about his death.

Whatever it was about the state of Arizona that had so corrupted Bolles's killers, that had made land fraud the state's biggest business, that allowed 200 recognized leaders and underlings of organized crime to find exile there, that prompted politicians and businessmen to look the other way—that was the real story.

2 | The State of Arizona

Arizona is a pristinely beautiful and sparsely settled state of just 2.3 million. Outside of metropolitan Phoenix (pop. 975,000) and Tucson (pop. 360,000) there are no other large cities in the state. The rest of Arizona is mostly uninhabited, consisting of desert and mountains. About a quarter of the acreage is taken up by nineteen different Indian reservations. Some eighteen percent of the state's total land is privately owned. The remainder belongs to the federal or state government.

Thus even in the last half of the 1970s, most of the state was as it had always been—open and wild.

Phoenix was a small, sleepy cowboy town until the post-World War II years brought the cost of air conditioning within the reach of the average person. In 1940, fewer than 65,000 persons lived there. From 1950 to 1960, the population increased threefold, to just over 400,000. By 1970, it was nearing 600,000 and was the fastest growing city in the 48 contiguous states. By 1980, Phoenix is expected to surpass 800,000 city residents. Tucson, though half the size of Phoenix, has experienced similarly dramatic growth.

But the shimmering glass skyscrapers and creeping pollution just beginning to settle in the mountain valleys of the state's two metropolises in 1976 belied their true roots. While the cities looked modern and grown-up, the old-west lifestyles and attitudes were still present. It was not unusual for a well-to-do Phoenician to take his wife out for an evening on the town, dressed in an expertly tailored four-hundred-dollar Western suit and wearing an old-fashioned six-gun on a carved leather belt, the holster tied gunfighter-fashion to his leg. In the daytime, in the heart of the city's financial district near the impressive Rosenzweig Center, shiny Mark IV's and silver Mercedes bear anti-gun control bumper-stickers attesting to the fact that ''No One Ever Raped a .38.'' In a downtown gun store the special of the week is advertised supermarket-style in boldy painted strips of window paper. One of the more favored sale items is the snub-nosed .22, a gun totally useless to sportsmen or target shooters.

Of the continental states, Arizona was the last to be admitted to the

Union. Thus, "old family," an Arizona term of high respect, applies to those who were there before 1912, when it was known as the Arizona Territory. Like Texans, Arizonans like superlatives. It is a state that boasts "the world's tallest fountain" in one desert land development and "the Original London Bridge" in another. And on the edge of Phoenix, in the middle of what was recently just desert, Phoenicians have built "Big Surf," a giant swimming pool equipped with mammoth fans capable of making ten-foot waves suitable for surfboarding. There is Tombstone, Arizona, "the town too tough to die," and Del Webb's Sun City, "the world's largest retirement village."

Arizonans don't like boat-rockers. In 1976, when a couple of young families with children moved into the over-fifty community of—believe it or not—Youngstown, they were literally run out of town by elderly citizens who threatened to put rattlesnakes in the children's rooms and burn their houses down.

Even the young people of Arizona seem of a different age. At night, particularly on a weekend, North Central Avenue in Phoenix is used for drag-racing by the city's teenagers, who congregate on street corners in *American Graffiti* scenes reminiscent of the 1950s in other American cities.

Phoenix began in the early 1860s as a small settlement along the banks of the Salt River, a rough and tumble town of drifters, miners, and cowboys. Back then, the river flowed full in the winter and spring, and its lush green banks were like a vertical oasis slashing through the broad desert valley that gave birth to the town. A few decades later, the river was diverted thirty miles to the northeast and a series of canals, originally etched out of the sand by the Indians hundreds of years before, were widened and expanded, thereby bringing water across the valley. Those same canals are in use today and the river, one of Arizona's most reliable, still provides the bulk of Phoenix's water supply, filling swimming pools, greening golf courses, and irrigating the desert.

Perhaps the state's most colorful character of the early years— besides the famous Indians, Geronimo and Cochise, and the gun- fighters, Wyatt Earp and Doc Holliday—was a reclusive miner by the name of Jacob Walz, "The Dutchman." It was Walz who allegedly discovered, in the Superstition Mountains some fifteen miles due east of Phoenix, a gold mine so fabulously rich that it is still the object of expeditions. Walz was a strange character. After his partner was killed by Apaches at the mine site, he went a bit daft. While he would return to his mine from time to time, he never fully developed it. Instead, he would take only enough gold to pay for his needs, though government records show the amount totaled over a quarter of a million dollars during one six-year period. And Walz never told a soul exactly where the mine was. Nevertheless, word of his discovery spread far. From the late 1860s to the mid 1880s, his ramshackle home on the edge of the Salt River was surrounded by a tent colony of gold seekers determined to find the old man's claim. When Walz went out in the desert, he was followed by hundreds of them, some on horseback, others riding mules, some on foot. Several dozen of his pursuers died violently over the years. Invariably, the cagy old Dutchman would lose his trackers at nightfall, only to reappear in Phoenix a few days later with a new supply of nuggets from his mysterious find in the Superstitions. Walz took his secret to his grave in 1891, and even today the Phoenix Police Department gets an occasional report from the area where Walz's home once stood that people are digging around in the middle of the night, searching for a clue to the Lost Dutchman Gold Mine.

In 1864, the noted traveler and journalist J. Ross Browne visited Arizona. What he found was '' . . . a place of resort for traders, speculators, gamblers, horse thieves, murderers, and vagrant politicians.'' There are those who find the appraisal still appropriate in 1976. ''Arizona is the native home of the scorpion, the rattlesnake, and the real estate speculator,'' goes a well-known and oft-cited local saying.

No one is quite sure when the modern version of the land scam started, though Don Bolles used to say that between the late fifties and early seventies over one billion dollars had been fleeced from unsuspecting Midwesterners and other cold-state residents who bought worthless chunks of desert touted in the land hustler's ads as ''sun-drenched estates.'' What is known is that of the nearly six million acres sold by the land hustlers, few, if any, are habitable. ''It's really rather pitiful to see what's happened to people who think they've bought a chunk of paradise out here,'' said a Mohave County planner in 1973. ''We're always having a little old couple from someplace up north walk in and say they bought a lot in one of those desert developments and now they want to build on it but can't find it. We tell them if they have a helicopter, they can probably get to it. If not, they'll just have to hike in. But they'll have to bring in plenty of water.''

Using the standard planning figure of three persons per household, if just half of the lot owners who purchased land in desert developments suddenly showed up in Arizona, the state's population would triple overnight, according to a study done by a University of Arizona researcher. Since the state's water table is dropping by as much as a foot each decade, there is barely enough water for the present population.

How does the scam work? A hastily formed land company purchases a huge chunk of wilderness, maybe 10,000 acres for $100 an acre. Next step is the bulldozing of crude dirt roads and the plotting of the land into lots. The 10,000 acres become 40,000 quarter-acre lots. Then, through fancy advertising and lots of slick blueprints, those 40,000 lots are sold nationwide for $1,000 a lot. That's a $40 million return on a $1 million investment. By the time sales commissions have been paid, engineering and planning costs met, and the heavy advertising budget absorbed, the actual profit is closer to $20 million.

The desert between Phoenix and Tucson is crisscrossed with narrow roads that neatly bisect each other to the horizon. The roads go nowhere and no one except Mexican aliens sneaking up from the border to pick Arizona citrus travels them. The roads are mute testimony to the promises of the land hustlers. The utilities, country club golf courses, and other amenities that lure the unsuspecting buyers seldom materialize. Arizona land companies have a long history of conveniently going bankrupt before it's time to deliver.

That's land fraud on its most basic level. But in Arizona, the practice has reached new levels of sophistication. In some cases, the same desert lot has been sold to as many as three different buyers. Sometimes the outfits don't even own the property they sell. Mortgage companies are often duped right along with the original lot buyer, extending loans to land purchasers who don't even exist. It's a grand hustle, made easy by notoriously lax real estate laws. Traditionally, Arizona has led the states in the list of land fraud complaints received by the Interstate Land Sales division of the U.S. Department of Housing and Urban Development.

Then there are the hoodlums. No one knows how many have emigrated to Arizona in recent years, though Don Bolles once wrote a series on organized crime called "The Newcomers" that put over two hundred Mafia members or associates in the state. Basically, hoodlums moved to Arizona for self-preservation.

Law enforcement back east had become extremely tough since the early sixties. Grand juries and special task forces of eager young federal prosecutors were locking up dozens of organized criminal hoodlums each year. The heat was heavy.

Arizona, a state already filled with legitimate immigrants from the East and Midwest, was a perfect spot for many of the harassed hoodlums to resettle. Besides the dramatic growth—which offered lots of "action" in the traditional mob money-making rackets of gambling, prostitution, and loan sharking—there was the more relaxed, less troublesome attitude of the state's citizenry. As in the days of the Old West, a stranger's business was his own. It was a state whose land laws were virtually a license to steal. The only heat hoodlums had to worry about in Arizona came from the desert.

There had been plenty of threats to *Republic* reporters like Don Bolles, Paul Dean, and Al Sitter, who investigated organized crime and land fraud. And the unmistakably Western heritage of the cowtown suddenly grown up did not fit with the new tactics of investigative journalism. Paul Dean remembered the threats. Once when he and Bolles were working on an investigative piece together, someone sent him a letter in the mail. It stated that if he wanted to learn his fate, he should place the paper under a kitchen tap and turn on the water. Dean followed the instructions—and the paper burst into flame.

Even after Don Bolles was cremated—his funeral was attended by the entire Arizona State Legislature—the reporters working the story were given cause to be afraid. John Winters returned home from a vacation weekend to find that his car had been burned in what looked like a case of arson. There was no way to discern whether the damage was in retaliation for his work on the Bolles case or just the work of random vandals. Al Sitter, who had been doing most of the *Republic*'s investigative pieces on land fraud, felt he had been followed on several occasions after the Bolles bombing. Then there were the "sickies," the anonymous calls from disturbed people telling whoever answered the city desk phone—"you're next." The fears—both real and imagined—caused the police to add extra patrols to the neighborhoods of some of the reporters. City editor Early ordered extra security guards for the *Republic* and *Gazette* building and instituted a rule that reporters must go in pairs when interviewing news sources. All such meetings were to be held in public places whenever possible.

The involvement of wealthy rancher Kemper Marley and his sidekick, Max Dunlap, the land contractor who had tried to set up an Adamson defense fund, offered *Republic* reporters still another theory for the homicide. Bolles had been interested in Marley, as evidenced by his background stories which detailed the prominent rancher's political connections and questionable dealings. How far had the reporter dug into Marley's past? Was he, at the time of his death, delving into the old man's current activities?

Kemper Marley, born in 1906 on a cattle ranch, was a well-respected and prominent Arizonan. He presided over a score of businesses from liquor to land, and owned cattle and sheep herds numbering in the tens of thousands. He was "old family," a Phoenician term of high respect. And in his ever-present Stetson, the tall, thick-waisted Marley clearly loved his John Wayne image.

But there was a lot more to Marley than met the public eye. A Phoenix police background profile completed a week after the Bolles bombing contained information which would have embarrassed a number of Marley's current business and political pals. According to intelligence sources of the Phoenix police, Marley was at one time directly connected to remnants of the old Al Capone mob, operating a national wire service for bookmakers. The service, first known as Transamerica Publishing and News Service, was originally established in 1941 for Capone's heirs by a longtime Phoenix gambler named Gus Greenbaum.

Greenbaum was a close pal of mobsters Bugsy Siegel, Jack Dragma, and Mickey Cohen, and, with the assistance of the three hoodlums' contacts in Las Vegas and California, he set up Transamerica to compete with the James M. Ragen line, which enjoyed a virtual monopoly with the bookmakers west of Chicago. Greenbaum was an efficient gambler, and the line soon prospered even beyond the dream of the Chicago hoods. By 1946, it was so successful that Greenbaum turned its day-to-day operations over to Marley, whom he had brought in as an assistant, and a gambler known as Alex G. "Fats" Cohen. Greenbaum then commuted between his Phoenix home and Las Vegas, where he concentrated on establishing such hotels and casinos as the Riveria, Dunes, Flamingo, and Royal Nevada. Phoenix police traced Marley and the wire service to two hotels and a bottling company before the service eventually disbanded in the 1950s, when improved mass communications made the odds and the racetrack winners instantly known.

In 1958, Gus Greenbaum and his wife were found in bed with their throats cut in their Phoenix home. This double murder inaugurated a series of grisly gangland-style slayings in the city.

Marley's alleged criminal background had never surfaced in print, and so he was able to intersperse his gambling activities with a number of political jobs. Bolles had come across allegations of wrongdoing in the way Marley acted in his old government posts. But did the reporter also know the initial source of Marley's power? Was he about to expose it?

The reporters trying to uncover the motive for Bolles's killing had no way of knowing. But they did know about two separate chains of murders. There had been eight obvious mob hits beginning in 1958 with the passing of Greenbaum and ending the previous November with the bombing of Louis Bombacino's car in Tempe, and there had been eleven mysterious deaths linked to Arizona land fraud.

And now Don Bolles, a newspaper reporter who had spent ten years of his life trying to expose the state's shabby side, was dead. "With the assassination of Don Bolles, the City of Phoenix realizes it has come of age," editorialized the *Arizona Republic*. "The slimy hand of the gangster and the pitiless atrocities of the terrorist are part of the current Phoenix scene."

The editorial was somewhat misleading. For the ills were not sudden. They had festered for decades, and, by 1976, they had become so much a part of the state that Arizona was rotting from within.

The story was too big for any one newspaper.

3 | IRE and Punishment

News reporters make enemies. It comes with the territory. They step on toes, malign reputations and, occasionally, write stories so sensational that people go to jail. Investigative reporters, columnists and radio and television commentators make more enemies than general assignment reporters. Revenge is a constant occupational hazard and not a few journalists have been martyred for their work.

Elijah P. Lovejoy was one of the first to die in the line of duty. Owner of the *Alton* (Illinois) *Observer*, Lovejoy was the prototype of the crusading editor. He began the small paper in July 1836, and soon afterwards lashed out against slavery on his editorial page. A mob of townsfolk reacted violently. They ransacked Lovejoy's office and tossed his printing press into the Mississippi. Antislavery news stories incited two similar incidents, and each time the *Observer*'s press was destroyed. On September 20, 1837, a fourth printing press arrived. A crowd gathered on Alton's main street as Lovejoy and a group of thirty supporters supervised unloading and installation. The crowd became ugly by the night of the following day and demanded that Lovejoy leave town. He refused, vowing to continue his support for abolition. The mayor urged him to surrender the press but he stood firm. The mob finally stormed the *Observer* and burned it down. Lovejoy was shot in the chest and died. His murderer was never discovered.

The martyrology of American journalism includes the following names:

Wesley L. Robertson, editor of the *Gallatin* (Missouri) *Democrat*, shot in 1919 by a local politician for linking him to bootleggers.

Don Mellet, editor of the *Canton* (Ohio) *Daily News*, shot in 1926 by a Canton policeman for exposing vice payoffs to city police.

Gerald Buckley, radio commentator on Detroit's WTK, shot in 1930 by three unknown assailants within hours after broadcasting his promise to reveal startling facts on the city's organized crime and corruption on future programs.

W. H. "Bill" Mason, radio commentator and sports editor of the *Alice* (Texas) *Echo*, shot in 1949 by a deputy sheriff after announcing on the air that the deputy's tavern doubled as a whorehouse.

Emilio Milian, the forty-five-year-old news director of Miami's Spanish-language radio station WQBA, was luckier than Don Bolles. Six weeks before the Phoenix incident Milian lost his legs in a similar car bombing. A Cuban himself, he had delivered a number of scathing editorials denouncing a rash of shootings and bombings that had terrorized southeast Florida's large Cuban population that spring. Miami police believe that whoever booby-trapped his car was retaliating for those radio editorials. Despite fifty thousand dollars in reward money, the case was never solved.

Until recent years, reporters had the public image of used car salesmen. Portrayed in movies as arrogant and compromising types with questionable ethics, they were perceived as scoop-hungry sensationalists never willing to let the facts stand in the way of a good story. But then, a number of things happened. A grubby little war that took fifty thousand Americans in Indochina was probably the catalyst. Almost overnight the press started catching our government telling lies. The first lies were about the war and our conduct of it. There was the My Lai massacre and the Pentagon Papers. Later, the lies seemed to spread everywhere. In 1972, there was a third-rate burglary whose cover-up was initially exposed in print; this was followed by revelations that the FBI and the CIA were not what they should be. On the local level hundreds of hometown reporters searched for mini-Watergates and found some. Government chicanery and corruption, unethical business alliances, organized crime and union racketeering were the targets of newsmen across the nation. Investigative reporters became our new folk heroes and Don Bolles had been one of them. His murder had scared those who practiced the craft.

On the afternoon of the bombing Arizona Attorney General Bruce Babbitt extended the chill even further. "It's a departure from the unwritten rule of organized crime that you don't harm members of the press, the cops or the judges," he said. "I suppose the message is, if it can happen to Don Bolles, then it can happen to anyone."

Later, Maricopa County Attorney Don Harris was even more direct. "The Bolles bombing was done as a gesture to the news media to stop looking into this community."

Nationwide, reporters got the message. And it made them both frightened and furious.

Ron Koziol was late for work the morning of June 3, 1976. State construction crews were repairing the expressway he usually traveled from his southwest suburban home into the city and he sweltered in his Gremlin in stop-and-go traffic all the way downtown. It was too damn hot for the first week of June in Chicago.

As he entered the huge city room of the *Chicago Tribune*, he sheepishly waved to the slot editors. The first edition deadline was over. It was time for coffee and a breather as the reporters and editors prepared for the second edition, three hours away.

"This ain't San Francisco, Koziol," hollered one of the deskmen, looking at his watch. "The Hearst case is over, in case you haven't heard. You're ours again."

Koziol thought the kidding would never end. From the time newspaper heiress Patricia Hearst was kidnapped in February 1974, to the day she was captured in the fall of 1975, Koziol had stayed on the story almost full time, at one stage living in a rented apartment in Oakland for three months straight. In all, he had made eight separate trips to California pursuing the story. His several nationwide exclusives won him the *Tribune*'s Edward Scott Beck Award for outstanding domestic reporting. Though the Hearst case had ended months before, Koziol was still razzed for his year-and-a-half on the company expense account.

He sat down at his desk, lit the first of the twenty cigars he smoked each day, and sipped a cup of coffee as he scanned the *Trib*'s first editions.

"Bomb Injures Phoenix Reporter," read the headline on page three. Below was an Associated Press account of the Bolles bombing.

"Holy shit," he muttered, spilling his coffee. Ron Koziol knew Don Bolles. They had met in Arizona four years ago while Koziol was putting together a series of stories on the Emprise Corporation's alleged connections to organized crime in Illinois. Bolles was the Emprise expert, the first investigative reporter to dig deep into the background of the sports concession firm. He was glad to help an out-of-town reporter and saved Koziol a lot of legwork.

The AP story quoted Bolles as saying "the mob . . . Emprise got me." Koziol felt his stomach tighten. At forty-three, Koziol was a veteran newspaperman, who learned his business in the most competitive newspaper town in America, covering police news for almost five years on the city's tough South Side before launching into investigative reporting in 1972. He had been threatened many times. But now another reporter who worked the same story he did was mutilated in a bombing. In early 1974, Koziol disclosed that the firm held the majority stock in a downstate Illinois racetrack. His story led to an intensive investigation into Emprise by the Illinois Racing Board. If Don Bolles was bombed for his reporting on Emprise, Koziol wondered whether he might be next.

But the more he thought about it, the more he doubted whether Emprise really had anything to do with it. It just didn't make sense. The scandal was too old and too many other journalists were involved. Koziol figured it was more likely that a minor hoodlum, angered by Bolles's reporting, decided it was time to even the score. And there were plenty of hoodlums in Phoenix. To hear Bolles tell it, half of the Chicago Mafia had moved to the sunny Southwest. Bolles had often telephoned Koziol in Chicago, asking him to check out the backgrounds of Illinois people who had turned up in Phoenix.

Tom Carlvin, the *Tribune*'s assistant wire editor, tossed an updated version of the AP story on Koziol's desk. He scanned it quickly and saw that it contained little new information.

"You knew this Bolles guy, didn't you?"

"Yeah, I knew him," said Koziol, realizing that they were already speaking of Bolles in the past tense. Carlvin shook his head and walked off, promising to send all the wire copy to Koziol so he could keep informed.

As he sat there staring at the story, Koziol realized he had been talking about Don Bolles just the week before, as he went over preparations for the first annual convention of a group of unique journalists. In January 1975, during the height of the Hearst case, Koziol suggested to a reporter for *Editor and Publisher*, a newspaper trade magazine, that investigative reporters around the country should get together more often as a group. As he envisioned it, once a year investigative reporters would gather to swap story ideas and voice common concerns in an informal atmosphere away from their beats. There were a number of problems peculiar to their craft. Rather than relying on public statements and on-the-record interviews, they had to immerse themselves totally in the subject they were looking into. Confusing public records needed to be perused, confidential and usually anonymous sources developed. Loners by nature, often resented by their own staffs because of their odd hours and independence from such mundane newspaper jobs as preparing obituaries and covering routine press conferences, the investigative reporter more often than not found himself alone on a limb. It would be nice, thought Koziol, to meet some others perched on the same tree. His remarks were printed in *Editor and Publisher*. Koziol was surprised to find his phone at the *Tribune* ringing steadily from other reporters who agreed with the idea.

There already were a number of press organizations. Sigma Delta Chi, a fraternal group for print and electronic newsmen, is the oldest and best known. The Reporters' Committee on Freedom of Information was recently formed to provide legal aid to newsmen who encountered difficulty in gaining access to public documents or who were subpoenaed to reveal the identity of one of their sources. The Fund for Investigative Journalism, supported by grants and donations from philanthropic foundations and civic organizations, was established to aid underfinanced projects like Seymour Hersh's original My Lai stories.

But those groups were rather formal. Koziol preferred a looser, more service-minded operation.

About the same time Koziol's proposal appeared in the trade magazine, a similar idea had arisen at the *Indianapolis Star* where reporters had received a $5,000 grant from the Lilly Foundation, the philanthropic arm of the huge pharmaceutical firm, to arrange for a caucus of investigative reporters. This meeting was held in Reston, Virginia, the weekend of February 22 and 23, 1975. Attending were such media heavies as syndicated columnist Jack Anderson and his associate Les Whitten; David Burnham of the *New York Times*; Len Downie, metropolitan editor of the *Washington Post*; Jack Landau, Newhouse Newspapers Washington correspondent; and Paul Williams, an Ohio State University journalism professor who won the Pulitzer Prize in the early seventies for his exposé of Boys' Town. The *Indianapolis Star* reporters, Harley Bierce, thirty-three, and Myrta Pulliam, twenty-eight, the daughter of the *Star*'s publisher and granddaughter of Nina Pulliam, the publisher of the *Arizona Republic*, explained the reason for the gathering.

After a six-month investigation into Indianapolis's 1,100-man police department, a special *Star* investigative team exposed widespread bribery and extortion by Indianapolis police officers in a lengthy series of articles. The series won the Drew Pearson Award for Investigative Reporting. But it also suggested the need for a national network of reporters. ''We found that there were trails involving local people which we couldn't follow because they went out of our area,'' explained Bierce. "Finding someone in another city or knowing where to look in another city was strictly guesswork."

The conclave closed with an agreement and a name: the group would be known as the Investigative Reporters and Editors Association. And the next step would be organization. Bierce, Pulliam, Williams and Ed DeLaney, an Indianapolis attorney who had assisted the *Star* reporters, were named to an executive committee. Though Koziol was not present at the Reston meeting, his *Editor and Publisher* piece had been read there. He was called during the conference and asked to sit on the executive committee which was already being referred to by its acronym, IRE.

The next year passed quickly for the new group. The Lilly Corporation endowed IRE with another $20,000. Plans were drawn up for a research center, where stories and material could be computerized for the membership. By May 1976, IRE was an official nonprofit corporation. Koziol was elected its first president and more than three hundred reporters from newspapers, radio and television outlets throughout the country had joined up. Don Bolles was one of the first members. Koziol had recommended Bolles's name to the board and extended the invitation himself. The IRE members were busy in May planning their first convention, a weekend-long gathering scheduled for June 19 and 20 in Indianapolis.

Just before Memorial Day, Koziol was called at the *Tribune* by David Offer, investigative reporter for the *Milwaukee Journal*. Offer was to chair a roundtable discussion on reporters' ethics at the convention and wanted Bolles on the panel. Bolles was delighted by the request but explained that he couldn't afford the trip unless the *Republic* paid his way. Offer then wrote Bolles's editors to say how highly IRE regarded their employee and what a valuable participant he would make.

Offer's call to Koziol was to say that he had just heard back from Bolles and the *Republic* had refused to pick up the expenses.

"I really wanted him," Offer said. "He would have been perfect. That guy's been through the wringer out there. His telephone was tapped during the Emprise thing, he's been threatened and sued and gone through hell, and yet he still keeps his cool. He really wanted to come, too."

The two discussed a replacement and hung up, promising to get back together the next week.

But on Thursday, June 3, Ron Koziol was reading a page three story about Don Bolles's being torn apart in a bombing.

Koziol rechecked the newspaper item and the wire copy. He reached for the telephone to call Phoenix, but didn't dial. *Republic* reporters were probably all working the story and he would just distract them.

Mike McGuire came over to Koziol's desk. The two were close friends: they had started out together as general assignment reporters for the *Tribune* in 1961. McGuire, after a two-year stint as bureau chief in Moscow, was now the *Trib*'s foreign editor.

He, too, was shocked by what had occurred to Bolles. "I'm sorry, I know he was a friend." Koziol shook his head. "No, I hardly knew him. We'd helped each other out on a couple of stories. That's all. It's just that it's hard to believe. Jesus, he was a reporter, just doing his job. I can't believe it."

McGuire agreed. "Aren't you the head of that new reporters' group?"

Koziol nodded. "Bolles was one of our members."

"You know, as an organization, maybe you people ought to do something. Send a delegation out there. Find out what the hell happened that would cause somebody to bomb a reporter."

McGuire left and Koziol relit his cigar. Maybe IRE could do something.

Koziol picked up the phone again. This time he called the *Indianapolis Star* and reached Bierce, who had become the group's secretary-treasurer. Bierce was aware of the bombing. It was on page one of that day's *Star*.

"Do you know that he's a member of IRE?" Koziol asked.

Bierce didn't.

"Shit, Harley, we should do something."

"Like what?"

"I don't know. At the convention. We should respond somehow."

Bierce said he would toss it around and be back in touch with Koziol. He, too, felt there should be some sort of response from IRE.

Koziol's next call was to Paul Williams, the Pulitzer Prize-winning OSU journalism professor who had been elected IRE's vice-president.

"I was just going to call you," said Williams. "Did you hear about Don Bolles?"

Williams wanted to know what Koziol thought IRE could do. A

reward offer for information leading to those who ordered the bombing was the first possibility, he explained. But the *Gazette* and
Republic, the two Pulliam papers in Phoenix, had already posted
$25,000. Koziol repeated McGuire's suggestion, that IRE send some
of its people to Arizona to find out the cause of the bombing.

"I like that idea," Williams replied. "Let's respond as journalists,
the only way we know how. Professionally. Let's go into that state
and turn it upside down if we have to, but let's find out what the hell
happened."

Nine days later, Don Bolles was dead. When the story moved
across the wire services, Williams called Koziol. "The convention is
just five days off," he said. "We've got to do something. I thought of
inviting Bolles's editor, Bob Early, to come talk to us but he's too tied
up handling the story."

"From what I've been able to find out, the cops have a pretty good
hold on the case," replied Koziol. "They've got this Adamson dude
pretty cold and it looks like the people who hired him are about to go
down."

Williams agreed. "I still think we have to do something as a group.
The case itself seems pretty well wrapped up. If we still send somebody out there, I don't think it should be just to investigate the Bolles
case alone."

"What do you mean?"

"I mean that the intent should not be to bring Don Bolles's killers
to justice per se. The cops and the local papers are doing that right
now. Instead, we should go into Arizona and describe the particular
climate that caused his death."

"In other words, we should carry on Bolles's work, do the kind of
stories that Don himself would have done if he had had the time and
resources?"

"Precisely."

The first IRE convention began on schedule. From the time newspeople began filing into Indianapolis's Atkinson Hotel Friday night,
little else was discussed but the Bolles case. Word had spread quickly
that there would be a resolution urging some sort of action.

Williams and Koziol talked Friday night about who could handle
the job of weighing the feasibility of such a project. There was only
one choice: Bob Greene, the Suffolk County editor of the Long
Island, New York, newspaper *Newsday*.

Greene was the undisputed expert on team reporting. An obese, grey-haired man of forty-seven, he was one of the nation's most respected investigative reporters. He came to *Newsday* in 1967, after sleuthing for the old U.S. Senate Rackets Committee and the New York City Crime Commission. His first investigation for the paper was into payoffs of various Long Island zoning officials. Three years later, the exposés of "Greene's Berets," as the team was known, had resulted in twenty-one indictments and the resignations of nearly three dozen public officials. *Newsday* won the 1970 Pulitzer Prize for meritorious public service.

Four years later, another Greene team was awarded a second Pulitzer for an unprecedented year-long investigation into the way heroin reached the United States. He and his reporters worked in Istanbul, Vienna, Munich and Paris. They were the first journalists to watch the harvest of poppy fields, observe the clandestine laboratories of Marseilles. The series, called "The Heroin Trail," later became a primer for U.S. Drug Enforcement Administration agents in Europe.

In between his two Pulitzers, Greene and his team produced a seventy-thousand-word series on former President Richard Nixon's questionable real estate dealings through his pal, Bebe Rebozo. Greene's prize was a spot on the White House enemies list and an audit of his tax returns. After his return from Europe in 1973 he had spent most of his time as a deskbound editor, contributing heavily to various seminars on investigative reporting but doing little himself. So Paul Williams figured Bob Greene was just itching to get back on the streets.

The possibility of sending an IRE member to Phoenix was broached officially at a Saturday afternoon meeting of the board of directors to which Greene had recently been elected. After preliminary business, Paul Williams brought up the idea of the Arizona project.

Koziol was watching Greene carefully for his reaction. Greene was seated to the left, his huge frame supported by a small metal folding chair that looked to Koziol as if it might collapse at any moment. A tight smile briefly crossed Greene's face and he rolled his eyes as Williams finished the presentation. Would he take the job and go to Phoenix for a quick feasibility study?

Greene said he wasn't sure; he would have to think about the idea a little more. He promised an answer by the next day. The meeting went on to other matters.

Later, before gathering for drinks in the hotel bar, Williams approached Koziol in a hallway.

"Well?"

"Prepare the resolution, Paul. He'll take it. It's too good a story for a guy like him to turn down."

By Sunday morning, the IRE delegates spoke of nothing else. While most reporters favored this direct response to the Bolles killing, a handful of others were strongly opposed, claiming that it was nothing more than exploitation of the reporter's death. Some contended that a collective effort by journalists from competing papers would never work, that editors would never release a reporter for such a time-consuming project in another state, even if he was writing for just his own paper.

Williams's resolution "to redouble our efforts to keep open the channels of communication to the people" in the wake of Bolles's death passed the board. "We are outraged at the apparent motives for Bolles's death and the obvious efforts to stifle and intimidate the free flow of information to the American people," it read.

Greene would go to Phoenix and see what could be done.

Back at *Newsday*, he conferred with his own editors and outlined the proposal. If there was to be a full-scale probe into Arizona, it would involve a number of newspapers which would have to put aside their natural competitiveness and work together on an identical story which would appear simultaneously in the participating papers. To be sure, nothing like this had ever been tried in the history of journalism in the United States. But if it worked, it would write a new chapter in newsgathering and be taught in journalism schools forever. Closer to home, such a project would give *Newsday*'s reputation a badly needed shot in the arm. Since Greene had gone on the desk after the heroin series, the paper's investigative efforts had been spotty and produced little national impact. Greene was sure to head such a team, giving *Newsday* an edge over the other papers in controlling the story.

His editors liked the idea and on June 29, nine days after the Indianapolis resolution was passed, Greene was in Phoenix.

He spent two full days there, talking mostly with *Republic* city editor Bob Early and Early's key reporters. "This is your story," Greene told him. "We are here to offer you our help, not to take the story away from you. If you don't want us, we'll stay away. It's your decision."

Early had his doubts. Greene and his recruits would be outsiders.

The whole proposal seemed like a journalistic gang bang, a posse of Eastern reporters riding into Arizona intent on doing the work the *Republic* itself should be doing. On the other hand, Early admitted that he needed help. His staff was good but small. Digging sixteen-hour days seven days a week since the bombing, they had so many leads to pursue that it would take years to run them down. Then there was the family connection. Myrta Pulliam, of the *Indianapolis Star*, was not only a founder of IRE but the granddaughter of the *Republic*'s publisher Nina Pulliam, as well as the daughter of the publisher of the *Indianapolis Star*. Such ties could not be ignored.

Early voiced his support and tentatively pledged his paper's cooperation. *Republic* staffers would continue to work the Bolles case independent of any team effort by other newspapers. But as far as a broader investigation into the corruption and fraud of the state went, it would work hand-in-glove with the team.

That was good enough for Greene, who immediately dipped into the *Republic*'s files, familiarizing himself with every aspect of the Bolles case and the problems of the state.

He quickly learned that *Republic* staffers felt Robert Goldwater, the brother of Senator Barry Goldwater, and Harry Rosenzweig, the former GOP boss in the state, were the secret power brokers behind most of the land fraud and political alliances in the state. Greene was amazed to find that despite these strong suspicions the *Republic* had never assembled a dossier on the backgrounds and business dealings of the two.

Greene also learned that federal, state, and local law officials held a don't-rock-the-boat attitude, probably stemming, *Republic* reporters thought, from the Goldwater-Rosenzweig friendship with former U.S. Attorney General Richard Kleindienst, himself an Arizonan. Again, there had been no investigations into law enforcement corruption by the *Republic*.

On organized crime, *Republic* staffers readily confessed that they were not too familiar with the modus operandi of the mob in Phoenix, though they were sure it flourished. The newspaper did not even know the hierarchy of its hoodlums though a virtual immigration of Mafiosi from Chicago, Detroit, and New Jersey had hit their city. They suspected that Phoenix was closely tied to the mob in Tucson, some 160 miles to the south, where the dominance of Peter "Horse-face" Licavoli, head of the old Detroit Purple Gang, and Joseph "Joe Bananas" Bonanno, the transplanted New York Mafia don, had long been established. Greene could not believe that a similar structure did not exist in Phoenix.

There were plenty of fertile areas to plow, Greene concluded. The next question was where to set camp for the team. The obvious location would be in the *Republic* itself. Early offered facilities but Greene decided it would be better to maintain separate headquarters. The management of the Adams Hotel, a large and comfortable downtown hotel just two blocks from the *Republic* office, volunteered cooperation. The Adams agreed to supply rooms at $500 a month each, considerably below its $34 daily rate. Most of the cost would be picked up by the reporters' own newspapers. A minimum of four automobiles would be required, office furniture and typewriters would have to be rented, telephones installed and a full-time staff of at least two secretary-stenographers would have to be hired. Greene guessed that extra help from college graduate students could be obtained free from the state's two journalism schools. Total office costs to be borne by IRE would be close to $25,000. The entire project would take a minimum of ninety days, maybe considerably longer. Persuading newspapers to pay the out-of-town expenses of their reporters for so long would not be easy.

On June 30, he returned to Long Island. Twenty days later he submitted his five-page feasibility study to the IRE board. It would be difficult, he wrote, but the success probability was better than 50 percent. He reiterated the purpose of the probe—to uncover the intertwined political corruption, land fraud and organized crime activities that existed in Arizona.

"The idea is to exert heavy pressure on every possible pocket of corruption whether it directly relates to the Bolles murder or not," Greene proposed, comparing the project to the response of law enforcement to a cop killing. "The minimum effect then, would be to give heavy exposure to the corrupt element in a community in which an investigative reporter has been murdered. The community and other like communities would reflect on what has happened, and hopefully would think twice about killing reporters. For all of us— particularly newspapers with high investigative profiles—this is eminently self-serving. We are buying life insurance on our own reporters. If we accomplish only this, we have succeeded."

IRE's effort would be essentially punitive, he noted. "It would be a concerted statement by the press of America and working newspaper people that the assassination of one of our own results in more problems than it is worth."

By August, the IRE board had approved the project. It would begin in late September or early October. Meantime, Greene began assembling files and choosing his team.

His first selection was Tom Renner, an old friend and a veteran of other Greene-led teams: At forty-eight, Renner was one of the American press's leading experts on organized crime and the Mafia. He had written three books on the mob. His police and underworld informants were distributed from coast to coast and his incredibly detailed files were as complete as most police agencies. Though Renner had recently been ill with a stomach ulcer, he readily agreed to Greene's solicitation.

The *Arizona Republic* assigned a full-time reporter and the *Arizona Daily Star* in Tucson detailed two of its best people. Myrta Pulliam from the *Indianapolis Star* would be available for several weeks of labor; Koziol from the *Chicago Tribune* could be counted on for help, and the University of Arizona (Tucson) and Arizona State University in suburban Phoenix agreed to create special intern programs which would free competent journalism students for minor team work. As publicity about the project appeared in *Newsweek* magazine and the various journalism journals, offers of help from two dozen newspapers poured into Greene's *Newsday* offices. While most could not send reporters to Arizona, they were willing to gather pertinent information in their own cities.

Slowly, the files thickened. Renner was sent out on the road for eight days in late August, picking up information from police and organized crime sources in a half-dozen states that pointed to a virtual mob fiefdom in Arizona, ruled primarily by the Bonanno family in Tucson. There were also strong indications that mob money was heavily invested in the multi-million-dollar agri-business in southern California and Arizona. Other files detailed Arizona's sudden emergence as the country's major narcotics corridor (via Mexico) and pointed to the involvement of some of the state's most prominent businessmen.

"I am convinced that before we leave for Arizona we could literally write a major series of the crime takeover in that state," Greene reported to the IRE board in early September.

Meanwhile, Renner was doing some recruitment of his own. One of his on-the-road forays had taken him to Michigan where he had gathered files on the background of racketeer Pete Licavoli, Sr., who migrated to Tucson in the 1940s from Detroit. While there, he telephoned Mike Wendland, an investigative reporter for the *Detroit*

News, America's largest evening newspaper. Wendland was out of town on assignment for his paper, so Renner left a message to telephone him back at *Newsday*. The two were friends, though they had never met in person. At thirty, Wendland had specialized in the mob and government corruption stories since the early 1970s. As frequently happens with reporters, he and Renner had met over the telephone while chasing identical leads on the disappearance of Jimmy Hoffa during the fall of 1975.

When Wendland returned the call, Renner mentioned the Arizona Project. Wendland was interested because he too had benefited from Bolles's generosity. In 1972 he had spent ten days in Arizona investigating land fraud and had called on Bolles, who characteristically provided several leads.

"How tied up are you for the rest of the year?" Renner asked.

Wendland was swamped. Besides his investigative reporting, he also wrote, on his own time, a column on the Citizens Band radio craze which was sweeping the nation. Syndicated in nearly two hundred newspapers across the country, the column led him to write one book on the hobby the previous spring. He was in the midst of completing his second book when Renner called.

"You've got to be kidding," he said. "Maybe I could get away for a week or two but that would be it."

Renner suggested Wendland think it over. After they hung up, Wendland opened one of his file drawers and pulled out a manila envelope marked "Arizona." He reread his old clippings on land fraud and his research notes, which reflected his contact with Bolles. Then he read the clippings he had kept on the Bolles bombing. Like the other reporters, he felt rage over the tragedy.

That night, he broached the subject with his wife, Jennifer. She was less than thrilled. The Hoffa-Teamsters case had kept him out of town for weeks; he was almost a stranger to their three young children. He gave her several articles about the Bolles killing. When she finished reading them she told him there was really no choice.

The next day, he cleared the idea with his editors and called Renner.

"I'm in," he said.

"I already knew," replied Renner. "In fact Greene already has you budgeted. Plan on three months. It's going to be a bitch, but it's good stuff."

The project would commence the first week of October.

4 | The Project Begins

The airplane began its descent and banked to the west, just over the distinctive mounds that gave Camelback Mountain its name. Below, a maze of twinkling lights stretched over the light brown landscape of the Valley of the Sun, affording Wendland his first view of the city that would be his home for the next several months. It was Monday, October 4, 1976. The sun was just setting and the city, while not yet dark, was not quite light either. Purples blended with greens and the mountains that encircled the valley looked like dark tidal waves about to engulf a small desert island. As the 727 dropped lower, the downtown area of Phoenix showed itself out the left window. Wendland was surprised by how sparkling new it appeared. Glass and steel skyscrapers didn't fit with the Western image he expected. Except for the palm trees, it looked from the air like any other city.

While waiting for his bags inside Sky Harbor Airport, he felt the first twinge of paranoia. In his telephone conversations with Greene, he had been cautioned to keep his whereabouts unknown. "Don't let your paper make any announcement that you're coming," Greene had warned. "We don't want the other side to know who our people are." Wendland looked about the terminal as he hefted his suitcases off the conveyor belt. This was silly, he thought, walking outside for a taxi. There was no one watching.

The route downtown threaded through the city's black and Mexican neighborhoods. The cabdriver wanted to know where Wendland was from.

"You got a lot of nigger problems back there in Detroit," offered the cabbie, a short, balding man in a light blue Ban-Lon shirt. "But let me tell you—here, we got niggers, Mexicans, and Indians. The niggers are bad but the Mexicans keep 'em in line. The Indians don't bother no one 'cause they're drunk all the time. But don't go walking around down here 'cause it ain't safe for regular folks."

Wendland wondered why so many cabdrivers sounded so much alike. "I'll tell you this much, the weather's a damn sight better than it is back in Detroit. When I left, it was only forty-five and they were talking about snow by the weekend."

37

"Yeah. We got good weather, I guess. It was ninety-four this afternoon."

The fare from the airport to the hotel was $3.25. Wendland gave the driver $4.00 and stepped out in front of the Adams Hotel, a block-square sandstone building that stood eighteen stories above the city. Scalloped concrete forms shielding each window from the sun gave it a distinctly Spanish appearance, though the forms looked to Wendland like some sort of giant eyelids. The desk had his reservation ready and he was quickly ushered to the nineteenth floor.

"Actually, you're only on the eighteenth floor," explained the bellman. "We skipped the thirteenth, so the superstitious won't get too upset. We call the thirteenth, the fourteenth, and the eighteenth, the nineteenth. Anyway, this is our top floor. You got a good view up here."

The bellman opened the door to a room midway down the west corridor. Inside were two suitcases, a pair of shoes, and a rack full of clothes. Hastily, he backed out of the room. "They screwed up downstairs," he apologized. "I'll be right back with a new key."

Great security, thought Wendland. Greene had said that everyone on the team would be staying at one end of the nineteenth floor. That way, the office and the reporters' rooms would be semicontained and immune from any overhead eavesdropping. Once the project got going, Wendland wouldn't want bellmen bursting into his room with the wrong key.

Minutes later, the bellman, still apologizing, was back with a new key and led Wendland to a room two doors down from the first one. This one was indeed vacant. Rust-colored shag carpet stretched to stucco walls adorned with two large photographs of Indians and desert scenes. Two double beds separated by a nightstand, a color television set, a chest of drawers, a small round work table, and a separate dressing area and bath completed the layout.

It took ten minutes for Wendland to unpack. He picked up the phone and asked the operator for Bob Greene's room. A woman answered.

"IRE," she said, then, explaining, "Investigative Reporters and Editors."

Wendland identified himself and asked for Greene. A moment later, and Greene's unmistakable Long Island accent was on the line.

"Where the hell are you? We've been calling Detroit all day. You were supposed to be out here today."

Wendland said he was in the hotel but, because of a full morning flight, had only been able to get reservations on a late plane to Phoenix.

"All your office would say was that you were not at your desk. When I asked if you were on your way out here, they just said they'd give you my message. I didn't think you were coming."

Wendland reminded Greene that it had been his idea to keep the Phoenix trip quiet. "My office was just following your instructions. If they had told you I was here, that would have blown it."

Greene laughed, surprised to be a victim his own plans. He gave Wendland the IRE room number and said everyone was just getting ready for dinner.

The office was in suite 1939, just two doors down and across the hall from Wendland's room. Already, it looked like a mini-city room. The bed and most of the standard hotel furniture had been removed. Four metal desks lined the right wall and a long wooden table cut through the middle of the suite. Typewriter stands, smaller desks, and tables and filing cabinets were scattered about wherever they could be squeezed in.

There were four people in the office. The woman who had answered the telephone was Myrta Pulliam from the *Indianapolis Star*, which was run by her father. She introduced herself to Wendland and then introduced him to the others. Alex Drehsler, a young, mustachioed reporter from the *Arizona Daily Star* in Tucson stood up and shook hands. With him was John Rawlinson, a tall, stocky, dark-haired man, also from the Tucson paper. The third man was Greene.

Wendland had never met Greene face-to-face and was unprepared for the present vision. A huge bear of a man who must have weighed at least 350 pounds stood up from behind a desk in the far right corner of the room and lumbered across to greet him, his massive belly gushing over his belt and partially showing itself pink beneath a blue pullover sports shirt that seemed to be bursting at the seams.

"Bob Greene," he smiled, stretching out his right hand and smoothing down a mop of modishly long gray hair with his left. "Welcome to Arizona."

Greene explained the layout. His sleeping room was next door, and the adjoining doors between the office and his room would be left open during the day, giving the reporters extra working space. A bank of telephones with four outside lines had been ordered, though until

Mountain Bell could get in at the end of the week to install them, they'd have to get by with just two hotel extensions, one in his room and one in the office suite. Two secretaries had been hired and would show up for work in the morning. Several interns from journalism schools in the area would be coming in to help out with office chores. Four cars had been rented and were parked in the hotel garage below. A Xerox machine was to be delivered the next day, tape recorders, transcription equipment, and an adding machine were on hand.

Security was a problem. "We don't have any," Greene explained, "though we don't want that to be public knowledge."

The suite had been carefully selected. There was a clean view from the window of 1939. Originally, Greene said, the hotel had wanted to put the team in the suite across the hall. But because windows from other downtown office buildings faced the hotel on the north side, Greene had insisted on the south side suite, where the view was panoramic and unobstructed all the way to the South Mountains, some eighteen miles away.

"We'll keep the lights on twenty-four hours a day," Greene said, "so it looks like someone is always in the office. And I'll be sleeping right next door. But let's not kid ourselves. That's all the security we have. If someone wants to burst in that door and mow us all down with machine guns, there's not much we can do about it."

Greene had spread the rumor that the IRE suite was wired with a sophisticated electronic alarm system and that it was guarded by a plain-clothes security officer. "We know that's obviously bullshit, but, for a while at least, nobody else will."

Wendland wanted to know when the other reporters working on the team would be arriving.

"John Winters from the *Republic* will be in tomorrow. And we've got Tom Renner, but I'm keeping him out of the office, deep and dirty so to speak. Renner's job is to get the basic background stuff we need, but quietly. He's out reading law enforcement files and tapping some of his sources. Right now, we don't want him connected with us. A lot of his sources would dry right up if it was known. So he's staying away from the hotel and floating around the state."

In all, Greene explained, about twenty reporters would be working on the project, though most would be short-timers, in for two weeks or so and then gone. There would be six full-time reporters whom Greene had scheduled for the entire project: himself, Renner, Winters, Rawlinson, Drehsler, and Wendland. Pulliam would be in and out.

The modus operandi would be standard. Each piece of information would be recorded in memorandum. Greene would read each memo and then mark it for various files. As the files grew, their contents would be meticulously indexed and cross-indexed on three-by-five cards. Already, several hundred index cards had been filed and fifty major files had been opened.

"That's what you people will be doing for the next week, reading those files. By the time you finish, you'll be as familiar with this state as a native. You're the full-timers and I want you completely briefed on each area we'll be going into. Later, we'll split up into different groups, with one group handling land fraud, another digging into the mob, somebody else handling the political power structure, and a group going after the narcotics traffickers. As new people come in, we'll put them on a specific group, which will always be coordinated by a full-timer. That way, we keep continuity."

The five reporters left the office and went downstairs to the hotel's Sandpainter Restaurant. Over drinks and dinner, the conversation carefully avoided any mention of the project. Afterwards, Greene and Pulliam decided to turn in. The Tucson reporters and Wendland were restless, and went out to get a feel for the city.

For a while, they drove around aimlessly, stopping briefly for a beer at a couple of bars and getting to know each other. Rawlinson had worked in his newspaper's Capitol bureau for a year and knew the Phoenix street layout. So did Drehsler, who had lived in Phoenix before going to work at the *Daily Star*. It was all Greek to Wendland. A little after eleven, they found themselves on North Central Avenue, passing the Del Webb Hotel and the Rosenzweig Center, the sprawling complex of office buildings and banks that formed the city's financial heart. Abruptly, Drehsler hung a U-turn and turned off on a side street. He pulled into the parking lot of the Clarendon Hotel.

The three reporters got out of the car. Rawlinson, looking down, walked slowly past a row of parked automobiles and then stopped.

"There," he pointed. "That's where Bolles was parked."

The only signs of the explosion were a black stain and a couple of small potholes in the asphalt. A Chevrolet station wagon with California plates and a kiddie car-seat was parked on the spot.

For a minute, the reporters just stood there. The darkened asphalt was what had brought them to Phoenix. It looked almost like an oil stain.

"Let's get back," Drehsler said, breaking the silence. They returned to the hotel. Over the next several months, they and other reporters who joined the project would revisit the Clarendon parking lot. Standing on the spot where Don Bolles last stood was a spiritual charge for them.

The next week passed quickly. John Winters came in the morning of October 5, 1976. A quiet, bespectacled reporter in his late thirties, he wore a full beard and a bolo tie, which, he explained, was the official Arizona State Tie by virtue of legislative order. Winters was the *Republic*'s organized crime reporter, the staffer to whom Don Bolles had turned over his Mafia files. He had spent most of the past three months working on the Bolles case and, until city editor Bob Early had assigned him to the IRE team, had been looking into a series of suspected mob arsons and firebombings that had occurred throughout Phoenix that fall at various bars and restaurants.

The secretaries also showed up. Marge Cashel, the petite, attractive wife of an Internal Revenue Service employee, had formerly worked as a secretary for the Arizona legislature. She became the office manager, receptionist, and head stenographer. Her assistant was Florence Hogan, a plumpish widow in her late fifties whose chief hobby was singing in her church choir. Carol Jackson and Nina Bondarook, two twenty-year-old coeds from Arizona State University's journalism school, came in as the first volunteers. In exchange for two credit hours, they would help index the project files.

Except for the lack of telephones, the office began to function. The two hotel phones were constantly busy with calls from inquisitive reporters. They were calling in not to offer the team their services, but to get a story.

Ever since word of the project's approval had been announced by IRE in Indianapolis, the project itself had become major news in journalism publications. *Newsweek* had run an article on the team just the week before, prompting a flood of requests from general interest publications. That Sunday night, the CBS television program ''Sixty Minutes'' had featured a report on Bolles's death and the impending IRE probe.

By midweek, it seemed as though every television and radio talk show host and half the newspapers and magazines in the country were after interviews with IRE reporters. A Public Broadcast System TV crew wanted to film the reporters at work in the office. A Swedish film crew called long distance to express similar interest. Newsmen from Canada's *Maclean's Magazine* and England's *Guardian* showed up knocking on the office door.

The IRE reporters backed off from all of these intrusions, trying to keep the lowest possible profile. There was nothing to report, they explained. After all, work had just begun. Some of the media accepted this response and let it drop. Others did not.

United Press International somehow acquired a list of the names of the reporters headed for Phoenix from IRE's Indianapolis headquarters and promptly identified them all in a national wire story. There went whatever secrecy Greene had hoped to maintain.

The *New York Times* ran a snooty piece quoting its executive editor, Abe Rosenthal, saying that the *Times* was not participating in the probe because if it wished to undertake such a project its own staff would be quite adequate. Besides, the *Times* chieftain pontificated, the use of reporters from different newspapers destroyed the competitiveness that made the American press great. He was echoed by Ben Bradlee of the *Washington Post*.

But there were little victories and a practical joke. The reporter who wrote the *New York Times* piece, Robert Lindsey, sent an apologetic letter to Greene, admitting that more favorable comments on IRE had been edited out of his story. Lindsey said he was angry at the deletions and personally believed in the team concept. And when Jim Bellows, a high-ranking editor of the *Washington Star* saw Bradlee's remarks, he telephoned Greene to voice full support and put the complete services of his staff on call to the Phoenix project.

The joke was at the expense of *Time* magazine, whose reporter kept badgering Wendland for the IRE room number. Several times Wendland explained that the team would like to keep its exact location a secret for security reasons. But the *Time* reporter kept pushing.

"Look, just tell me what floor you are on," he pleaded. "I won't print it, but at least I can tell my editor that I know it."

Wendland smelled a con job. Recalling the hotel bellman's story about superstitious guests, he pulled his own con and told the *Time* correspondent that IRE was headquartered on the thirteenth floor.

The October 18 issue of *Time* magazine showed that both Wendland's "off-the-record" information and a bit of Greene's earlier rumor-spreading had become gospel. In a piece entitled "Arizona Invasion Force" that ran in the magazine's press section, *Time* called the project "the most remarkable journalistic joint effort since Woodward met Bernstein."

But it began by saying, "On the thirteenth floor of the Adams Hotel in downtown Phoenix, there is an unmarked suite, guarded by a security man. . . ."

The outside telephone lines were installed on Thursday and, with the media calls dropping off, the team settled into a routine that left the reporters with strained and bloodshot eyes.

Reading the files was a monumental task. On Thursday night, Pulliam and Rawlinson had fallen asleep in the office around midnight, court depositions and real estate records still in their laps. They were awakened by snores coming from Greene's room next door. With Wendland and Drehsler, they kept reading until two in the morning.

By Friday, the reporters had finished most of the background files. And from them, they had a clear idea where they were going. They were now ready to gather their own information.

Greene had compiled a list of corporations the team needed to research from the files. Thanks to a computer printout of more than twenty thousand land firms and their corporate officers, run for the team by a business professor at Arizona State University, the reporters had more than three dozen target companies to look into.

That morning, the reporters fanned out across the city. Rawlinson and Pulliam went to the Arizona Corporation Commission to check the annual reports and original articles of incorporation filed on many of the target companies. Wendland and Drehsler were sent to the Maricopa County recorder's office to pull all real estate records on the firms. Winters prowled through the morgue of the *Republic* for newspaper clippings on a number of persons and firms.

Record checking is the backbone of investigative reporting. Few people realize how much of their lives are documented on public records. From birth to death, from marriage to real estate purchases and disputes with neighbors and business associates—public records enable a good reporter to put together a complete profile on just about anyone. It is a long, boring, and tedious job, but if you know what you are looking for, there is not much about a person that can't be found out. Divorce proceedings, probate court estate hearings, tax assessment records, mortgage contracts, and applications for such things as drivers' licenses and business permits yield a vast amount of personal information. That was what the reporters set out to gather in the second week of the team's investigation.

All good reporters must be familiar with record checking. Though certainly the least glamorous aspect of their job, it is probably the most important. Some enjoy the task, comparing it to the completion of a jigsaw puzzle. Others do not.

Drehsler was in the latter category. He was a street reporter, who much preferred the person-to-person contact of interviewing.

"We've been here a full week now and we've yet to talk to a real person," Drehsler complained to Wendland, his notebook surrounded by a stack of two dozen microfilm tapes at the recorder's office.

At twenty-eight, Drehsler was one of the top newsmen in the Southwest. The year before, he had written a series on drug trafficking on the Mexican border that won him the coveted Arizona "Newsman of the Year" award from the Phoenix Press Club. That must have surprised a lot of people who knew his background.

Born of German citizens who brought him to the United States when he was six years old, Drehsler had probably the most interesting personal history of any of the team's reporters. He quit high school six weeks short of graduation to join the U.S. Army in 1967, hoping to go to Vietnam as a combat photographer. Because of his German citizenship, however, he was turned down and made a supply clerk, stationed at Fort Bliss in El Paso, Texas. That wasn't for Drehsler, who wanted adventure. So, borrowing five dollars from another GI, he went AWOL, crossing the border into Mexico and spending exactly half his grubstake for a bus ride south to Chihuahua.

The next morning, he awoke in a sleazy downtown hotel and took stock. He had the clothes on his back and, after paying for his room, not quite two dollars.

He walked around Chihuahua for a while until he came to the German consulate. Suddenly he was inspired. He went inside and told the consul that he was a free-lance writer-photographer on assignment from a German magazine to produce a feature piece on Mexico. Drehsler said he had just arrived that morning and had been victimized by a sneak thief who dashed out of the bus station with his suitcase. The consul was shocked and apologized repeatedly, shutting down the small office and personally escorting Drehsler to the property room of the Chihuahua police station. He asked Drehsler to look around to see if he recognized any of his property. Drehsler said he did, picking out a couple of shirts, slacks, a jacket and sweater, a pair of boots, and even a suitcase to carry the new wardrobe in. Back at the consulate, his host beamed at his ability to assist his stranded countryman. Dipping into the consulate's emergency fund, he gave Drehsler twenty-five dollars' worth of pesos and bid him farewell, urging Alex not to let his "bad experience" affect the article he planned to write on Mexico.

Armed with a tourist map, Drehsler set off on another bus, deter-mined to see the country. Several days later, near a small mining and university town in the interior, he met a young English-speaking Mexican girl, who asked what Drehsler planned to do. This time, he introduced himself as a schoolteacher from Texas who had decided to take a year off to travel. The young woman had an idea. She knew of many young Mexican girls, the daughters of rich miners, who would welcome a chance to learn English. Would Drehsler consider staying in her city awhile, tutoring her friends? He certainly would. Staying at the home of two of the young woman's brothers, he picked up fifty pesos a week from half a dozen young women, learning Spanish while teaching English.

This Mexican odyssey lasted over two years. After the tutoring job, he continued traveling the country, working as a ranch hand, a tourist guide, and a swabbie on a couple of shrimp boats.

Back in Phoenix, he settled his problems with the army and knocked about for a while, pumping gas at filling stations and toiling as a janitor at Sky Harbor Airport. In 1970, he was fired from the airport job after trying to unionize his coworkers.

At the time, Drehsler had been reading a lot of Jack London. London's background intrigued him. He figured that being a reporter wouldn't be a bad profession, so he went to the Phoenix office of the Associated Press. He claimed education at a number of Mexican universities on his application; for work experience, he made up an impressive list of Mexican newspapers, giving himself titles such as "executive editor" and "assistant publisher." The scam worked and he was hired and sent to run the one-man Tucson AP bureau, located in the same building that housed the *Arizona Daily Star*.

The only problem was that Drehsler didn't know how to type. When his ninety-day probationary period ended, he was fired, effec-tive May 1.

No problem. Drehsler had met a number of people at the *Daily Star*. While serving out the last week on the AP job, he began bad-mouthing his employers, telling a couple of editors at the paper that he was thinking about quitting. He'd much rather work for a newspaper, he explained. Again, the con worked. He was offered a job with the *Star*, beginning May 1.

Drehsler almost blew his newspaper job the first day. Assigned to cover crime news from four in the afternoon until one in the morning, he bumped into a group of Mexican women at the Tucson police department the first Friday night on the job. The women were from Nogales, some sixty-eight miles to the south, and they had missed their return bus. Drehsler promptly loaded them all into his car and drove them back home. But instead of immediately heading back to Tucson, he decided to celebrate his new job in Nogales' infamous red-light district. The celebration lasted four days.

When he returned to the *Star*, he freely admitted his fling. Somehow, he kept the job.

Over the next three years, he found his niche. Drehsler loved reporting. His varied experiences, which he called "adventure collecting," gave him an insight into how the other side lived. His stories were detailed and uncommonly well written. His disarming charm and sympathy gave him a wealth of news sources, among both criminals and the police. In 1976, married to a Mexican girl and the father of an eight-month-old daughter, he was a thoroughly rounded and mature news reporter with an impressive stack of reporting awards.

But that didn't mean he had to enjoy going through public records. By Friday afternoon, he had had enough.

"There's got to be an easier way," he said to Wendland, who similarly had been running through thousands of pages of microfilm records and then meticulously writing down the information they needed in notebooks.

Drehsler looked at the sheet listing the particular real estate transactions the pair were interested in, as well as the microfilm pages they appeared on. Putting them all on a new piece of paper, he took it to a clerk in the office.

"We want copies on all these," he explained.

The clerk, a middle-aged woman who still hadn't lost her Brooklyn accent despite ten years as a Phoenix resident, studied the list. "You want all these?" she asked, her eyes registering surprise.

Drehsler smiled and nodded.

"It's going to take some time, then. And it's going to cost. We'll have to charge you a quarter a page. It's going to take three of us all afternoon to do this."

"Okay," Drehsler said. "We'll come back."

When the two reporters returned late that afternoon to pick up the Xeroxed documents, they had a three-inch-thick stack of 600 pages and a copying bill of $150 waiting for them.

They paid the bill from their expense accounts and took the stack of documents to Greene for reimbursement from the IRE account.

"One hundred and fifty dollars!" Greene exploded. "You had to have copies? You couldn't have just taken notes like everyone else?"

"We would have been there until December," Drehsler replied. "Besides, this way we don't have to rely on notes. We've got the complete documents."

Reluctantly, Greene paid the reporters the $150 they had shelled out. Rawlinson and Pulliam shook their heads. They had been taking hand notes. But before they could speed up their record pulling by similar means, John Winters from the *Republic* worked out an arrangement with the various government offices to provide microfiche copies of key records. The group borrowed a special microfiche reader that allowed examination of the filmed documents in the IRE office. The machine freed the reporters to schedule interviews during the day and complete their records research at night.

Like Drehsler, Wendland was not fond of record checking. But from the files already compiled and the new documents they had dug up at the county recorder's office, he had come across a company whose background stirred his interest. For one thing, it had a direct tie to Detroit, which would surely please his editors back at the *News*. More importantly, the firm was run by the biggest names in Arizona.

The corporation, called Goldmar, was a many-tentacled enterprise named after its principal owners: Robert Goldwater, the senator's brother, and three members of the Martori family, one of the state's most prominent clans. On the board of directors was Harry Rosenzweig, the former state GOP boss and political power broker who had masterminded Barry Goldwater's political career since the late 1940s.

Goldmar was involved in apartment rentals, land development, and real estate investments, but its prime business came from the growing and selling of citrus. Goldmar's main citrus orchard, a sprawling series of groves just north of Phoenix known as Arrowhead Ranch, particularly interested Wendland. For Arrowhead Ranch had originally been formed by a couple of Detroiters back in June 1955. And the Detroit incorporators were not just average businessmen.

According to the documents on file in the recorder's office, Joseph Zerilli and William Tocco had started the Arrowhead Ranch. Zerilli was known back in Detroit as "Papa Joe." According to U.S. Senate testimony, he was the chief don of the Detroit Mafia. Tocco, a.k.a. "Black Bill," was one of Zerilli's lieutenants.

The records showed that Zerilli had owned the ranch for almost four years. He had sold it in January 1959 to Del Webb, a Phoenix entrepreneur whose land development firm would become one of the largest in the nation. Webb, in turn, didn't hold onto the land for very long. A little over five years later, Arrowhead became the property of Goldmar.

The sale prices raised Wendland's eyebrows. When Zerilli unloaded the land to Webb, he was paid nearly four million dollars. But Webb, a few years later, sold the ranch to Goldmar for just a one and a half million dollars. Wendland may have been new in Arizona, but he knew that valuable irrigated farmland like Arrowhead Ranch did not normally depreciate in value. Yet the real estate records indicated that it had done just that, losing about two and a half million dollars in five years.

Studying the documents more closely, Wendland spotted the name of Carl Jarson, another Detroit man who had been involved in the original purchase of the ranch. Jarson, the records showed, was still in Arizona, running a citrus brokerage firm known as Western Growers Distributors. He decided to pay a visit to Jarson.

Jarson was extremely cordial on the telephone. Sure, he'd be glad to talk to a reporter from his old home-town, giving Wendland directions to the cramped office he rented in a run-down old white frame house in Glendale, a northern Phoenix suburb. Jarson was in his unmarked office waiting when the reporter arrived. He beckoned Wendland to sit down on a battered old couch with oozing stuffing and promptly produced a display of yellowed newspaper clips that sketched his career in the fruit business. An affable, cigar-chomping man of sixty-five, he had spent a half century in citrus brokering, beginning at Detroit's old riverfront produce terminal. It was there that he had met and become partners with Joe Zerilli.

"I figured that's why you wanted to see me," Jarson said. "I didn't think you just wanted to talk about produce and citrus."

So Wendland asked him how the Detroit Mafia leader had come to own the Arrowhead Ranch.

"It was just an investment," Jarson said. "Hell, I don't really remember. We just decided to branch out a bit. It started with a small grape vineyard and pretty soon we had the whole ranch." As an investment, the ranch was more trouble than it was worth, he claimed. "Mr. Zerilli just didn't want to have the headaches, so, after a while, we sold out." Jarson said that he had fallen in love with the state of Arizona while visiting the ranch and had decided to remain there. He and Zerilli had parted company amicably.

"Look, I know what you must think," Jarson interjected, "but I'm no fuckin' Mafia. All I know about is produce. I loved Mr. Zerilli. He was always a gentleman. I haven't talked to him in years. I'm afraid to call him. Every time I see him, I'm called a hoodlum, a Mafia associate. Ain't that a bunch of shit?"

Jarson stood up. "Come on, I'm taking you for a ride."

They got in Jarson's car out front, and he drove around Glendale for half an hour, pointing out various citrus packers he did business with.

Then he said he wanted Wendland to see his biggest buyer—Goldmar.

Inside the huge Goldmar packing house, Jarson was treated as if he owned the place. He brushed by a number of office workers, who respectfully greeted him by name, and led the reporter to the packing area, where fifty Mexican workers sorted and graded grapefruit off a long conveyor belt.

"This is my life," Jarson said, picking up a softball-sized fruit. "Citrus is what I sell. What do I know about the Mafia?"

They returned to Jarson's office, and Wendland thanked him for his time. The interview hadn't been a complete waste of time. At least the reporter knew that Goldmar had been doing business with a Zerilli associate.

There were other things about Arrowhead Ranch and Goldmar that needed checking. In the batch of newspaper clippings brought back by Winters from the *Republic*'s morgue, Wendland had spotted a couple of two-year-old news stories dealing with a suit brought against Arrowhead and a number of other valley citrus growers alleging that they wittingly hired illegal workers from Mexico, thereby contributing to the high unemployment among American farm workers in the area. The suit had been dismissed, and the allegations seemed to have died as quickly as they had been raised. Wendland was suspicious.

Back at the office Monday afternoon, October 11, Wendland called the Phoenix Legal Aid Society, which had been identified in the clips as a party to the suit. No one there recalled anything about the abortive legal action. They suggested he try the United Farm Workers Union, where he unearthed the name of Lupe Sanchez, a former union official supposedly knowledgeable about the Arrowhead case. Wendland left a message with Sanchez's wife, and Sanchez returned the call the next morning.

"Oh, man, I'm all done with that," Lupe said, after Wendland asked what he could tell him about Arrowhead Ranch.

"Look, all I want to know is whether they still use illegal aliens out there," Wendland asked.

"If that's all you want to know, you sure as hell don't have to call me. Of course they do. Anyone could have told you that."

"What I want is a complete picture. How many? What do they pay them? Everything."

Lupe sighed. He had heard about the IRE team and was curious about what it was doing in his state. "Okay, man, look, I'll come talk to you. I got to come downtown anyway. But I want to get it all done today. Tuesdays and Thursdays are the only days I have any free time from school. I'll see you in a couple of hours."

He was at the IRE office door at two o'clock sharp. They went in Wendland's room to talk. A short, stocky man, Lupe knew all about Arrowhead Farms. He had practically lived there for the better part of a year, trying to convince the wetback laborers that they were being exploited and should support the farm workers' union. He guessed that upwards of 300 wetbacks picked at Arrowhead during the peak of the citrus harvest. Lupe said that he had been threatened and chased by ranch foremen during his visits there. He told of two of his coworkers who had been captured and then kicked and beaten in front of the wetbacks as an example of what the foremen would do to those who questioned the Arrowhead operation. He told of wetbacks who died at the farm from their work, of rumors of a mysterious wetback graveyard in one of the orchards, of incredibly low wages and a total lack of living facilities.

"They don't even have shelter," he said. "They live in the middle of the orchards—worse than dogs. They camp there, without heat or water, sleeping on the ground."

Wendland asked how the workers got to Arrowhead.

"Ah, that's the worst of it. They're recruited down in Mexico, promised all sorts of riches if they'll just pay the service fee to the coyote who brings them across."

"What do you mean, 'coyote'?"

"Coyote. That's what the guide or recruiter is called." The coyote's fee ranged from a low of $75 to as high as $150. "You must understand that these are *campesinos*, landless peasants, and that fee may be half their annual income.'' After the payment was made, the wetbacks were smuggled across the border at night.

''The lucky ones are driven north,'' he continued, ''in special vans and station wagons that have had all but a small seat for the driver torn out. I know of as many as eleven wets jammed into one station wagon. The unfortunate ones make it all the way to Phoenix on foot, crossing the desert and using remote trails. Some of them actually die on the trip. Believe me, the desert is filled with the bleaching bones of many an unlucky wet.''

Once camped in the orchards of Arrowhead, the aliens are virtual slaves, Lupe said. ''They are told that if they leave the fields, they will be picked up by the border patrol.'' Lupe said he had talked to wetbacks who had been shipped to other states against their wishes and forced to work in order to pay off outrageous bills they had supposedly run up for clothing or food.

''This is a way of life out here,'' said Lupe. ''You have no understanding of what it is like. It's pathetic. But no one cares. We've been screaming about it for years. No one listens. The newspapers don't care. The courts don't care. It remains the same.''

Wendland told him that if all he had said was true, the team of reporters certainly would care. ''But we have to verify everything you said. We'll have to see it ourselves.''

''That could prove to be dangerous.''

''Why?''

''I've told you about the beatings. The word is that there are phony workers in some of the orchards. They're there to keep the wets unmolested by Legal Aid people. When I was going out there regularly, I was warned that there was a guy planted in the orchard who was supposed to knife me. This guy was going to stick me and split. Then, if the cops came round, the foreman would just shrug and say it must have been a wetback gone crazy. And believe me, it would have worked. They would have said the wet got scared and ran back to Mexico. And that would have been the end of the investigation.''

''If all you've said so far is true, we're still going to have to go there ourselves. Will you take us?''

Lupe shrugged. ''Why not? Let's go.''

Wendland wasn't sure he had heard right. ''Did you say you will?''

''Sure. I've got a couple things I have to do first. Pick me up over at the Laborers Union in about an hour.''

''Today?''

"Sure, why not? Unless you've got something else you have to do. Otherwise, I can't make it until Thursday."

No, Wendland's schedule was clear. They'd visit Arrowhead that afternoon.

5 | The Goldwater Ranch

Lupe was waiting out in front of the union hall. Wendland had brought Drehsler along for the ride, and the two of them listened intently to their eager passenger. "It's been quiet out there for over a year," Lupe explained as they drove along Black Canyon Highway. "Nobody from Legal Aid or anyone else has been around. So they're not going to expect us. But that's no reason to let our guard down."

Drehsler was appalled that local reporters had never visited the ranch.

"The press in this town is part of the problem," said Lupe. "We've told them what the situation is, but they refuse to get involved. The people who own Arrowhead own this town, too." Lupe handed Wendland a sheaf of legal papers. "These are some of the affidavits we collected when we were trying to clean up that place. Read 'em. That's what you're going out to see."

The affidavits were from young wetbacks. They painted a grim picture.

The story of Demetrio Diaz, a skinny young worker from the village of Guameo Chico, in the state of Michoacán, Mexico, was not untypical.

Diaz's odyssey began when a man named Alberto came to his house and asked if he wanted to go to work in the United States. Alberto was a coyote, or recruiter, who scoured the poor villages and farms of central Mexico for peasant laborers.

"He said he had work lined up working in the oranges for at least $20 [a day] and that he would get us across the border and that we would walk for two days to reach the ranch," the affidavit quoted Diaz. "He said that he would charge me $100 to take me to the ranch."

It was a lot of money for Diaz, but he managed to raise it all by borrowing from relatives. One night soon after Alberto's visit, he was on a bus with twenty other young men, heading for the border and their promised fortunes. The bus stopped at a farm just outside the tiny village of Altar, Sonora. The men were let out and told to wait. About 2:00 A.M., Diaz said, they were loaded into two pickup trucks and driven to a desolate spot on the border.

They hopped the fence and set off across the desert, following Alberto. By midmorning, they were several miles into Arizona.

"One young short boy hurt his leg," recounted Diaz. "The leg was so swollen that the boy couldn't walk. Alberto gave him some marijuana to make the boy walk, but the boy couldn't get up. Alberto wouldn't let us carry him, so he was left in the desert, unable to walk, an entire night's walk from the U.S. border."

The journey lasted for four days. What little food the wets had with them was soon gone, forcing several of the men to kill a javelina, a desert pig, to eat. Several times the men spotted human skeletons and bones beside rusting water cans on the trail, said Diaz.

Finally, late the fourth day, Diaz said, the aliens reached the southern outskirts of Casa Grande, Arizona, a small farming town about seventy-five miles north of Tucson. There, the affidavit claimed, they were met by a foreman from Arrowhead Ranch, who drove the twenty men to Phoenix. They spent the night camped in the ranch orchards.

"The food we ate was brought to us by the foreman," said Diaz. "Then at the end of the week, money was taken out of our checks. One time we got a bag of flour, two dozen eggs, salt, and three cans of beans. The foreman charged us twenty dollars for this."

Instead of the big wages he had been promised, Diaz claimed his salary was less than forty dollars a week. For that, he worked twelve hours a day, seven days a week.

Diaz said that the foreman told the aliens that they were never allowed to leave the orchards. If they tried, the foreman would alert the border patrol, which would send the worker back to Mexico without his pay.

After finishing the affidavits, Wendland had the same question as Drehsler. "You mean to tell me that the *Republic* or *Gazette* never got their hands on these?"

"Sure, they saw them," replied Lupe. "They just didn't bother to investigate any further."

"Hasn't anyone from the local media ever dropped in on that place?"

Lupe said that he had twice escorted newsmen to the ranch for a firsthand look. "But both of them were not real reporters, they were from small, community-type newspapers, activist groups really." On one occasion, an Arrowhead foreman cut the microphone wires of a reporter interviewing a wetback. On another, Lupe and the reporter were chased off the land by club-wielding farm supervisors. "It was a good story, but their little newspaper had a reputation for being a radical underground sheet, and nobody paid any attention to it." The publication had since folded.

"What about the Goldwaters?" Wendland asked.

"The ranch is really owned by the Martori family and Bob Goldwater," Lupe replied. "But everyone suspects that Barry has an interest in it. We can't prove it, but by putting two and two together, it's obvious that Barry wants Arrowhead to keep making money." Lupe told of an overseas trip the senator had taken a couple of years before, plugging the benefits of Arizona-grown citrus. "That certainly has the appearance of using his public office to plug his family's business interests."

During the height of the union's organizing campaign at Arrowhead, Lupe crashed a testimonial dinner to Barry Goldwater. "I stood up and asked Barry how come his brother was exploiting wetback laborers when able-bodied farm workers right from here were going begging for picking jobs," he recounted. "Well, right there, in front of all those people, Barry looked me right in the eye and said that if all my people, the Mexican-Americans, weren't so lazy and would get off their butts and work for a living, his brother wouldn't have to hire wetbacks. And he was cheered. A bunch of goons carried me off and tossed me out on my ass."

It took them about a half-hour to reach the ranch, located at the edge of the foothills to the north of Phoenix, just off Bell Road on Fifty-ninth Avenue. In every direction, all the reporters could see were neat rows of fifteen-foot-high citrus trees. Three miles down the road, Lupe told Drehsler to slow down.

"These are lemons," he said, pointing to a section of the orchard where the trees were heavily laden with small, greenish-yellow fruits. "My guess is that this is where we'll find the camps. It's too early for oranges."

They passed a house trailer and a short dirt service road that led to a couple of frame houses and an equipment storage building. "Just to the south of that little drive is where we want to go," Lupe said. "There's water there, and the wets will be as close to it as they can. They'll be under the trees a dozen or so rows in."

He had Drehsler drive a mile north, where the Arrowhead land ended and the Thunderbird County Park nestled against a small mountain. "We'll park the car here," he said, grinning at Wendland, who was overweight and obviously out of shape. "Sorry, but there's no other way but to walk in. We can't risk being spotted by the foremen."

Thunderbird Park was empty except for a picnicking family roasting some hotdogs on a charcoal grill. Their small black dog, leashed to the door handle of their car, yipped furiously at the newcomers.

The sun was just setting as the reporters and Lupe got out of their car and began walking towards the ranch. The land was virtual desert, broken only by an occasional clump of sagebrush. Lupe pointed out a scorpion and cautioned the reporters to watch out for rattlesnakes.

"He's kidding, isn't he?" asked Wendland, who had never had to worry about such creatures in Michigan.

Drehsler just laughed.

Arrowhead Ranch was a strange contrast to the barrenness of the land surrounding it. Kept green and lush by a series of deep wells, pumps, and irrigation ditches, it loomed ahead like an oasis. The three men crawled under a barbed-wire fence and made their way into the groves.

"These are grapefruit trees," Lupe explained. "They won't be ready for picking until December." Even so, it was clear that people had lived under the trees before. A circle of small rocks marked off an old campfire site. A tattered shoe, rusting tin cans, and scraps of paper bags and food packages defined the rest of the camp Lupe said had been used the year before.

The groves were filled with insects. Horseflies and fruit flies were everywhere, swarming into the trio's faces, tangling in their hair.

They walked on for about fifteen minutes, shielding themselves from view behind the trunks of trees, slowly making their way towards the small dirt service road they had seen on the way in. When they reached it, Lupe raised a hand and slowly crept forward, peeking around a tree.

"There are some people off to the left," he said. "If we cross now, they're sure to spot us."

They waited, watching two men smoke cigarettes and lean against an old pickup truck. Somewhere closer, a dog began barking. An elderly man in faded blue overalls emerged from one of the storage buildings and shouted at the animal, quieting it down. It was getting darker by the minute. Finally, one of the men got in the truck and drove off. The other two walked out of sight behind the storage building.

It was fifty yards across the service road, and it was open all the way. Lupe told the reporters to walk slowly, as if they were field hands. Midway across, the dog began barking furiously. "Don't run. Just take it easy," Lupe reminded. The dog was still barking as they entered the protection of the groves. They stopped for a breather. Lupe didn't think they had been spotted.

Two quick gunshots rang out. Stunned, the reporters whirled around. They listened, crouched beneath a lemon tree. For a moment all they could hear was the buzzing of the flies. Then, behind them and back towards the road, they heard voices and another shot, followed by far-off laughter.

"Target practice. Maybe a coyote," Lupe said.

It didn't make the reporters any more comfortable, realizing that there were men with guns nearby.

Slowly, they started to walk up one of the rows. It was almost completely dark in the orchard. Wendland spotted something moving ahead. He stopped for a moment. It was a man. Wendland waved, hoping to look friendly. When they reached him, the reporters were amazed. The man was reed-thin, maybe forty years old. He was with his wife, a heavy woman in a tattered green dress. Two young children were squatting in the dirt, trying to eat some sort of soup. Their faces were covered with open sores. Flies floated in the soup and coated the sores.

The family had fashioned a camp between two lemon trees. A fruit packing case lined with old blankets served as a shelter for the children. The husband and wife slept on the ground, their heads partially protected by a sheet of black plastic stretched between the two trees.

Lupe talked to them in Spanish. They were Mexican aliens who had come to Arrowhead the week before to pick lemons. The work was slow. It was still too early for the good picking, though they had been told that they would earn big money. They had been driven to the ranch in a car by a man who charged one hundred dollars to smuggle them across the border, the woman said. The hundred dollars was all the money the couple had. They had even had to borrow some of it from an uncle.

"But we have been here a week already and all we have earned is ten dollars," the man said. "That is not enough. I don't know what we will do."

A small sign in Spanish was tacked to a tree in front of their camp.

While Lupe conversed with the family, Drehsler translated it for Wendland.

It read: "This little house is occupied. Beware of the dog."

There was no dog. The sign was meant to frighten other field hands who came around looking for something to steal, Lupe explained after the three walked away from the family, bidding them good luck.

They moved deeper into the orchard, going slowly to avoid tripping over the tree roots in the darkness. Suddenly, Lupe stopped, raising a hand. "Listen," he said. From their right came the sound of splashing water and muffled voices. They headed towards the sound and discovered two naked men.

Their clothes were hung neatly over the branches of a lemon tree as they tried to bathe in the copper-colored water of an irrigation ditch. One of the men grabbed a three-foot-long stick.

Lupe greeted the men in Spanish, telling them they had nothing to fear. The man with the stick seemed to relax, though he continued holding onto it.

They had just arrived at Arrowhead, the man with the stick said as his partner continued bathing. They had no money. Work was slow. It was very difficult, but they hoped that things would soon improve. They had come to Arrowhead with four friends who were camped elsewhere in the orchard. They had taken the train from their small village in the interior of Mexico to the border, where they had squeezed into a van for the trip north. Each man had paid $125 to come there, they said.

"Already we are losing money," said the bather. "We owe the foreman twenty dollars for food."

What kind of food?

"Some flour and beans," he said. "But that is not so bad as some of our friends. One man owes thirty dollars for a pair of trousers."

The men said they would work their debts off as soon as the fruit ripened a bit more. Meantime, they were having trouble just getting by.

Lupe and the reporters said goodbye and moved off towards the main road to the east. Ten minutes later, they spotted the flickering light of a small fire shared by a group of six men.

The aliens were preparing their dinner. A concoction of beans sizzled in a fire-blackened skillet. Another frypan was filled with toasting tortillas, expertly rolled out on a tree stump with a short stick by a slightly built Mexican in a straw cowboy hat. The only shelter in the camp was a sheet of black plastic strung between two trees. Sleeping blankets were spread on the ground.

It was cold in the orchards. With the sun down, the ground surrendered its heat rapidly. It was still October and a light jacket provided sufficient warmth, but Wendland wondered what it would be like in December and January, when the temperature in Phoenix dipped to freezing on many nights.

They talked with this group of aliens for nearly half an hour. The men complained bitterly of the long hours they had to put in to earn a dollar. One of the workers produced a green checkstub from Goldmar, showing earnings of less than forty dollars for what he said was nearly two weeks' labor. Noticing that the deductions section of the stub identified the alien with a Social Security number beginning with a series of zeros, Wendland asked if he could have the stub. The worker shrugged and handed it over. Wendland knew that genuine Social Security numbers never began with zeros.

This group of workers said they had walked all the way to Arrowhead, guided by a coyote who had charged them $125.

"There were twenty-four in my group," said the tortilla-maker. "Only twenty-three of us made it. We were crossing an arroyo on our third day when one of the men was bitten by a rattlesnake. The coyote said we had to leave him behind. I don't know what happened to him."

Another said he had seen a human skeleton on the trail.

"It is a very rough walk," he said. "Many things can happen in the desert."

Wendland and Drehsler exchanged glances, recalling the affidavits Lupe had shown them on the way out. These men had just verified the earlier information.

Lupe thanked the men for their time and led Wendland and Drehsler out of the groves to the main road. "It's dark now. We can take the road back to our car."

The walk back was quiet. The sky was a deep black velvet, illuminated by a maze of incredibly bright stars. From the road there was no way to discern the hidden life that went on inside the groves. As Wendland stepped into the car, he noticed something sticking to the bottom of his boot.

"Shit," Lupe said, pointing at Wendland's foot. "Human shit. There are no toilets in there. You have to watch where you step."

The visit had been depressing. The misery in the Arrowhead

groves was worse than the reporters had anticipated. During the drive back to Phoenix, they made plans to return to the ranch on the following Thursday to search for a large camp the aliens had said was located in another section of the groves.

The U.S. Border Patrol, a division of the Customs Bureau, is the government agency responsible for the enforcement of all laws regarding illegal immigrants. Early the next morning, Wendland was on the telephone setting up a meeting with Raymond Feld, head of the local office of the border patrol. He could hardly wait to get the government on record with some tough questions about Arrowhead.

Feld was a tall, slim man of forty-six, neatly dressed in the bright green border patrol uniform he had worn for the past twenty-one years. He was clearly nervous. But he was also more than willing to talk. In fact, he had just about had it with government service. Much of his dissatisfaction stemmed from the way his superiors had handled the Arrowhead case, he said, pulling out a sheaf of file cards which indicated that the ranch was the site of more wetback arrests than any other grower in the valley.

"Look, let me ask you this," he said, putting down the cards. "How many men do you think I have in this office?" Before Wendland could reply, he answered himself. "I'll tell you how many. Exactly four. That's right, four men. And I've got a 36,000-square-mile area to cover. That's as big as some states, all the way from here to the Utah border. We do what we can, but there's no way we can really keep Arrowhead or any other ranch clean."

Wendland asked why Feld didn't request extra help.

He laughed. "A few years back, I did. And on a couple of occasions, my district office in Tucson would send me a detail of a half-dozen agents for special enforcement. But we'd go out to Arrowhead expecting to make a complete roundup and the place would be as clean as a whisker. Nothing. Not one wet to be found on the whole place."

Feld later learned that spies from Arrowhead had somehow been tipped off on the impending raids and that Arrowhead supervisors secretly monitored the conversations of border patrol agents over government radios. "They even had people watching our office and the motels the extra agents stayed in. They knew every move we were going to make before we made it."

Since then the agency had been caught in a budget crunch. The U.S. Congress had made border areas the top priority, thereby relegating more distant offices like Phoenix to second-rank status. "All the money is being spent down in Tucson near the border. I couldn't get extra help up here for anything. But that's just part of the problem."

"What else is there?" asked Wendland.

Feld tensed. Then, with a sigh, he stood up and began to pace around his office. "A couple of years ago I wouldn't have said anything. But the service is damn well aware of what's going on out there. So I'll tell you. Maybe you guys in the media can do something."

Feld explained that alien arrests were easy to make. "We take them into custody and ship 'em back home. Next week, they're right back up here." The charge he wanted to make was harboring, getting to the organizers who profited by the smuggling and procuring of illegal workers. He had found such a case earlier that year. "The guy's name was Frank Sanchez. The workers call him Pancho. He's the number one foreman for Arrowhead."

That spring, Feld had developed an undercover informant, a local man who ran a mobile concession service that trucked coffee and sandwiches out to various farms for the fieldworkers. The man knew Frank Sanchez and, in February, reported to Feld that he had been approached and asked to transport wetbacks. Feld told him to go ahead and the trap was set.

"The informant was to be paid $150 a head. He agreed and met Sanchez after dark one night not far from Arrowhead. They piled eight wetbacks in my man's truck and off he went. All the way to Idaho, where Sanchez had set up a drop not far from Twin Falls. Okay, now my informant kept me posted every step of the way. As soon as the deal was set, I notified the patrol up in Idaho. They said they'd take care of it. We had the name of the ranch Sanchez had sold the wets to and everything. So what happens? Nothing, absolutely nothing. My man's back the next day and Idaho tells me they don't have the manpower to go search the ranch. I get on the phone with my superiors in Tucson and tell them. I beg and plead and offer to go up there myself to do it. They say no, that I can't work another district's territory."

Several days later Feld's informant was again approached by Sanchez and asked to make another run. Feld decided to trust that his agency would come through this time and authorized the second trip. Meantime, he had gathered telephone company records which proved

Sanchez was in contact with the Idaho ranch. The informant met Sanchez as before and drove to a secluded spot in the orchards. They got out of the informant's truck and Sanchez whistled in the darkness. Soon, a half-dozen wetbacks emerged from the trees. Sanchez was furious. He had told eight workers to meet him.

"But, señor, Jose and Juan say they do not want to go to Idaho," one of the wets explained, according to Feld's informant.

Sanchez told the informant to wait, that he would be right back. A half-hour later, the thick, muscular Sanchez returned, pushing two pathetic looking aliens ahead of him. One of them had obviously been beaten. He loaded all eight into the informant's truck, and they left, heading for another ranch in Idaho.

This time, the informant arrived at the drop-off point only to be met by the ranch foreman, who told him that they did not need so many workers. The foreman took only two of the men, leaving the informant with six others. The informant drove them to the Twin Falls office of the border patrol, dropped them off, and returned to Arizona.

Again, Feld was on the telephone, explaining the situation and requesting help in arresting Sanchez and the Idaho ranchers who had contracted with him for the illegal laborers. Again nothing happened.

"I had a solid case that would have busted a major alien smuggling ring," Feld said, providing Wendland with copies of the reports he had written and forwarded to his superiors. "They totally ignored it."

According to Feld, Sanchez was probably one of the state's biggest smugglers. "I personally know that he makes over $150,000 a year just running wetbacks." Sanchez was currently waiting deportation, said Feld, thanks to some nosing around by Phoenix agents, who had come up with a birth certificate proving that he was not an American citizen as he claimed, but a Mexican, born in the small town of Imuris, Sonora.

"But even that deportation is doubtful," Feld remarked disgustedly. "It's being appealed and won't be settled for a couple of years, at best. And you'll never guess who Sanchez's lawyers are. He's represented by the Martori law firm. And the Martoris, with Bob Goldwater, are the people who own and operate Arrowhead, Sanchez's own employers."

"Why is it that you are getting so little cooperation from your superiors?" asked Wendland.

"Who knows? I've tried to figure it out myself. All I can do is wonder if somebody high up has told the service to lay off Arrowhead."

"Somebody like Senator Barry Goldwater, for example?"

"Exactly. That's the only thing that could explain why the situation is so totally ignored. Goldwater's certainly got the clout. All I really know for sure is that the service is doing everything possible to ignore Arrowhead and keep me down."

"What do you mean, keep you down?"

Feld sat down. "I've told you this much, I might as well tell everything."

Feld had once had a drinking problem. It had developed the year before, and he had long since straightened it out, taking a leave of absence and coming to grips with himself. But back on the job and in the midst of his investigation into Arrowhead, the ax suddenly fell. "I was hauled in for a disciplinary action," he said. "They gave me a short suspension. I think the whole deal was intended to put pressure on me to not take my job so seriously, to lay off a bit."

The interview continued for another half-hour. Feld had kept good, solid records on his investigations and he allowed the reporter to make notes on them. After Wendland finished, Feld stood up and took him to a back room of the building where there was a coffeepot and a small hotplate. Feld filled a paper plate with beans he had cooked in a crockpot and treated the reporter to a lunch of beans and toasted tortillas.

"Look, I don't know what you are going to do with all this," he said as Wendland prepared to go. "Just remember one thing. What's going on out there at places like Arrowhead is not much better than slavery. Those wetbacks are being used and exploited. They are the real victims. And it's the big corporations, the agribusinesses who make millions because of the cheap labor, who deserve the punishment. Right now, that's not happening. They're just getting richer and everyone is turning their back to what's happening. *The Grapes of Wrath* was a Garden of Eden compared to the misery in those citrus fields."

Back at the Adams, Wendland spent the rest of the afternoon writing a memorandum on the Feld interview. He made a number of telephone calls to civil rights groups, legal aid workers, and various social agencies which came into contact with illegal aliens and the border patrol. In each case, Feld was described as an honest, compassionate man, hamstrung by a lack of manpower. Wendland contacted the informant Feld had used to infiltrate Sanchez's smuggling operation. The informant verified the story, adding one significant detail. "We were riding around the ranch one day and I asked Sanchez if Barry Goldwater was involved in Arrowhead—it was just idle conversation, really. Sanchez's face turned red and he slammed on the brakes. He turned to me and said to forget that name. He said if I ever mentioned it again, he'd break both my legs."

The next day, Thursday, October 14, Lupe was waiting out front of the union office at the arranged time. Because the three men were concerned about the health of the children they had seen during the first visit, they decided to bring along a nurse Lupe knew, a woman named Ann Morales. A tall, blonde, Anglo woman originally from Minneapolis, she was married to a UFW organizer and devoted herself to public nursing. From what Lupe had told her of the family's living conditions, she was worried.

Again they left the car in the county park just north of the ranch and made their way in beneath the barbed wire. There were no problems crossing the service road, and they were soon inside the groves at the camp where they had encountered the family. But the family was gone. The little sign warning of the nonexistent dog was still tacked to the lemon tree. But the blankets had been removed from the packing crate. The campfire ashes were cold.

The six men in the camp further in and towards the main road were still there. "Jesus," said Drehsler as they approached the camp, "I feel like a soldier in one of those old war movies. I feel like we ought to be bringing these poor people some chocolate bars or something."

They were greeted like old friends. The apprehension the wets had felt during the first visit was gone. Lupe introduced the nurse and asked them what had happened to the family. "They have gone back to Mexico," said one of the aliens. "The children were sick and there was no money." No one knew how the family would make it back, though the men assumed that the border patrol would spot them and they would be picked up. "On the way home, we do not hide," said another of the wetbacks. "The border patrol will give us a ride back to Mexico."

They chatted for about a half-hour before Lupe, Ann, and the reporters set off to find the large camp. It was supposed to be across the main road, deep within another section of the orchard.

"This is what you will never believe," said Lupe. "It is like an entire village."

"Good lord, I can't believe this," said Ann. "I thought I'd seen rotten living conditions, but this is the worst. This place is crawling with disease. Living like this with no sanitation facilities, these people can't help but become ill."

Wendland stopped her and pointed to the ground. She was about to step in a pile of dung. A brown-stained leaf from a lemon tree, used as toilet paper, partially covered it.

"I made that mistake the last time," he said.

"But, you see, those leaves are probably covered with parasites," she said. "They wipe themselves with the leaves and they get infected by them. I bet these people all have ringworm and intestinal infections."

They continued walking, scurrying across the road into the other side of the orchard. Ten minutes later, they found the main camp.

It was impossible to say how many people lived there. In the darkness, they could only see those they passed. But small campfires were everywhere for three and four rows across, a hundred yards long. Wendland tried to count just the men he could actually see. He stopped at a hundred. They were, as Lupe had predicted, standing in the middle of a small village. Thick, sweet-smelling smoke from mesquite logs filled the orchard. Workers lay or sat on the ground, chewing on tortillas and talking in low voices. A few of them had made shelters out of packing crates. Most slept beneath the trees, under sheets of plastic. As Lupe began talking with the men, a crowd slowly formed. Wendland offered one of them a cigarette. A flurry of hands appeared and the pack soon emptied.

The workers were not particularly upset about the sudden invasion, only curious. Lupe introduced Ann, who had been hungrily watched by a couple of them, and said she had come to help out the children. "She is a nurse," he said, looking straight at one of the watchers, who then cast his eyes downward. "And these are journalists, here to learn how hard you all must work."

Their stories were no different from those of the other wetbacks.

"I have a small farm," said one. "The coyote who came to my village said I could earn more here in a month than from my land in a year. So I came here. I make nothing, not even enough to feed my children one week. I will go home soon. But I don't know what to do. It is too late to seed my own land this year. I have nothing, señor, nothing."

The visit lasted for half an hour. Wendland was able to collect a couple of other Goldmar checkstubs, further documenting the low wages paid the wetbacks. Drehsler joined Lupe in questioning the men in Spanish, getting more information on Arrowhead's recruitment practices.

Despite the miserable conditions and obvious abuses that the reporters had observed, they would have to come back to Arrowhead at least one more time. They had to document what they had seen with photographs.

Meanwhile, new reporters were appearing at the IRE office in the Adams. By the start of the project's second weekend, Norm Udevitz of the *Denver Post* had arrived, and Harry Jones of the *Kansas City Star* had also checked in. Both men were in their late forties, slim of build with horn-rimmed glasses, and both were seasoned pros. Udevitz was the first westerner from outside of Arizona to work on the team. A native of Cheyenne, Wyoming, he had been a reporter for twenty-seven years, at one time owning and operating the *Wyoming Buffalo,* a small weekly that eventually folded for want of advertising. Since 1970, he had headed the *Denver Post*'s investigative efforts. Earlier in 1976, he had dispatched a team of *Post* reporters to the town of Trinidad, Colorado, exposing widespread corruption among public officials there. As a result of the *Post*'s reporting, a grand jury had indicted fifteen town leaders. Udevitz had never met Don Bolles in person, though he had often spoken to him on the telephone.

Jones, from Kansas City, also had wide experience in investigating organized crime and political corruption. He was a quiet, soft-spoken man who went to his room each evening at exactly six o'clock to change into a comfortable blue jumpsuit for his evening file reading. An excellent records man who had a reputation for dogging a story until he dropped, Jones was frequently the last reporter to leave the office and the first to arrive the next morning.

Both were assigned by Greene to back up Wendland and Drehsler on the visit to Arrowhead planned for the next Tuesday. Mike Padgett, an ASU student volunteer, would also go along as photographer. Married and in his mid-twenties, Padgett had worked at several small Phoenix-area newspapers as a reporter-photographer and knew his camera well.

Tuesday morning Wendland went through the Phoenix yellow pages, trying to find someone who would rent several walkie-talkies for use on the Arrowhead visit. He dialed half a dozen firms but struck out on each one'. Though they carried walkie-talkies, they would only lease them for extended periods of time.

"Look, all I need them for is about five hours," Wendland pleaded with the seventh man, the owner of an East Phoenix radio supply shop.

"Buddy, I don't care how long you want 'em for. These are expensive pieces of equipment. The only way I get to make any money is with long leases. It'll cost you fifty bucks each, whether you keep them a day or a month."

There were only two other companies listed in the phone book that he hadn't tried. This time, he took a different tack. Wendland's syndicated CB radio column was carried in the *Phoenix Gazette*, the city's morning paper. When the next shop owner came on the line, Wendland introduced himself as the CB writer. The shopkeeper recognized his name. Explaining that he was in Arizona to do some radio tests out in the desert, Wendland asked to rent three ultra-high-frequency walkie-talkies to keep in touch with his research assistants. The shopkeeper was delighted to cooperate. By three that afternoon, the Arrowhead team was equipped with three hand-held radios which could reach out for five miles, more than enough range for the job.

The reporters drove out in two cars. The first stop was at the western end of the Arrowhead groves, where a small white cross and a pile of rocks marked the spot where an illegal alien had died.

"He was picking fruit on a ladder," Lupe explained, as Padgett got out to photograph the grave. "Somehow, he slipped and came into contact with some power lines. Arrowhead just called the sheriff's office and asked them to remove the body. We found out about it from some of the other wets and took up a collection in the union to send the poor guy home for burial. Otherwise, he would have been planted in the unclaimed section of the county cemetery."

After Padgett had finished, the two cars made a U-turn and headed towards the section of the groves where they had found the main camp on the previous visit.

That's when they picked up the tail.

As the reporters' cars passed, a shiny new yellow pickup truck eased out from between two lemon trees. It had been parked there, rear first, as if the driver was waiting for someone. It stayed back a hundred yards or so, turning when the reporters turned, accelerating when they went faster, slowing down when they did.

"I'm going to lose this guy," crackled the voice of Drehsler over the radio in Wendland's car after about fifteen minutes. "Let's split up."

Drehsler turned east on a road that led to Black Canyon Highway, the main north-south route out of Phoenix. Wendland's car took a dirt cutoff a mile to the north, past the Arrowhead groves.

The man in the pickup paused, making up his mind. As the reporters hoped, he decided to stick with Drehsler.

Wendland's route wound its way past mesquite and cactus towards a range of small mountains. Lupe had been down the road before. "Keep going for another half-mile or so, then stop. We can hoof it to the groves," he instructed.

Twenty minutes later, Drehsler, the tail shaken, joined up with Wendland's group. Lupe picked up a stick and sketched out in the sand their rough position in relation to the main camp. It was five o'clock, time to get moving.

Again they divided. Lupe, Wendland, Drehsler, and Padgett would walk into the groves. Jones would stay where he was with one car, on the watch for anyone following the reporters into the orchard. Udevitz would take the other car and drive around to the opposite end of the groves, where he would have a clear view of anyone coming in from the front.

Lupe led the way. Four hundred yards out, there was a slight rise. He turned around to tell the group to stay down. Scrambling up it on hands and knees, he peeked across. On the other side was another pickup; the driver was waiting, watching.

"Shit," he said. "Those bastards are expecting us."

Lupe led the reporters south, roughly following the rise which divided the Arrowhead groves from the desert. They had walked for a quarter-mile when, some two hundred feet in front of them, they spotted a lone figure on foot. The man had just materialized, stepping out from between a couple of scrubby mesquite trees. Cradled across his arm was what was unmistakably a rifle or shotgun. He stood there, facing the opposite direction.

The reporters and Lupe dropped to the ground, hoping to take advantage of the low brush.

"Who is he?" Wendland asked. "A hunter?"

"He's a guard," said Lupe.

The reporters had two choices. They could turn around and go back to Jones, or they coud make a break for it, hoping to clear the rise before the gunman spotted them. If they called it off, there would not be another chance. The security was out in full force. It was now or never.

They were over the rise in seconds and kept running until they were well inside the groves. Then Lupe doubled back to see if the gunman was following. He returned a minute later with a smile.

"Let's go take those pictures and get the hell out of here," he said.

But the main camp was gone. It had been moved, obviously in a hurry. Sheets of plastic were still strung between the trees, and neat piles of kindling wood were stacked next to campfire ashes. But it was abandoned.

The reporters poked around as Padgett took photographs of a packing crate once used as a bed. They were about to move on when the walkie-talkie in Wendland's rear pocket crackled with static.

It was Harry Jones. "I've got company and he's got a gun." It was the same gunman the group had spotted moments before. He had stepped out of the brush a hundred feet behind Jones's parked car and was heading his way. "I'm not sticking around for any introductions," radioed Jones. "I'm going to join Norm."

He drove off, only to find his way out blocked by a light blue pickup truck. Jones stopped. He looked in his rear-view mirror and spotted a dark blue Volkswagen coming after him. It was the gunman. He looked around, hoping the desert sand was firm enough to get his Nova past the pickup. But just as he was about to try, the pickup slowly drove off, heading west. Jones didn't waste any time.

The Volkswagen continued following him. Jones turned north on Fifty-ninth Avenue. Then the pickup suddenly reappeared, joining the gunman in a caravan after Jones. Udevitz's car was on the shoulder of the road at the far northern edge of the groves. Jones pulled up next to him. As Jones got out of his car and walked over to his companion, the Volkswagen and the pickup slowly passed, only to turn around and stop a few hundred yards behind them.

"Look, we might as well be out front with this thing," Udevitz said. "Maybe we can get these guys to think we're border patrol or cops."

Udevitz and Jones got out of the car. Jones carried a walkie-talkie and pretended to be talking on it. Udevitz placed a pair of binoculars to his face, as if he were reading off the license numbers of the Volkswagen and pickup.

The ruse worked. The two observers drove off, heading back towards the Arrowhead offices.

Inside the groves, Padgett had finished taking his pictures of the abandoned camp.

"What I figure is that some of the wets told the foremen about our last visit," Lupe said. "So they busted up the main camp. Now, they sure as hell can't make that many men disappear. But what they probably did do was move them to other spots in the orchard and have them divide into smaller groups. All we got to do is find them."

It was Drehsler who first noticed the airplane.

A small, silver, single-engine craft with red fuselage striping, the plane was little more than five hundred feet above the trees, methodically following a nearby row of lemon trees across the orchard. It was definitely looking for something.

"Get under the trees," Lupe shouted as the plane swept by directly overhead.

Wendland got on the radio to Udevitz. "Watch that airplane."

A couple of minutes later, Udevitz had a message. "It's turning around, headed back your way."

This time it was even lower. Again it passed by.

"There are two people in it," radioed Udevitz, who was watching it from the road with his field glasses. "The passenger has binoculars and he's using them."

Time and time again, the aircraft buzzed the orchard. On each pass, the reporters ducked beneath the trees. Finally, as darkness enveloped the groves, it flew off.

For the next half-hour, the reporters explored the orchard, trying to find the aliens. There was nothing but darkness. They made their way to the main road and were about to cross it to search the other side when Udevitz again radioed them.

"A pickup, headed into the groves."

The reporters ran back into the orchard a few hundred feet, crouching beneath the trees. "It's shining its lights down the rows," informed Udevitz. "Stay down."

But the truck, too, soon departed, after making a half-dozen such looks. Ten minutes later, the reporters were across the orchard.

The six aliens they had talked to on the previous visits were still there. They were also clearly apprehensive about being visited again.

"The foreman, he told us that you are bad men, that you come to hurt us, to steal our things," said one of the aliens. "He said we should run away and tell him when you come back, that he will take care of you."

Lupe explained that they were reporters, who meant no harm.

"They come to see for themselves how hard you work and what little you get," said Lupe.

The alien shrugged his shoulders. Padgett hurriedly snapped a roll of pictures.

"Hey," said Padgett after he had finished, "I thought I had counted six of them."

Drehsler looked around. There were only five. Obviously, one had slipped off. "Little guess where he went," he said.

Thanking the workers, the invading party made a hasty path for the main road, where they were picked up by Udevitz.

For the next hour, the reporters waited in Thunderbird Park. Drehsler and Wendland drove off in one car to a small store back on Bell Road and returned with a twelve-pack of beer and some snacks. As a coyote howled off in the hills nearby, the group filled their stomachs, waiting for the Arrowhead security people to quit their search. The guards now knew they had been in the orchard. The flash from Padgett's camera had lit up a large area.

They set off again a little past nine, this time slowly cruising the roads that crisscrossed the ranch, looking down each row of citrus for light. Far off in the orchard's western section, they found a large camp of perhaps seventy-five aliens. As Lupe tried to banter with the men, Padgett took his photographs. The workers were not openly hostile, but it was clear that the presence of the strangers put them on edge. It was hard to tell who was the happiest to see the reporters leave, the wetbacks or the newsmen.

IRE had its photographs. The reporters could now document what they had seen inside the Arrowhead groves. That part of the story was wrapped up.

But there was much more to Goldmar, the firm that owned Arrowhead, than the exploitation of alien workers. And Goldmar was just one story.

6 | The Friends of Barry and Robert Goldwater

The team was rapidly settling into the investigation by the end of the second week. Groups of reporters were working a dozen different stories and the files were growing so rapidly that three women were hired to index the various reports and memorandums.

With just one exception, everyone got along famously. Reporters, particularly the investigative kind, are not renowned for their humility. The team's organizers had wondered at the beginning whether so many fragile egos could coexist within the confines of such a project. The reporters literally lived and worked together twenty-four hours a day. The nineteenth floor of the Adams resembled a college dormitory, with newsmen wandering in and out of each other's rooms around the clock.

The only exception was Peyton Whitely, a handsome, six-foot-four-inch young reporter from the *Seattle Times* who arrived just after the Arrowhead escapade. Whitely and Greene just did not hit it off. Whitely considered Greene too secretive and arrogant. Greene thought Whitely, who had the annoying habit of saying "huh," not as a question but as an exclamative, whenever someone spoke to him, a prima donna. For a few days, the two warily skirted one another. At dinner, Whitely's "huhs" constantly interrupted Greene's long, detailed stories. Whitely voiced skepticism on the progress of the investigation and complained to other reporters that Greene had blown up at him when he once tried to correct some minor inaccuracies in the files. On another occasion, Greene caught Whitely Xeroxing an IRE file that he had planned to send to his editors back in Seattle. Whitely lasted less than a week. For some time after he left, the other reporters found themselves saying "huh" a lot. The habit was catching.

Tom Renner, *Newsday*'s organized crime expert, remained "Deep 'n Dirty," Greene's expression for undercover. Special memos prepared by Renner on his various travels around the state would come into the IRE office almost nightly. Since nobody except Greene had laid eyes on him, the other reporters began to speculate on what he really looked like. Drehsler and Wendland kidded around by pointing

to a derelict on the street, winking, and whispering to colleagues—
"Tom Renner, he's a master of disguise." They continued the game
for weeks, fingering every strange looking character they spotted for
the elusive Renner. Gradually, Renner became a fixation with some
of the office workers. The only signs of his existence were an
occasional phone call and the amazingly comprehensive memos he
dispatched for the files each day. His "Deep 'n Dirty" status inspired
the reporters to draw up a design for a special T-shirt, depicting a
heavy-set, trench-coated reporter furtively scribbling in a notebook.
A local sports shop took the design and printed the shirts. But Greene,
promising to send one along to Renner, refused to let anyone wear
them outside the office until the project was done. Drehsler then
proposed a second T-shirt, to be given to all IRE news sources. "All
it will have on it is a giant bullseye," he smiled.

During the late evenings, some of the reporters had laid claim to a
small room off the hotel's downstairs bar. It was there that the
"Babaluba family" was born.

Weary of reading the exhaustively detailed background reports on
organized crime families, one night the reporters decided to create
their own, disguised as a memo from Renner. The mythical family
was headed by "Bobby (Bubba) Babaluba, of Burbank, who is big in
barbiturates, barbut, broads, booze, and bookmaking." The family's
hit man was "Bill (Bang Bang) Brown, a black, who was known to
use a Baretta, baseball bat, and blade, and was linked to the following
unsolved murders: Buster Bancom, a Barstow banker; Barney Bioff,
his brother; and Beatrice Bankoff, who Bang Bang bang-banged."
The memo was placed on Greene's desk the next morning. It ended
up, amid much laughter, as a special introductory file for all IRE
initiates.

Later, reporters wrote an obituary for their mythical mobster:
"Bobby (Bubba) Babaluba, 64, died last night while imbibing at the
Balboa Bay Bistro near Burbank with a big, boisterous banker from
the Bahamas. The bulbous bad guy reportedly barfed his last three
bonbons, blinked several times, and bent over the buffet bereft of
breath."

Not to be outdone, Diane Hayes, a schoolteacher hired to help out
with the indexing, and student volunteers Carol Jackson and Nina
Bondarook added a follow-up report on the activities of Babaluba's
wife: "Following the burial of her beloved Bobby Babaluba, a
bereaved Betty (Booby) Babaluba bopped back to Bisbee (Ariz.) for a

brief break from her bitter bereavement. While basking in the bright Bisbee sun Booby bumped into Bernard (Baby Face) Burgleburp, a butcher from Baskerville. As fate would have it, Booby and Baby Face became bosom buddies . . . browsing the boulevards buying big bottles of brandy and bouquets of buttercups to bind their budding affair. . . .''

The phony memo-writing continued. Harry Jones of the *Kansas City Star* took first prize for this parody of the typical dry style, including coded news sources, that each reporter used for legitimate memos:

QS-112, a knowledgeable source, has just returned from St. Louis, where he interviewed QS-113 surreptitiously about the mob's ties to the B.V.D. Co., which manufactured IRE's T-shirts.

B.V.D., he says, stands for Bianco-Vitale-DiGiovanni. The Biancos are very big into agribusiness in California. Vitale is a St. Louis mobster of long standing. The DiGiovannis of Kansas City (Scarface Joe and Sugarhouse Pete) are heavy into wholesale and retail liquor.

Cotton for B.V.D. comes from a twenty-acre plot south of Arrowhead Ranch near Phoenix. This twenty-acre plot is owned by Pablo Fellicinio, a half-Mexican, half-Sicilian son of an Apache squaw who is rumored to have married into the C. Arnolt Smith family back in the early 1920s. Fellicinio began as a cotton-picker but won ten of the present acres in a high-stakes poker game in 1931 from a nephew of Al Capone. The nephew's name is not known. Incorporation papers were destroyed in a hotel fire in Terre Haute, Ind., in 1948.

The cotton Fellicinio grows is processed through a Greek-Negro originally from St. Paul named Sambo Zarros, who has ties to Detroit's Black Mafia leaders from the late 1960s. Zarros originally was involved in the smuggling of hot piccolos and flutes from Vienna into New York, where several musicians fenced them to members of the Phoenix Philharmonic Orchestra, a major contributor to which has long been Barry Goldwater.

A Demaris-Reid book on organized crime, *The Cotton Picking Mafia*, relates that T-shirts were first invented in the southernmost province of Sicily in 1942; were brought to the U.S.A. by Lt. Col. Archie Tromboni, a U.S. Army officer who helped liberate Sicily during World War II (with mob help). Originally known as "underwear shirts" in Sicily, they were named after Tromboni, thus T-shirts.

Tromboni tried to set up a nationwide T-shirt syndicate but made the mistake of using Las Vegas as his headquarters. It was about this same time in the same city that Bianco, Vitale, and DiGiovanni (B.V.D., remember?) were in the process of importing Nevada sand to beaches near San Diego. Once they had formed and bled that company of its assets, they entered the washing machine business (probably to help them wash illegal gambling profits). This brought Vitale into contact with the ex-colonel, Tromboni, whose nephew, Thomas (Tootie) Tromboni, promptly married Vitale's daughter by an earlier marriage. The nuptial link was not enough, however, to prevent a Vitale hit man from drowning the elder Tromboni in a late-model washing machine in 1959, enabling Vitale to acquire majority stock ownership in T-Shirt Enterprises, which became B.V.D. Co. in 1964.

Of major interest now is how IRE happened to contract with B.V.D. for its Deep 'n Dirty T-shirts, and whether they will shrink when washed.

No one topped Jones's memo, which remained tacked on the IRE bulletin board for the duration of the project.

Nonsense aside, the project was moving along rapidly.

Good, solid contacts had been made with the Intelligence Unit of the Phoenix Police Department, the so-called "I Squad," an elite, twenty-one-man division of police detectives who specialized in keeping track of mobsters and organized crime. Renner had returned from his forays with high praise for the unit. "We can trust them," he told Greene not long after the project began. "Their reputation is spotless." Incredible as it sounded, in a state torn apart by organized crime, the I Squad was the only outfit of its kind in Arizona. Greene and Drehsler made quiet contact with the unit.

Operating out of a series of cramped, cubbyhole offices filled with file cabinets and cardboard boxes jammed tight with reports, the squad's organized crime operations were directed by Lt. Glenn Sparks, a political science graduate from ASU. Dapper of dress and soft-spoken, the slightly-built, forty-three-year-old Sparks listened carefully as Greene made the pitch.

"We obviously need help," Greene explained. "You're the man and this is the unit that can provide it. What we need is cooperation."

Sparks was actually glad to see the team come into his state. Though he knew the reporters' findings could seriously damage Arizona's national reputation, perhaps this group of outsiders could put things in perspective. Things were way beyond control. Organized criminals had been flocking to the state in recent years. The squad was hopelessly undermanned. Despite many unsolved murders, rampant land fraud, and obvious signs of political corruption, nobody in authority seemed to give a damn. Yeah, he told Greene, he'd help, he'd do whatever he could.

For starters, the reporters were interested in learning more about the status of the Bolles case.

Sparks then told them about a small white card with a childish code.

From this clue the reporters not only learned more about the conspiracy that led to Bolles's murder, but, more importantly, came to understand the hopeless position law enforcement in Phoenix had found itself in during the summer and fall of 1976.

Lonzo McCracken was a forty-two-year-old detective with the Phoenix Police Department. He worked with Sparks in the I-Squad and was a good friend of Don Bolles. Besides a sort of professional bond stemming from McCracken's work in investigating land fraud, an area Bolles himself had once concentrated on, the two were bound by something much more personal. Each had a child with severe hearing problems. They saw each other frequently as members of a parents' group for the hard-of-hearing child. Another member of that group was Mickey Clifton, a Phoenix attorney.

It was Clifton who provided police with the card. And how he got it shed significant light on the Bolles killing.

A moderately successful lawyer who did a lot of his drinking in the same North Central Avenue cocktail lounges frequented by Adamson, Clifton was more than interested in the Bolles case. He knew both the victim and the suspect. So he was surprised when, shortly after the Bolles bombing, Adamson approached him with an incredible tale. Whether Adamson was looking for legal advice or just shooting off his mouth, Clifton never really knew. But Adamson wanted Clifton to know that he had planted the bomb beneath the reporter's car.

Further, Adamson said he had been hired to kill one other person, a man named Al Lizanetz, a colorful local character known to police and the news media as King Alfonso. Once an employee of rancher Kemper Marley, Lizanetz had devoted the past two years to a campaign of letter writing and pamphleteering, accusing Marley and a handful of Phoenix businessmen of graft and corruption. Most people had written Lizanetz off as a harmless crackpot, since his allegations were both vague and unsupported.

But the person who hired him to kill Bolles, Adamson told Clifton, also wanted him to murder Lizanetz. That person, said Adamson, had given him a small white card to use if he ever needed lawyers or cash. Then, incredibly, Adamson gave Clifton the card, explaining only that he didn't want it anymore.

At the top right side of the card was a code name for the man Adamson said hired him: "John Smith." To the left of the code name was written ''Yellow 782'' and ''White 286.'' These were references to the page numbers in the telephone directory's yellow and white pages where Adamson could reach two contacts for ''John Smith.'' Adamson said he was supposed to call these contacts not only for money and legal help, but also if he had some message to pass to ''Smith.''

Apparently, this simple code was too complicated for Adamson. Thus, the full names and phone numbers of the contacts were written in right below the code. The first name was ''Dwight Charles Flickinger—258-8831.'' Flickinger was also an attorney, a law partner of James Colter, the chairman of the Republican Party for the state of Arizona. Under Flickinger's name was written ''Max Dunlap— 265-5914.'' Dunlap, who had used a third partner in the Flickinger-Colter law firm, Benton L. Blake, as his attorney, was the Lake Havasu contractor who was the business partner and protégé of rancher Kemper Marley.

After Adamson showed him the coded card, Clifton didn't know what to do. He recognized the significance of the names he had seen. This could be proof of a conspiracy. Adamson had not asked him for legal advice. So technically there was no counsel-client relationship. Clifton was sickened by the coolness with which Adamson had confessed the killing but he was also frightened. Now he knew. Was he in danger? Briefly, Clifton debated whether he should keep Adamson's admission secret. But he had known and liked Don Bolles and, in good conscience, could not remain silent. He called Detective McCracken.

He was almost in tears. For one thing, he was frightened. Adamson had come to him as a friend. He gave the information to McCracken, asking for anonymity.

The card and Adamson's remarks to Clifton pointed to one man: Kemper Marley.

McCracken turned over a full report to the department's Homicide Division, which was handling the Bolles investigation. And Intelligence was told to stay out of the case.

All of this had transpired the week after the Bolles killing, Sparks told the reporters. It was now mid-October. And Adamson was still the only person charged in the case.

''Jesus,'' Drehsler said. ''I can't believe it.''

Greene wanted information on the Maricopa County prosecutor's office. Specifically, he wanted to know about Moise Berger, who had suddenly resigned as County Attorney a few weeks after the Bolles killing. Greene had heard that the police had a tape recording in which Berger laid open the problems the office was having.

There was indeed such a tape, secretly recorded by Detective McCracken on August 4, 1975, when Berger came to the I-Squad to discuss the frustrations lawmen were experiencing with organized crime prosecutions. According to his long, rambling conversation, Berger was a bitterly disillusioned man.

"I think what's going on is this," the tape transcript quoted Berger as saying to McCracken. "I think, this is my own personal belief and it's not professional, but I think you guys are being held back."

"Like a, City Council or a . . . ?"

"Yeah, I think they are secretly keeping you from getting the people you need, and I think the reason is they know damn well, if you had a large enough staff—some of the people you would get. I think this is true over on our side, too. I think those guys on the Board of Supervisors feel the same way, that if we had the people they would be afraid of what we would be doing."

"Yeah," McCracken agreed. "I thought about that. I wondered why the state, even at the state level, why they don't put twenty investigators on it."

"Yeah, you been frustrated a lot of times on cases," Berger acknowledged. "And I've been frustrated the same way. See, I know these bastards are out to get me."

McCracken wanted the prosecutor to be more specific. "You mean the Board of Supervisors, or a . . .?"

"It's not just the Board. You know, I feel like there's a coalition out there of people." At the head of the power structure Berger put Harry Rosenzweig, the longtime GOP power broker and chief financial backer of Barry Goldwater. "It starts with Rosenzweig," Berger continued on the tape recording, "who's pissed off first of all because I didn't do some favors for them. They wanted me to drop some cases, reduce some charges, and I wouldn't do it."

"Yeah," said McCracken, wanting him to keep talking.

"Rosenzweig, he calls up the Board and tells those guys, don't give the county attorney anything because he's not playing ball. Okay, so that's the way that goes. Then we start finding out that Rosenzweig has got himself involved in some of this."

"Yeah, involved," offered McCracken, keeping Berger going.

"Yeah, prostitution, I feel that prostitution in this state is being allowed. Now I'm not a moralist, you know what I mean. You know, probably in a lot of respects prostitution is in some ways a good thing.''

"Yeah."

"But on the other hand, we do have it on our books as against the law," Berger said. "And we have a lot of it going on involving some very prominent people. Some of these people are guys like Rosenzweig, who's been involved in it. And I don't think these things are by accident. I think everybody in power, back there behind the scenes, is working together. There is a power structure out there.''

Briefly, the conversation turned toward Berger's own problems in getting additional manpower and a proposal then being debated before the Maricopa County Board of Supervisors which would appoint a special prosecutor outside of Berger's office, staffed with six investigators.

"But why have it that way except that those guys would not be answerable to me," Berger told the police officer. "They would never investigate Rosenzweig or any of these other things. Now they are getting scared. Because you see what's happening. With you working and gradually developing any of this stuff, more and more of it is kind of leaking out, it's coming out front.''

"Well," said McCracken, "just keep pecking away at it. It's about the only thing we can do, you know.''

"Yeah. But you end up with the same damn frustrations for years.''

"Yeah."

"And the reason is very simple," said Berger. "The goddamn lid is on the son-of-a-bitch all the way from the very top.''

Berger did not know the conversation with McCracken was being taped. But the officer did so for good reason. Under Berger, organized crime prosecutions had dwindled to a mere trickle. While the police could make the cases, the prosecutor's office was not taking them to court. McCracken submitted a formal report, dated January 19, 1976, with a complete transcript of the secret recording.

Concluded the officer: "These statements by Berger clearly indicate that he is not his own master and he is told what cases are not to be prosecuted. Considering this is true, it goes a long way in explaining Berger's actions as the County Attorney and his track record.''

The tape transcript gave the reporters several major new leads and a shopping list of details that needed confirmation.

The first person the team wanted more information on was Harry Rosenzweig. For Rosenzweig, a stately, gray-haired man nearing the age of seventy, was clearly the "Mister Big" of Arizona.

Rosenweig was "old family," a native Phoenician born and educated in the city when it was still a dusty cowtown. In October 1976, he and his younger brother, Burke, ran Rosenzweig's Jewelers, a venerable old firm opened by their father in 1912, the same year the Arizona Territory was admitted into the Union.

Harry's business, civic, and political biography filled two type-written pages. He was a founder of the North Central Development Company, which immodestly named its impressive downtown financial development the Rosenzweig Center. He was on the board of the Phoenix Art Museum, helped found the city's Better Business Bureau, raised funds for Phoenix's leading charities, served as president of the Downtown Merchants Association, and belonged to the prestigious Phoenix Country Club and the old-line Arizona Club.

It was Rosenzweig who masterminded the successful 1952 Senate race of his boyhood chum, Barry Goldwater. Since then, he had been Goldwater's chief financial backer and fund-raiser. He was one of Goldwater's closest advisers during the senator's unsuccessful run for the presidency in 1964 and was a national Republican committeeman, state GOP chairman, and Maricopa County Republican Committee finance boss. Rosenzweig was the only person by Goldwater's side the night the senator's presidential ambitions ended in the crush of Lyndon Johnson's landslide. In state and local politics, Rosenzweig's word was law, thanks to the dozens of legislators, county supervisors, and judges who owed their political existence to his power.

Rosenzweig's open second-floor office, its walls filled with "Man of the Year" awards and autographed photographs of his political pals, overlooked the main floor of his downtown jewelry store. Each afternoon he could be seen holding court up there for those who needed favors, while below, nervously pacing between the diamond showcases, the next petitioner waited.

But the IRE files also painted a different picture of Harry Rosenzweig.

Back in 1952, the year he ran Goldwater for the Senate, Harry had done a big favor for a friend of his, a man known as William Nelson. A reporter from the *Arizona Republic* had discovered that "William Nelson" was really Willie Bioff, a convicted pimp and extortionist living under an assumed name given him by the FBI after Bioff's ten-year sentence for labor racketeering had been reduced in exchange for testimony against five members of Al Capone's old gang. The reporter, who was tipped to the hoodlum's identity by an anonymous caller, had written a story exposing Nelson-Bioff. The story never ran, thanks to Harry Rosenzweig's power.

For a man supposed to be in hiding, the stocky, bespectacled Bioff had been extremely visible, lunching three times a week with Rosenzweig, hobnobbing with the elite of Phoenix society at the stodgy old Arizona Club, and wheeling and dealing his way between Phoenix and Las Vegas as a virtual commuter.

How Harry Rosenzweig had met Nelson-Bioff no one could find out. Reporters who had uncovered the relationship years before were simply told that Rosenzweig had always known him as an honorable gentleman whose past was old history. Indeed, when Nelson-Bioff came to Rosenzweig in 1952, telling him of the impending newspaper story, Rosenzweig said he was shocked and saddened. He said he believed that Bioff had reformed. So Rosenzweig went to Gene Pulliam, the crusty, conservative owner of the *Republic* and persuaded him to spike the Bioff story.

A grateful Bioff then gave Rosenzweig $5,000 as a "contribution" to Goldwater's senate race.

Their friendship blossomed and grew by two: Senator Goldwater and Gus Greenbaum. Soon Bioff was accompanying Goldwater to various social events around the state, often flying aboard the senator's private airplane. Greenbaum, who had come to Phoenix in 1928 from Chicago and had become the controlling power in Arizona gambling, eventually hired Bioff to help him in Las Vegas, where Greenbaum took over the mob's interests in Las Vegas gambling, first at the Flamingo, then at the Riviera. Goldwater several times visited Greenbaum in Vegas.

The foursome lost one of its members on November 4, 1955. That's when Bioff's mob associates, angered by his past history of informing and his carelessness with funds, planted a bomb in his pickup truck and blew him to bits. At the inquest into the murder, which remains unsolved, Bioff's widow, Laurie, named Rosenzweig as one of her husband's closest friends. Attending the funeral with Rosenzweig was Senator Goldwater. Questioned by reporters, Goldwater first maintained he knew nothing about Bioff's background. Later, he claimed to be using Bioff as a source of information about labor racketeering.

Rosenzweig, reporters later discovered, had borrowed $10,000 from Bioff several days before the murder. He had used the money to finance a cotton venture he and the senator's brother, Robert, were undertaking in Fresno, California. Rosenzweig said he repaid the loan to Mrs. Bioff a few days after the killing.

Meanwhile, the fast-talking Greenbaum continued as the guardian of the mob's Vegas interests. For a while, he did well. But then he began drinking and gambling like there was no tomorrow. His lifestyle of booze, broads, and blackjack eventually took its toll on his health. A Vegas doctor gave him heroin to soothe his jangled nerves. Addiction followed.

Back in Phoenix for a rest, on December 3, 1958, Greenbaum and his wife were found with their throats slit. Again, there were no arrests, though police learned that the mob had tried to pressure him to retire from Vegas. Unfortunately, Greenbaum was trapped: if he ever did leave, his successor would surely discover the skimming he had done at the Riviera to cover his gambling losses.

Goldwater and Rosenzweig attended his funeral, as they had Bioff's. Rosenzweig even volunteered to serve as the appraiser for the Greenbaum estate. Confronted by reporters after the funeral, Goldwater said once again that he had no idea of Greenbaum's background.

There were other mob associations in the backgrounds of both Rosenzweig and Senator Goldwater which IRE reporters dug up in old police files and court records.

Clarence "Mike" Newman, a childhood friend of both Rosenzweig's and Goldwater's, had inherited Phoenix's gambling action when Greenbaum and Bioff moved to Las Vegas. In 1959, Newman was arrested by federal authorities in a crackdown on the widespread gambling activity in Phoenix. On the day that Newman was sentenced by Federal Judge David M. Ling, Harry Rosenzweig was in the courtroom, observing the proceedings. Court officials later admitted that Rosenzweig and Senator Goldwater had personally intervened on behalf of their friend, persuading the judge to hand down a light sentence. Newman drew just a six-month prison term.

And then there was Morris B. "Moe" Dalitz, the contact man between the mob and the rich Teamsters Union pension fund, who helped consolidate mob control in the Southwest in the late 1940s with the likes of Meyer Lansky, Bugsy Siegel, and Peter Licavoli, Sr. Identified in the 1950 Kefauver hearings as a top U.S. gangster, Dalitz was a golfing partner of Robert Goldwater, and he invited the

Goldwater brothers, who were then running the family department store, to open a branch store in his Desert Inn in Las Vegas, a venture which proved extremely lucrative for the Goldwaters.

If the information contained in the McCracken-Berger tape was accurate, it appeared that Harry Rosenzweig, Barry Goldwater's close friend and associate, Phoenix's "Man of the Year" in 1975, might be involved in criminal activities like prostitution and in influencing the prosecution of certain criminal cases as the head of a "coalition" of men who ran Phoenix.

On October 15, Greene and Drehsler decided to pay a call on Don Harris, Berger's appointed successor in the office of county attorney, to see where he stood on the issue of political corruption. A slim, dark-haired man in his late thirties, Harris had been born in Brooklyn and had moved to Arizona with his family at thirteen. As a lawyer, he had done well for himself in private practice, earning upwards of $100,000 a year handling mostly corporate and business clients as well as representing professional athletes in contract negotiations. Since taking the interim appointment, he had appeared on the CBS television program "Sixty Minutes" and had consented to dozens of interviews with magazine and newspaper reporters investigating the Bolles case. In many instances, his remarks extended beyond the case into the nebulous area of speculation. His frequent comments provided plenty of ammunition for Adamson's defense attorneys, who were sure to charge that pretrial publicity had jeopardized their client's chance for a fair trial.

Greene and Drehsler picked Harris up at his office for lunch. Harris suggested Durant's Restaurant on North Central Avenue. IRE files identified Jack Durant, the owner of the restaurant, as a past associate of the murdered hoodlum Gus Greenbaum. Greene and Drehsler exchanged glances as they drove to the crowded, single-story eating spot.

For several minutes, the reporters made small talk, explaining who they were and why they were in Arizona, that they were looking into gambling, organized crime, official corruption, land fraud, and narcotics.

Harris quickly volunteered that he had given up his high-rolling habits in Las Vegas for the duration of his appointment. "I've told the people who provide me with the junkets to stay away until my term is over in ninety days," he said.

He was asked what he knew about Gus Greenbaum. "Nothing,"

Don Bolles, the reporter whose murder was the catalyst for the Arizona Project.

Downtown Phoenix. In the rectangular building at center was the Adams Hotel office of the IRE reporters.

Border fence between Nogales, Arizona, and Nogales, Sonora, Mexico. The bottom of the hill is known as "smuggler's gulch" because of its heavy narcotics traffic. The twin cities of Nogales are seen in the background.

United Press International Photo

Wide World Photos

These are the men linked to the murder of reporter Don Bolles. *Top left* is John Harvey Adamson, the confessed killer, who lured Bolles to his death. Adamson said the killing was ordered by millionaire Kemper F. Marley (*top right*) through land developer Max Dunlap (*bottom left*). *At bottom right* is Adamson's pal James Robison, who detonated the bomb under Bolles's car. Adamson, Dunlap, and Robison have all been found guilty of first-degree murder. Marley has not been charged, though the investigation is continuing.

The mob and a judge. *At top left* is Joseph (Joe Bananas) Bonanno, and (*top right*) Peter Licavoli, Sr., Arizona's major organized crime leaders. *At bottom left* is Bonanno's son Joe, Jr., whose jury conviction for conspiracy to murder was mysteriously reversed by Chief Federal Judge Walter E. Craig (*bottom right*).

A long string of death. *At top left* is Ned Warren, Sr., the self-styled 'godfather'' of Arizona's land fraud racket, who owes his start to former (now dead) State Real Estate Commissioner J. Fred Talley *(top right)*. A number of Warren's associates have met sudden death in recent years. *At bottom left* is Anthony Serra, killed in prison after promising to tell all to an IRE source. Warren's accountant, Edward Lazar *(bottom right)*, was shot to death the day after he appeared before a grand jury investigating his boss.

he replied. "I was too young when he was around. All I know is that he was the biggest bookie in the state."

Slowly, the reporters steered the conversation towards Harry Rosenzweig, who had been so close to Greenbaum.

Harris was eager to talk about Rosenzweig, whom he described as a "highly respected man." He confessed to Greene and Drehsler that Rosenzweig and Barry Goldwater, whom he called "Mister America," had been his boyhood idols. Harris was proud of serving on a couple of civic groups with Rosenzweig.

The reporters then brought up the police tape of Moise Berger. The existence of the tape had not been entirely secret. Reporters from the *Republic* had written a story about it several months earlier, though Rosenzweig's name had never made it into print.

Harris said he had not read the *Republic* story, nor a later piece run by the *New York Times*. However, he had read a *Time* magazine article which referred to Berger's remarks and to an allegation that Berger had been romantically involved with a secretary who worked for a land sales company owned by Ned Warren, the swindler and land fraud artist Berger had been unsuccessfully prosecuting before he left office.

Greene wanted to know whether the taped remarks by Berger might warrant an investigation into Rosenzweig's influence.

"I don't know about any admissions by Berger," said Harris, as his tone suddenly chilled. "Look, I have only been in office since August 11."

Drehsler pointed out that the publicity over the tape had appeared after Harris took office.

"I told you, I haven't seen the article."

"But you knew that such a tape had apparently been made, or at least that it was being discussed," countered Greene.

"I don't know what the hell is supposed to be on any such tape."

"Then don't you think you should find out, be more aggressive in seeking out the tape and finding out what it contains?" asked Greene.

Harris, looking over his shoulder, became angry and defensive. "Look, I am not going to be a puppet for you guys. If you can show me evidence that there is a tape of some kind, then I'll call a grand jury investigation on Monday morning because Berger may have committed crimes."

The reporters knew that the actual tape recording had been destroyed by the police. But a transcript existed. And the reporters had a copy of it. "There is such evidence," Greene said. "We have some information that clearly indicates there was a tape."

"Fine, bring it into my office this afternoon."

Greene realized that Harris was pulling a fast one. If he was sincerely interested in pursuing the tape, he could simply order the police to provide him a copy of the transcript. No—Greene and Drehsler believed that what Harris really wanted was to get them into his office and trip them into some sort of comment which could later be used to discredit the IRE investigation. The only tape that would come from such a meeting, Greene believed, would be Harris's recording of it.

"We're tied up this afternoon," said Greene, "but maybe we can work something out with you next week so you can see what I have."

"Fine."

But there was something that Harris had said a moment before that the reporters wanted to pick up on. "Look, you said that if such a tape existed, you'd want to investigate Berger. But if what Berger was supposed to have said on it was true, wouldn't Rosenzweig be equally guilty of a conspiracy? What we're wondering, quite frankly, is whether this lack of aggression on your part is due to the fact that Rosenzweig is a sacred cow around here?"

Harris vehemently denied it, repeating that if the reporters could show evidence of such a tape, then he would call a grand jury to look into the matter.

Again, the reporters felt it wasn't their job to provide the tape transcript. They were newsmen, not volunteer prosecutors. Besides, if Harris really wanted it, he knew where to look.

The interview ended without lunch. Harris said he was late for an appointment and had to return to his office. As they dropped him off at the downtown county building, Harris said he wished he had more time to spend with the reporters and would have to invite them out to his house for dinner and a long, uninterrupted talk some night. The reporters agreed, realizing full well that no such invitation would be forthcoming.

So far, there was no reason to suspect that the secret transcript they had obtained was unreliable. But to be sure, there was one other person who had to be contacted: Moise Berger, the former county attorney.

Berger had left Phoenix in August under a cloud. He had been accused of hiding a large stack of documents indicating payoffs to state real estate officials by land fraud artist Ned Warren, Sr. Berger denied any knowledge of the whereabouts of the missing documents, which had been provided to the county attorney's office by a Warren associate. He claimed that the papers had been "lost" by one of his assistant attorneys. Then the *Time* magazine story had intimated that he had been involved with one of Warren's secretaries. None of the allegations had ever been proven, but, together with his failure to nail Warren, the state's most infamous swindler, they had seriously damaged his reputation. After relocating in California, where he quickly passed the bar examination, he obtained a job as an instructor at the Western State University College of Law.

On October 24, Harry Jones, the *Kansas City Star* reporter, flew to San Diego.

Arriving at Berger's new office at the college, Jones found that he had just missed his source. A secretary said Berger had left for home fifteen minutes before. Jones got Berger's address and home phone number and killed a half-hour walking the downtown streets to give Berger time to get home.

He dialed the number from a pay telephone booth. Berger answered the call. Jones identified himself, going easy, hoping not to spook his source. He suggested that they meet face to face that evening or the next morning, a Saturday.

"Sure," said Berger, "I think I can swing it tonight. Let me check with my wife."

So far so good, thought Jones as he waited for Berger to come back to the phone.

A couple of minutes passed. Then Berger returned, explaining that he couldn't locate his wife, who must be across the street visiting neighbors. Could he call Jones back in half an hour?

"No, I'm in a pay phone. Let me call you." Jones had been that route before, when a source promised to call back and then never did. This was a bad sign. Once a source agreed to talk, it had to be followed through with immediately. Otherwise, he could too easily change his mind.

And that's exactly what had happened when Jones called back.

"Look, I've thought it over and I really don't want to see you," said Berger. "I don't know anything that would be of any help to you anyway."

Jones couldn't let it drop there. He asked about the police tape. Yes, Berger was now aware of its existence. No, he had never bothered to request a transcript; he was sure it was accurate. Beyond that, he had nothing more to say.

Bingo. Jones had at least gotten Berger to confirm the meeting with police and the fact of the tape.

"On the tape, you said that you had been approached by Rosenzweig and asked to drop some cases," said Jones. "Which cases were they?"

Berger hesitated. He didn't want to answer. Jones kept pushing.

"I really can't remember. Oh, wait, there was the Erskine case. Yeah, Rosenzweig came to me and asked me to ease up. I wouldn't do it. It really didn't make any difference. The case finally went to a jury and the kid was acquitted."

The "kid" Berger spoke of was John Erskine, a nephew of Barry Goldwater's, who had been arrested in 1975 on a charge of selling marijuana to undercover police officers.

A telephone is the worst possible medium for interviewing a reluctant news source. It always works to the source's advantage. In in-person encounters, a reporter can usually press a subject as far as necessary. Only rarely does the source cut it short. There's something about personal contact that compels most people to be polite.

Berger obviously had nothing more to say. Jones thanked him, gave him the IRE phone number in Phoenix, and urged him to call if there was anything more that he could think of. Berger could not have hung up faster.

Meanwhile, other reporters were either en route or arriving daily. As October entered its final week, George Weisz joined up.

At twenty-five, just graduated from the University of Arizona in Tucson with a Master's in public administration, Weisz could have chosen any one of several careers. His father is William Weisz, the Motorola Corporation's board president. George's future was assured if he wanted to go into business. But he didn't. George wanted to be a cop. His thesis was a 400-page dissection of Tucson's notorious organized crime structure. During the nearly three years spent preparing it, Weisz had made contact with a large number of journalists throughout the West. It was Dick Lyneis, a reporter from the *Riverside* (Calif.) *Press*, who first thought of Weisz when the IRE project started. An IRE board member, Lyneis was familiar with Weisz's knack for research and analysis. He knew that the kid had just graduated the past summer and was job hunting, hoping to hook up with a police agency. Lyneis tracked him down in Chicago, where

Weisz was staying with his parents, and asked him if he would like to join the IRE team as an analyst-researcher. Weisz was ecstatic. Now he had a chance to do some real work, to follow through on some of the leads he had been developing from school. He accepted on the phone.

However, there was one hitch. IRE had no money to pay him. He would have to cover his own expenses. "My father may be rich, but that doesn't mean I am," Weisz explained. "I supported myself through school. Everything I've done, I've paid for." And he was just about broke. He told Lyneis that he just couldn't afford the trip.

For two days, he was thoroughly depressed. The IRE people were doing what he had always dreamed of—investigating organized crime and political corruption with a free hand. This was an opportunity that would not happen again. Besides, he hadn't earned anything from the thesis research. What was a few more months of free work? He telephoned Lyneis back and said he'd come after all. He found a free place to stay in Scottsdale at the home of a fraternity brother, and was in Phoenix with four huge boxes of research notes the last week of October.

Greene was delighted. Weisz was just the sort of person the team needed. Though he wasn't a journalist, he had the keen mind of an accountant. He could sort through hundreds of pages of corporate and financial records and plot out A to Z. There were a number of individuals and firms that needed such analysis. Weisz was very welcome indeed.

After the excitement of the Arrowhead Ranch escapade, the reporters were ready for more. Most newsmen like the world to think they are fatalists and seldom aroused. In truth, like small boys chasing firetrucks, reporters crave action.

They were disappointed to learn that Greene had more record checking in mind.

"Now we've done well so far," he told the group at the morning staff meeting the day after Weisz arrived. "But where did the leads come from? The files, that's where. So right now, we're going back to them. We've got a lot of holes to fill."

One of the first had to do with Arrowhead, its origins and owners. After a few days of record checking and analysis, the reporters had filled these holes.

The first transaction the IRE team examined occurred in 1955, when Detroit mobsters Joseph Zerilli and William "Black Bill"

Tocco and produce broker Carl Jarson purchased the ranch. In his interview with Wendland, Jarson had intimated that the hoodlums had been minority partners in the Arrowhead operation. But files dug out of musty county recorder offices showed otherwise. Reporters found telegrams from Zerilli and Tocco which dictated the arrangements under which Arrowhead would be set up. The telegrams showed they were clearly in command.

Around the same time as the Arrowhead purchase, Zerilli, Tocco, and Jarson joined with several other men to form a fruit marketing association. One of their new partners was John Curci, a California and Arizona grower.

But further research produced even better information. The records indicated that on July 21, 1955, the Zerilli group first bought 3,900 acres, paying $2.6 million, or about $658 per acre. The terms of the purchase called for a $1.8 million mortgage, a down payment of $550,000, and the remaining $710,000 due on January 3, 1956. All that was standard enough.

What happened next wasn't. For according to the records, on the very same day that Zerilli's combine made its initial purchase—July 21, 1955—it sold 975 of the acres. Zerilli's selling price on his newly bought land was $1,258 an acre, or almost double the per-acre price he had just paid.

Who was the buyer foolish enough to pay so much? None other than one Arnold S. Kirkeby of Los Angeles. Kirkeby was an international financier with big mob connections. Before his death in a 1962 plane crash, Kirkeby was linked to Chicago mob interests. He was also the former owner of the National Hotel in Havana, Cuba, where mob moneyman Meyer Lansky had his office and operated the hotel gambling casino. Kirkeby and Lansky also knew Zerilli.

Zerilli's sale to Kirkeby meant that, in effect, he didn't have to pay a cent for Arrowhead. Under the terms of the agreement, the 975 acres were sold for $1.2 million. Zerilli got a down payment of just over $750,000—or $200,000 more than the down payment he had to come up with in the first place. The balance of Kirkeby's money was due on January 3, 1956, and thus would help to cover Zerilli's second payment, due that same day to the ranch's original owners.

The next owner of Arrowhead bought in some four years later. He was Del Webb, probably Phoenix's best-known citizen. Originally a carpenter who moved to Arizona in the 1920s, he became a respected national developer of shopping centers, retirement communities, office complexes, and hotels. For twenty years (1945–65) he was a part-owner of the New York Yankees. A personal friend of former presidents Franklin D. Roosevelt and Dwight D. Eisenhower as well as of ex-FBI head J. Edgar Hoover, Webb was a self-made man and financial wizard, eulogized after his death on the Fourth of July, 1974, as the "personification of the American success story." He was the Roy Rogers of the land development business. Yet there he was in a puzzling business deal with two well-known Mafia hoodlums.

The deal was puzzling for a couple of reasons. Greene had Les Whitten and Larry Kraftowitz, two of syndicated columnist Jack Anderson's best reporters, go through the Securities and Exchange Commission records in Washington, since Webb's company was a public corporation. They reported back that SEC records noted a purchase price of $3.8 million. But newspaper clips from the *Arizona Republic*'s morgue contained an announced price of $5 million. Reporters scouring through public records put the price at $3.4 million.

It appeared that there were three different price tags for the ranch.

One thing was clear: the Zerilli group had made at least $2 million for land it never had to put up anything for.

Webb kept Arrowhead until 1966, when it was sold to Robert Goldwater, the brother of Barry Goldwater, and Joseph F. Martori, the aging patriarch of the prominent Martori family. And again, the IRE reporters found a confusing second real estate transfer which allowed Goldwater and Martori to secure the bulk of the cash needed for a down payment on the ranch.

This time, Henry Crown, a Chicago investor, bought 360 acres of land owned by Martori a dozen miles from Arrowhead. The cost was nearly a million dollars, or an unusually high $2,778 per acre. A week later, on September 22, 1966, Martori and Goldwater purchased the main Arrowhead Ranch from Webb for just $685 an acre, only $27 more per acre than Zerilli had paid for it eleven years before.

All this led reporters to the ranch's current status. In November 1976, it was a part of the giant Goldmar corporation, owned by Robert Goldwater and the Martori family. Old Joseph F. Martori had died in 1973. Harry Rosenzweig, the Goldwater brothers' chief business and political associate and the man Berger had referred to as head of the Phoenix power structure, was a recent member of the board of directors. So was John Curci, one of Detroit hoodlum

Zerilli's partners in the fruit brokering business originally set up in 1955 to market Arrowhead citrus. And Carl Jarson, an original co-owner of Arrowhead with Zerilli, had bragged to Wendland that Goldmar was one of his biggest customers. Thus, while mobster Zerilli, at seventy-three, lived in Michigan and was ostensibly out of Arizona, some of his associates still had business interests in Arrowhead.

Putting it all together, IRE had established links between the Goldwater brothers and Rosenzweig and organized crime figures going back more than two decades—associations which were still beneath the surface in the fall of 1976.

7 | The Appearance of Ned Warren, Sr.

On Monday, October 18, 1976, John Harvey Adamson went on trial for the murder of Don Bolles.

Two hours into the jury selection, Judge Frederic Heineman's long description of the case was interrupted by a messenger who presented him a written note. He glanced at it and then put down the pile of notes he was using to instruct the prospective jurors.

"Ladies and gentlemen," he said, seemingly with a sigh, "we've had a misunderstanding. The trial will not proceed now."

The note concerned security. The courtroom was too difficult to guard, according to the sheriff's deputies. There had been several threats against Adamson. While they were too vague to act on, they couldn't be ignored. For maximum security, the case should be moved to a smaller courtroom. The county could not stand the embarrassment of a Jack Ruby-type killing.

The next day, interim County Attorney Donald Harris blew it.

According to the code of legal ethics, the prosecuting attorney must keep silent as to the direction an investigation is taking, particularly at the beginning of a trial, when prospective jurors can easily be exposed to publicity about the case they may soon be asked to hear. So it came as a surprise to reporters and a shock to the judge that Maricopa County Attorney Donald Harris was shooting off his mouth about the theories on the case on the second day of jury selection. His remarks made page one news in the *Los Angeles Times*.

Harris said his office was close to bringing charges against six other persons in the Bolles case. No, he said, he didn't think the killing necessarily involved the Mafia. Instead, Harris thought it was more likely that the conspiracy involved the elite of Phoenix, "the country-club set." Judge Heineman declared a mistrial without delay, citing excessive pretrial publicity which then made the selection of an unbiased jury impossible. The following day, in an unprecedented move, Raul Castro, Arizona's Democratic governor, stepped into the case and ordered it transferred from Harris's control to that of Arizona Attorney General Bruce Babbitt.

Babbitt, a young lawyer elected the previous year, had tracked down the governor in a Tucson hotel. Babbitt claimed that Harris's bungling had ruined his own case. He told the governor of Harris's lust for seeing his name in print, of the sensational statements he had given newspapers and magazines, and of the interview he had done with CBS's "Sixty Minutes," in which he flatly stated that he believed Bolles had been killed because he was getting too close to a figure of local prominence. Although no one else had been charged in the killing, Harris was spouting off about other conspirators. Those were not the kind of things a prosecutor said when he was about to try the only person so far implicated in the murder. Castro agreed and signed a letter giving his attorney general the authority to bump Harris.

On the night of October 21, after Harris had gone home, Babbitt ordered police into the county attorney's office to remove all files connected with the case. Harris was furious. He would appeal the governor's order, he told reporters at a hastily called press conference. Meanwhile, Adamson was returned to solitary confinement in the county jail. The date for his new trial was tentatively set for the first week in December.

Babbitt confided his disgust with Harris to IRE reporters. "What he wanted to do, besides seeing his name in print, was to make a big splash, bring everybody even remotely connected with the case in. Charge them all in a bunch of shotgun indictments and then hope that maybe a couple of charges will stick."

Babbitt was one of a handful of state and local figures that IRE team members trusted. As they had done with a few officers with the Phoenix Police Department's intelligence unit, they had made informal contacts and secured pledges of cooperation from Babbitt's office.

Harris, Babbitt said, was about to form a grand jury to investigate the Bolles killing. "That's the worst possible thing right now," the attorney general explained. "In the Adamson case, witnesses are at a premium. That is, their testimony is. If a witness testifies before a grand jury, you can bet your ass his identity is going to be made public. If that happens, there exists the very real possibility that he will be killed. Then, no matter how good his testimony before the grand jury was, it's all void. However, if we make a case not by grand jury but by regular charges, we get the witness to talk in open court at a preliminary hearing. That way, no matter what happens to the witness, the testimony can always be used."

"Do you really think a witness would be killed to prevent him from appearing?" Babbitt was asked in a briefing with IRE shortly after he had taken over the case.

"You bet I believe it."

After the initial interview with Greene and Drehsler, Don Harris had clearly been skittish of IRE. Of late, he had begun bad-mouthing the team, telling local reporters that IRE was on a wild-goose chase, only interested in winning journalism prizes and making a name for its members. Dick Levitan, an award-winning reporter for WEEI-Radio in Boston and the only broadcast reporter with IRE, was assigned to visit with Harris to get his views on the mistrial and the subsequent removal of the case from his office.

"Babbitt is a four-eyed prick, a real fuck-up," Harris told Levitan for openers. Sitting in his office, which was decorated with eight medals he had won as a Marine in Vietnam, Harris conceded that he wanted to call a grand jury. He was convinced that Kemper Marley, the wealthy rancher and political shaker, had contracted Adamson for the job. He also believed that Max Dunlap, Marley's protégé, was the middleman. There were others involved, he said, who had assisted Adamson, but those were the big three.

Rocking in his leather swivel chair and fondling his Western-style shirt, Harris changed the subject to the hundred thousand dollars a year he had raked in as a private attorney. Levitan steered the conversation back to the Bolles case. "Do you think that if you get the case back you'll still order a grand jury into the Bolles murder?"

"Who gives a fuck?" Harris shot back. "Frankly, the case is so botched up now that I don't want it back."

Harris had refused to cut any deals with Adamson. There were no promises in exchange for testimony. If Adamson wanted to talk, the only thing Harris would do would be to ask for a life sentence rather than the death penalty. That wasn't much of an inducement for Adamson, thought Levitan as he returned to the IRE office. Even if he were sentenced to death, Adamson knew the odds against dying in the electric chair were overwhelmingly in his favor.

Meanwhile, the IRE team was deep into its various investigations. As October began to turn to November, suite 1939 at the Adams was the scene of constant activity. The original glamour had faded. Now, they all seemed to be working for a single newspaper, trying to cover dozens of different news stories. The phones and the mail daily brought news tips from the general public. Some of the contacts were fruitful, some not. Others were rather unusual.

For example, a former Phoenix resident now living in California wrote Greene a 200-page letter complaining that her invention had been stolen. The woman's invention was a revolutionary new brassiere that purported to increase the bust size by three inches and still appear natural. Her story was full of betrayal, hardship, near victory, and bad times again. Things had been so rough once that her family existed by stealing food from a Phoenix zoo. During this period the woman's husband deserted her because, she said, "he didn't like monkey food." The woman wanted the IRE to help her get her bra back.

A very interesting and mysterious source contacted Wendland and Drehsler early in the investigation. A part-time private eye and real estate speculator, the man had dozens of leads which he rattled off while chain-smoking cigarettes in the Adams Hotel coffee shop. He showed up daily for a month. His tips were never detailed, merely suggestions to look up certain people who might be connected with various types of wrongdoing. But unknown to him the names he kept raising were also showing up in the IRE files in precisely the same context he hinted. His motives for seeking the reporters out were selfish. He had been blacklisted from selling real estate by local bankers and politicians who, he claimed, were angry at him for not making kickbacks from his sales. He wanted to expose the corruption. There was a grain of truth in most of his accusations. But he never produced anything more than the barest details. Because of his rapid-fire conversation and one-line leads, Wendland and Drehsler dubbed him their Henny Youngman informant.

He was insistent on one particular point. From the time the reporters first began talking with him, he was concerned about the *Arizona Republic*'s connection with the team. "You got a *Republic* reporter working with you. I'm telling you, you're being had. The *Republic* has no intention of ever printing the stuff. They've sent the guy just to keep an eye on you."

Wendland and Drehsler didn't believe it. They both had worked with John Winters, the bearded, bolo-tied reporter from the *Republic*, who was currently investigating land frauds with other IRE men. Winters was not simply an observer. He was an active participant who had come up with several good pieces of information. Besides, *Republic* city editor Bob Early was another IRE backer. Early had stopped by several times and voiced strong support.

"Look, I know what you guys are thinking," said Henny. "But mark my words right here. The *Arizona Republic* won't print a thing. The only reason they're here is to find out what you're doing here and who you're talking to."

"How do you know?" asked Drehsler.

"Never mind how I know. I just know. I'm telling you this for your own protection, that's all."

"We know the *Republic* reporter. He's solid. So's his city editor," vouched Wendland.

"Sure they are," said the informant. "That's because they don't know a thing about it. It goes much higher than the reporter or the city editor. I know this for a fact. There was a meeting held over there among some really top people. At it, they decided to play along with you guys."

"Why? And who was at this meeting?" pressed Wendland.

"I told you, I can't say any more. But why do you think they wouldn't cooperate? Because the people you guys are investigating are the people they've protected over the years, that's why. Just don't ask me any more. I'm telling you, they won't print the stories you guys write and they'll try to derail you."

Henny's allegations disturbed Wendland and Drehsler. They mentioned the conversation to Greene.

"Forget it," said Greene. "The *Republic*'s with us all the way. Your source is way off."

Wendland and Drehsler considered bringing the matter up with Winters. But if the source was right, Winters wouldn't know about it anyway. There wasn't much they could do about the tip except hope it wasn't true.

The dilemma was temporarily forgotten when, on October 29, Drehsler came into the office to find a phone message from a most unexpected source.

It was from Ned Warren, Sr., the self-styled "godfather" of the state's billion-dollar land fraud business, who at that moment was under investigation by IRE. Warren, an ex-con who had migrated to Arizona with his wife, his mistress, and his pet dog some twenty years before, had become a millionaire by selling worthless desert land as "vacation homesites." In 1967, he received his first widespread attention when Don Bolles uncovered a massive swindle which Warren masterminded through a firm known as Western Growth Capital Corporation. A thousand people throughout the United States had been taken in the scam that sold land through a series of mostly dummy corporations for five percent down. Once the money was turned over, salesmen then split a twenty percent commission with the buyer, who then promptly defaulted. Warren raked his money off the top, bankrupting the company and escaping prosecution. The "godfather" then went into more than three dozen other Arizona companies, peddling worthless land and mortgages. Each time, before the top caved in, he unloaded the firms themselves to legitimate buyers, who then had to stand the losses. Although he had been charged with hundreds of counts of land fraud and assorted other offenses, including bribery, he had never been convicted in Arizona, a fact generally attributed to his talent for cultivating prominent and powerful politicians. One of Warren's boosters was Senator Barry Goldwater, who wrote a glowing letter on the state of Arizona to potential Warren customers.

Warren's swindles also had the odor of death. A string of eleven corpses, all former associates of the "godfather," had been laid to rest since 1972. The most recent obsequies had occurred just a year earlier, when Edward Lazar, Warren's chief accountant, had been shot to death the day before he was to testify before a grand jury investigating Warren's operations.

Drehsler, who had interviewed Warren in the past, was very mindful of that string of deaths when he returned the call.

Warren wanted a meeting, right now, with no one else except Drehsler. Drehsler wasn't to tell anyone. He was to drive out to Warren's spacious home on exclusive Camelback Mountain. Alone, stressed Warren, who refused to say what he wanted to discuss.

Stalling, Drehsler said he wasn't sure when he could get away. He said he would see if he could get out of a couple of appointments and call Warren right back.

He told Greene of the request from Warren.

"Tell him no dice," said Greene. "The son of a bitch just wants to pump you to see what we've got on him."

"I don't think so," said Drehsler. "That's not his style. He's got something. Or at least he wants me to think he does."

Greene agreed to the meeting. "But you don't go alone. You're covered all the way. You meet him in a public place where we can observe the whole thing."

Drehsler phoned Warren back. The meeting was arranged for the Compass Room, a circular bar in the Hyatt Regency Hotel, just across the street from the Adams. Warren would be there at four o'clock.

John Rawlinson, the *Arizona Daily Star* reporter from Tucson, and Myrta Pulliam, from the *Indianapolis Star,* were assigned as backup crew. They would pose as a couple on a date and sit as close to Drehsler and Warren as possible. Harry Jones from the *Kansas City Star* would be on standby at the office with a waiting car, in case Warren and Drehsler were to leave the Hyatt for any reason.

Rawlinson, Pulliam, and Jones had been working upwards of fourteen hours a day on Warren since their arrival at the beginning of October. They knew him probably better than Warren knew himself and were anxious to get their first look at him. Besides spending hundreds of hours tracing Warren's background and untangling the maze of shell corporations he used to cover his land fraud schemes, they also had an informant, a highly talkative one.

The Warren snitch was Richard Frost, a former partner of Warren's who had become Warren's chief detractor in the fall of 1976. Frost was one of the dozens of businessmen duped into a partnership with Warren.

A paunchy, white-haired man of fifty-five, Frost was a native of Michigan and a highly successful businessman, comfortable in the upper reaches of Detroit's automotive money and Democratic politicians. He was appointed director of the Port of Detroit in the mid-1950s. But in 1957, his wife in ill health, Frost gave up the job, moving first to Kansas City, Kansas, where he opened a successful consulting firm, then in 1963, after his wife's death, to Phoenix, where he hooked up with the gigantic Del Webb Corporation.

Phoenix was a boom town at the time. And the boom was in land. Frost soon left Webb and jumped into real estate. Not long afterwards he started the immediately successful Arizona Land Corporation. His sales director was Ned Warren, Sr. Frost stated that he had no idea of Warren's background until it was too late. That was in 1968, when Frost uncovered documents showing that Warren had been making widespread payoffs to state real estate officials and had secretly formed two corporations of his own to sell nonexistent ALCO lots. Frost quickly bailed out of the company, realizing that Warren had, in effect, taken control. He was a bitter man. So, gathering up the documents linking Warren to fraud, Frost turned them over to the Maricopa County Attorney's office. Soon, ALCO was bankrupt, bled dry by thousands of phony sales contracts Warren had sold to unsuspecting investors. Frost was a ruined man. The money he had

successfully parlayed from his days in Detroit was lost in the dust of
ALCO. What little assets he had were tied up in dozens of civil suits
arising from the bankruptcy.

In September 1975, Frost was a main witness against Warren in an
extortion trial in Seattle, Washington. Warren was convicted on two
counts, but after posting bond and filing an appeal, left the state
without serving a day behind bars. In Arizona, Warren had been
indicted on three occasions. Each time the so-called ''godfather'' of
land fraud had seen the legal proceedings dropped, either through
inaction, government incompetence, or procedural errors. The Seattle conviction wasn't enough for Frost. He was obsessed with exposing Warren's swindles.

Frost himself had some legal difficulties stemming from a job he
held briefly with a firm known as New Life Trust Co. In October
1975, a month after the Warren case in Seattle, Frost was among
those members of the company indicted by the federal government in
connection with land fraud, though he maintained that he had only
worked there for a few weeks after the ALCO debacle and had quit
when he suspected that New Life was also cheating its customers.

Frost had spent dozens of hours with IRE reporters Pulliam,
Rawlinson, Winters, and anyone else on the team who would listen,
briefing them on everything he had learned about Warren and land
swindles. He had brought in nearly 2,000 pages of depositions, court
transcripts, and personal notes that he had collected in his campaign
against Warren.

One of his main charges was that the incriminating documents he
had turned over to former county attorney Moise Berger during the
ALCO bankruptcy in 1968 had disappeared from the prosecutor's
office. The incident was one of the many things that forced Berger to
resign in August, 1976. It came to light during a 1974 land fraud trial
against Warren and two of his associates, James Cornwall and Tony
Serra. Charges against Warren were dismissed by Berger's office,
though Cornwall and Serra were convicted. Berger, asked about the
ALCO evidence after dropping charges against Warren, said he knew
nothing about the documents. He conceded, however, that they had
somehow been misplaced by someone on his staff.

Again, Frost was enraged. So he went to the Arizona State Prison
in Florence on August 10, 1976, with his attorney and a court
stenographer and questioned Serra. Frost provided the IRE reporters
with a copy of Serra's deposition in which Serra said he was in fear of

his life. But not included in the deposition, because the court stenographer had not yet set up his equipment, was a statement Frost said Serra gave him as soon as they began talking.

"He said that he himself had removed the ALCO records from Berger's office," Frost told the reporters. "He told me that he had some help. He said that Berger and Warren were in on it with him."

Frost said Serra had voiced fear that he was going to be murdered in prison because of what he knew about Warren.

"He's terrified, petrified for his life," Frost told Wendland several days before Drehsler was called by Warren. "Look, I know Warren. He's smooth. He's sharp. And he can be quite charming. But he's a dangerous man. Look at the deaths involving those who were in a position to testify against him."

Wendland, while not working the Warren investigation, had, like the other reporters, frequently been cornered by Frost. And like his coworkers, he was not prepared to accept Frost's statement that Serra knew where the missing documents were. If it had been on the deposition, he explained, it at least would be quasi-admissible in court. But as it stood then, all the team had were Frost's allegations.

"Look, Dick, it's not that we don't believe you," said Wendland. "But right now, it's just your word. And your word isn't good enough. You're awaiting trial on land fraud charges yourself."

Frost was frustrated. "I understand all that. But you don't understand. Serra's going to be killed. They're going to get to him in prison. They'll kill him. I know it."

Unfortunately, Frost was right.

The meeting with Ned Warren, Sr., on Friday, October 29, was carefully planned. Alex Drehsler and Myrta Pulliam left the Adams about the same time. Drehsler went into the Hyatt first, taking a seat in the lobby outside the Compass Room. Pulliam waited outside for ten minutes, allowing Warren and Alex to meet and select a table. But when she entered, Drehsler was still alone in the lobby. She had hoped to pick a table near Warren and Drehsler in order to observe the discussion. There wasn't much that could be done now, so she walked past Drehsler into the Compass Room.

She was alone for about five minutes. Then Warren, a short, tanned man in casual clothes, walked in with Drehsler. He looked around the sparsely occupied lounge, his eyes sweeping past Pulliam without a second glance. With Drehsler in tow, he selected a table on the opposite side of the circular room, out of Pulliam's sight.

According to the carefully orchestrated surveillance outlined by Greene, Rawlinson was supposed to join Pulliam in the lounge, bearing a box of candy as if he were late for a date. He was not to enter, however, until Warren and Drehsler sat down. But like Pulliam he encountered Drehsler still waiting in the lobby. So, he went back outside and walked around the block, stalling for time. Then he almost ran into Warren, who was hurrying through the lobby. Quickly, Rawlinson turned his back without being noticed. He gave Warren three minutes to meet Drehsler. Then he went to buy his box of candy. But the hotel giftshop didn't carry boxes. He settled for a candy bar and a small roll of breath mints.

Pulliam cracked up as the straight-faced Rawlinson entered the Compass Room and presented her with the candy. Discreetly, they changed tables so they could keep their eye on Warren and Drehsler, ordered drinks, and began chatting like two infatuated lovers.

Warren, meanwhile, said nothing until the waitress took their drink order. When she left, he cleared his throat.

"You got a body bug on you?" he asked Drehsler.

"Of course not," replied Drehsler. "You want to go in the bathroom and check?"

Warren shook his head. "Look, what I got to say will only take a couple of minutes. Then, we'll take a short trip. Okay?"

Drehsler said nothing.

"Okay, look. Here's the deal. I'm here speaking on behalf of John Adamson. And his wife, Mary. Now I don't want you to get any ideas. I'm not really that close to Adamson, you understand? He's not my type. Let's just say I've known him casually for a few years. He and his wife have been out to my house a couple of times. But my wife wouldn't have anything to do with him. See this one time, Mary, Adamson's wife, said the word 'fuck' in front of my wife, Barbara. Now Barbara is a very straight lady, you understand. Later she says to me, 'Ned, I don't want those people here anymore. I don't like that kind of talk. They sound like they are hoodlums.' Well, since then, I haven't really seen them much."

Warren was starting to ramble. "Get to the point, Ned."

"Yeah, okay. I just wanted you to understand the picture. Here's the deal. Adamson wants to talk. He's ready to give the cops the names of everyone involved in the Don Bolles bombing."

"How do you know this?"

"From Mary, his wife. She tells me that these other people comprise a ring."

"Wait a minute, Ned. Where are you getting all this from, Adamson or his wife?"

"From his wife. She told me that John decided to wait ninety days after his arrest, to see what would happen, if his friends would take care of him. But they haven't. She told me that everyone has deserted him."

"If Adamson wants to talk, how come he doesn't just talk? How come you're mixed up in this?"

" 'Cause John trusts me. He told his wife to come to me, to let me handle the negotiations. He's afraid to go directly to the cops. He wants to protect himself with some intermediaries."

"Okay," Drehsler asked, "what does Adamson get out of the deal?"

"Four things," said Warren. "He'll talk if he gets out of jail in ten years. More time than that and he says nothing. He wants a television set in jail. He wants the state to take care of his wife financially. And he wants conjugal visits from Mary once a week. After all, a man gets used to a regular piece of ass. You can't fault him for that."

"So much for Adamson. What does Ned Warren, Sr., get out of all this?"

"Nothing, nothing at all. I've been asked to do this and I agreed, that's all. I'm just doing a favor for the wife, really. The only thing I want is for the state to stop fucking with me. I mean if anyone has evidence of something really criminal I've done, okay, I understand they got to file a case against me. Otherwise, they ought to stop fucking with me on chicken-shit cases like they've been doing."

"Ned, why the hell are you telling me all this? What am I supposed to do?"

"You're on that task force of reporters, aren't you?"

"Yeah, but we're not looking into the Bolles case at all. We're looking into other things."

"That doesn't make any difference," said Warren. "I want you to act as a go-between. I want you to go to Bruce Babbitt and tell him I can get the names and circumstances of the persons involved in the Bolles killing."

"Why don't you go yourself, Ned? Or send Mary. Why me?"

"Look, I'm not stupid. If I go, who else knows that I was involved? No one. They can take the information and put the screws to me if they want. With you involved, they'll have to be more careful.

Babbitt wants to be governor some day. He won't fuck around with this if he knows the press is involved.''

"What's to stop Babbitt from going right to Mary?''

" 'Cause Mary won't talk to anyone unless I say it's okay. And Babbitt knows he can't make me talk. It's either this way, or no way.''

"How sure are you that Adamson wants to talk?''

"I'm positive. Now I'll tell you what we're going to do. I'm going to go make a phone call. Then we're going to go see Mary Adamson. I want you to meet her. She'll assure you that I'm speaking for her and her husband.''

Warren excused himself and left the table. Drehsler waited a minute and was just about to run over to Rawlinson and Pulliam and tell them to get ready to follow him when Warren walked back into the room.

"The phone's busy,'' he said. He sat back down and sipped on his drink. "This has been one hell of a week.''

"What do you mean?''

Warren sighed. Good lord, thought Drehsler, it looked like he was about to cry. Tears were welling up in Warren's eyes.

"My dog,'' Warren said. "He died the other day.''

"I beg your pardon?''

"My dog, my Doberman. He died. He was twelve years old. You have no idea how attached my wife and I were to him. Our own kids are grown. I guess the dog was like another kid to us.''

Drehsler was dumbstruck. This was Ned Warren, Sr., the state's leading swindler, a man whose associates over the past few years had died in a bizarre series of coincidences.

"It's been hell,'' he continued. "I just paid two hundred and fifty dollars for the Doberman's burial plot at this little pet cemetery. That includes the tombstone. I also bought another plot for our other dog. He's just a mongrel, really, but he's getting up in years, too. It's so sad to lose a pet. I guess we can buy another Doberman puppy. But it just won't be the same.''

Drehsler was getting uncomfortable. "Say, what about that phone call?''

"Oh. Yeah. I'm sorry to burden you with this. I'll be right back.''

Drehsler waited again. He got up and looked around the corner. Warren was on the telephone, deep in conversation.

Quickly, he rushed over to Rawlinson and Pulliam, who were into a game of backgammon, played on a portable board Myrta had stuffed in her purse before leaving the Adams.

"Get a car," Drehsler hissed.

"Do what?" asked Myrta.

"Get a car. We're leaving. Be out front."

"Why?"

"We're meeting someone. Hurry up."

Pulliam got up and dashed out of the room, leaving Rawlinson to cover for her.

"Who are you meeting?" Rawlinson asked Drehsler.

"Mary Adamson," replied Alex, darting back to his table before Warren could return.

At the Adams, Pulliam ran into Harry Jones, who was waiting in the lobby with the parking ticket for an IRE car. Rawlinson had phoned the office right after Myrta left, hoping to save time.

"Who the hell are they meeting?" Myrta asked Jones as they entered the elevator for the garage.

"Rawlinson said some guy named Harry Anderson."

"Who the fuck is Harry Anderson?"

Jones didn't know. That was the message. They hurriedly located one of the rental cars on the third floor of the Adams parking garage, wheeled it out to the street, and made their way to the front of the Hyatt. Pulliam spotted Rawlinson standing between a couple of bushes near the entrance. She parked on the street, leaving the engine running and the lights out.

Rawlinson ran across the street and jumped in the car, just moments before Warren and Drehsler came out of the hotel and got into Warren's Oldsmobile.

With the reporters following, Warren drove to North Central Avenue, turned right, and headed to a run-down bar called Fonzie's, located about two miles north of the Adams. He pulled his car up in front as Pulliam turned into a parking lot across the street.

"You wait out in front," Warren told Drehsler. "She's in here, drinking. But I don't want you to go inside. If someone were to recognize me with you, it could leak out what I'm doing. If that happened, I'd need protection from dusk to dawn."

A couple of minutes passed. Then Warren, accompanied by a tall woman with long black hair and tight white pants came outside.

"Are you Mary Adamson?" he asked her after taking her over to Drehsler.

"Yes, I am," she replied in a soft voice.

"Okay, honey. Now I'm not going to introduce you at this time. I just want this man to be sure who you are and that I'm acting on your behalf. Do you have a driver's license you can show him?"

The woman looked confused for a moment. She shrugged her shoulders, fished around in her purse, and handed Drehsler her license. She was Mary Adamson.

Warren thanked her and said that they'd be back in touch. She went back to her drinking and Warren returned Drehsler to the Adams.

Drehsler said he wasn't sure what, if anything, IRE would do with Warren's information request, but that it would be forwarded to Babbitt.

"That's all I can do," he said. "If we are going to pursue this anymore, I'll be back in touch."

That was good enough for Warren. The two shook hands as Drehsler said goodbye.

"Say, Alex, one thing," Warren said. Drehsler turned around. "Back at the Hyatt, you said you guys on that reporting team weren't looking into the Bolles killing. What are you doing then?"

Drehsler couldn't resist the opportunity. "Lots of things, Ned. We're looking into just about everything else. Especially land fraud. In fact, I'm sure we'll be talking to you soon about that."

Warren laughed. "Yeah, I'm sure you will." With that, he left.

It was the last weekend in October. Drehsler and Rawlinson, as was their weekend habit, drove home to Tucson to visit their families.

Wendland flew back to Detroit for a couple of days. Sunday was Halloween, which, next to Christmas, was his kids' favorite holiday. He was homesick. His wife, Jennifer, accepted the long absence but still was angry. News stories were always complicating their family life. The birth of their second child, in 1972, had to be induced because the city desk had assigned Wendland to an out-of-town political story and he hadn't wanted to be absent when Jennifer delivered. And he had almost missed the birth of their third child, born in October 1975, during the middle of the Jimmy Hoffa disappearance because he was staked out around the clock in a crosstown motel waiting for a break in the case. So after a month in Arizona, he want home to take his three kids trick-or-treating and to tell his wife that the story had no end in sight.

Over the weekend Bob Greene drafted a confidential letter to Attorney General Bruce Babbitt. He specified Warren's deal and reiterated IRE's intent not to involve itself in the Bolles case.

The reporters decided to avoid any middleman role between Adamson and Warren and the authorities. For one thing, Warren was a major object of IRE investigations. Were they to work with Warren on this, they would be hard pressed to suddenly turn on him when it was time to go into his own land fraud activities. Another reason was simply a matter of propriety. Reporters have to walk a fine line between observation and participation. It was one thing to meet with Warren and discuss Adamson and the Bolles murder. It was another to cooperate with him, on Adamson's behalf, in negotiating a deal.

Babbitt, meanwhile, was elated by the news that Adamson wanted to talk. He understood the reporters' feelings about not getting involved. And he was not concerned that Adamson would only talk through his wife. That was nothing more than jailhouse bravado. If Adamson wanted to deal, he must be feeling alone and unprotected. Babbitt figured that it was just a matter of time until Adamson broke. And when that happened, so would the entire Bolles case.

8 | Frontier Sex

It's an old saying in Arizona that what money won't buy, sex will. And the saying is not without merit. For in almost every aspect of the state's business dealings being investigated by the visiting reporters, sex—in the form of well-paid prostitutes or carefully kept mistresses—played a major role. Without seeking it out, the reporters kept stumbling across example after example: a couple of extremely prominent lawyers who staged weekly sex-party poker games for their well-heeled business clients; a land fraud huckster who bought a Phoenix tavern for his mistress; a Tucson drug dealer who kept two Las Vegas hookers on annual retainers; an elderly judge whose vice was young girls; and a well-known Phoenix politician and businessman whose kinky sex habits were paid for in diamonds, thus earning him the nickname "Diamondman" in the trick book of almost every madame in the Southwest.

Throughout October and into the first week of November, the sex stories reporters kept uncovering from their growing number of news sources were often the highlight of the day, boisterously swapped over late-night drinks in the hotel bar. For the most part, interesting as they were, the stories were totally without news value. Thus, notes were seldom kept. But, taken as a whole, the stories nevertheless illustrated an old-fashioned and crudely exploitative business attitude out of step with the rest of the country in the open and sophisticated 1970s. In Arizona, it was still chic to have a mistress. That's what the successful, big-time businessman had. Not a girlfriend or a lover, but a mistress, bought and paid for just like his thousand-dollar turquoise belt buckle.

The IRE reporters would soon find that the sex stories they had been halfheartedly collecting would, in at least one very major case, become the subject of intense investigation. The story would be uncovered by the team's newest arrival.

Ron Koziol, the cigar-chomping *Chicago Tribune* reporter and the president of IRE, flew in late in the afternoon of Friday, November 5. Since the project had begun, he had been asked to check out dozens of leads in Chicago, and he came to Phoenix with nearly a hundred

pages of notes. Koziol was amazed at what he saw. The hotel suite
resembled a War Room, he thought, with maps, graphs, reports, and
law enforcement documents marked "confidential" scattered
everywhere. The index card boxes and files were filled to overflow-
ing. Telephones rang incessantly even late at night, and reporters
hustled in and out of the room.

"Hey," Koziol said upon surveying the scene, "this ain't too
shabby. Not too shabby at all."

Like the Seattle reporter's "huh" the month before, "ain't too
shabby" soon became the most overused expression heard in suite
1939.

Greene briefed Koziol on the major developments in the investigation over a long boozy dinner in the hotel restaurant. About ten
o'clock Drehsler, who had been drinking with a police source since
five, stopped by the table. As Greene headed back upstairs, Drehsler
invited Koziol for a nightcap.

They went to a place known as the Foxe au-Disco, a small, cozy
bar located a few blocks west of North Central Avenue on Camelback
Road. The place was a frequent hangout for the IRE reporters, not
because of its charms—which were few—but because of those who
frequented the place. Owned for the record by a short, gregarious
transplanted New Yorker by the name of Joey Ferrero, it was really
run by Jack Duggan, a convicted gambler and a man identified to
reporters by police as an extortionist, drug financier, and organized crime associate.

IRE had already established Duggan's intimacy with some pretty
powerful mobsters. A confidential U.S. Drug Enforcement Administration report, in IRE's possession, detailed a meeting between
a Mexican lawyer, a Phoenix judge, and Duggan at which plans were
discussed to bring in several kilos of heroin. Reporters had observed
Duggan meeting and socializing with several notorious hoodlums
from the Joseph "Joe Bananas" Bonanno crime family in Tucson.
And offers to buy cocaine, women, and hot automobiles had been
extended by Duggan's pals to reporters. John Adamson, himself a
close pal of Duggan's, was a frequent hoister at the Foxe, as were
dozens of the minor-league lawyers and businessmen who nurtured
the state's land fraud racket.

So the reporters, particularly Drehsler and Wendland, did a lot of
drinking at the Foxe. They made no attempt to disguise their identity.
Duggan, a well-built, handsome man in his mid-thirties with a Van-

dyke beard, seemed actually to enjoy their presence. The reporters never discussed their investigations and seldom asked questions, trying to create the impression that they were simply hanging out there because they needed to unwind after a long day. Duggan was always playing the good host, inviting the reporters to after-hours parties and introducing them to his friends. By keeping their eyes and ears open, IRE reporters often picked up information. Not that Duggan or his pals volunteered anything. Indeed, it was just the opposite. Duggan was forever complaining about how unfair it was that police considered him a hoodlum He was merely a struggling businessman who was drawing law enforcement heat because he did not hold past mistakes against his friends. But, like Brutus, Duggan protested too much. And by watching him and his associates, the reporters came to know who was who in the Phoenix underworld.

The Foxe was full when Drehsler and Koziol arrived. A long-haired kid was playing disco records in the other room and the dance floor was crowded. Joey Ferrero spotted Drehsler and came over to say hello.

"With us again? You newspaper people really like to drink, huh? Nothing wrong with that."

Alex introduced Koziol, and Joey was amazed at the way he talked.

"You sound like you're from Chicago," he said. "You talk like those gangsters in the old Al Capone movies."

They chatted for a few minutes. When Drehsler got up to use the restroom, Joey motioned for Koziol to come closer.

"Listen, you come back in a day or so. I might have something to tell you. I don't want to talk to Alex about it 'cause he knows me, you understand? But I'll tell you if you keep it just between us."

Koziol shrugged. "Sure, Joey, no problem."

Ferrero turned around. "Hey, see that broad?" He pointed at a young woman in a tight-fitting sweater-vest that emphasized her huge, round breasts. "Silicone tits," said Joey. "But that's okay 'cause she's one hell of a piece of ass." He snapped his fingers and the girl came over, put her arms around him, and gave him a long, open-mouthed kiss.

"Mandy," said Ferrero, "I want you to meet my friend, Ron. He's from Chicago."

Mandy was pleased to meet him. "I always like older men," she remarked suavely.

Joey whispered something in the woman's ear, clapped Koziol on the shoulder, and said he had to leave for an appointment. "Get to know my friend Mandy," he said. "She'll show you what a great city Phoenix is."

Mandy seemed more than eager to stay with Koziol. They made small talk while Drehsler sipped on a beer. When she excused herself to go to the restroom, Koziol told his partner that she had offered to drive Koziol back to the hotel.

"Okay," said Drehsler. "Let's play along—it's an obvious setup."

Drehsler would follow Koziol and the girl when they left the bar.

Mandy returned. "I'm ready if you are," she said, noticing that Alex had left.

Out in the parking lot, she wanted to know if Koziol would rather go to her place. "Don't worry, I've got shaving stuff and an extra toothbrush if you're too tired to go back downtown tonight."

"That's a great idea, honey, but, see, we got this rule that we can't stay out of the hotel," Koziol lied. "Like football players, you know? Our boss worries if we're all not accounted for every night."

It made no difference to her. "I haven't been in a hotel for a long time," she said, starting her car.

On the way downtown, Koziol tried to get her to talk about her relationship with Joey and Duggan.

"Close friends," she said. "They like to party and I like to party." She didn't volunteer any more. Instead, she wanted to know who the other people were that Koziol was working with in Phoenix.

"There's lots of us," he said. "There's people from all over."

"How many?" she asked, trying to sound nonchalant.

"I'm not supposed to say, but, what the hell, you're certainly nobody I have to worry about. Right now, there are seventy-five of us. But don't tell anyone, okay? It's a secret."

She wouldn't breathe a word. "And you're all staying at the Adams?"

"Heavens, no. Only some of us. The others are staying all over. They're undercover, you know."

"Uh huh. That's really exciting. I really like writers. What kind of things are you guys, like, doing? I mean are you investigating somebody or what?"

"Baby," said Koziol, "we're investigating everybody."

"I mean like anyone in particular?"

"Lots of people in particular."

"Oh. Well, like who?"

"Well, I'll tell you. There's this one guy who we're really after. I don't know if I should even be saying this. But he's really heavy. His name is Millard Fillmore." Koziol bet himself that she had never heard of the long-dead president.

"Who?"

"Millard Fillmore. You mean you haven't heard of him?"

"It sounds familiar. Is he in real estate?"

"He's in everything," replied Koziol.

"Yeah, I guess I know who he is after all."

Koziol figured that would confuse whoever it was who had tried to set him up with the woman. As they neared the hotel, Mandy pointed to a tan Nova just ahead of them.

"Say, isn't that your buddy, Alex?"

Koziol looked closer. It was Drehsler. What a great tail, he thought. Drehsler was supposed to be following him, not vice versa.

At the Adams, Mandy was about to park the car when Koziol cut her off. "No, not tonight, baby, maybe some other time."

"But I don't understand," she said. "It won't cost you anything, you know. I really like you. Really."

"No, can't do. It's been a rough day."

"I can make it a nice night."

Koziol got out of the car. "Yeah, I bet you could." He stuck his head back inside. Mandy started to lean across the seat. Instead of kissing her, Koziol flipped down the ashtray and squashed out his cigar, filling the car with smoke. "See you around," he said, slamming the door and walking into the hotel.

"You asshole! You prick!" she screamed after him.

Back in his room, he had just undressed when the telephone rang. It was Drehsler.

"Where did you go? I couldn't find you."

"Just back to the room. Don't worry. But thanks for looking out for me."

Reporters are far from immune to the pleasures of the flesh. In fact, because of the varied people they come into contact with daily and the glamorous aspect of their jobs, they are not known for having low sexual drives. Thus, when a number of ego-centered reporters used to the good life of an expense account find themselves on an indefinite assignment away from home in a fun-loving convention city like Phoenix, celibacy is a difficult state to maintain.

But the Arizona Project was different from most out-of-town stories the reporters had covered.

"You must be constantly aware that a setup is something the other side will certainly consider doing to you," Greene told the reporters on several occasions. "I'm not telling you that you can't get laid while you're working on this story. I'm just telling you to be extremely careful. Those whom we can hurt the most by our reporting would like nothing better than a chance to discredit us. And if they can do it by our behavior, then believe me, they'll do it."

On Sunday, November 7, Bob Teuscher from the *St. Louis Globe* arrived. This tall, stocky, forty-three-year-old document mole would spend the rest of the month on the team. Unlike the other reporters, who had readily taken to the casual, Western-style clothing of Phoenix, Teuscher was immediately noticeable by his dress. He was always immaculately attired in a vested suit and tie, day or night, seven days a week. He looked as though he had just stepped out of a haberdashery display window.

Teuscher had gotten into the newspaper business in 1960, shortly after his discharge from the army. Before joining the army, he had studied for four years at Concordia Seminary in St. Louis, planning to become a Lutheran minister. But he had done a bit of public relations work in the service, found he had a flair for writing, and instead landed his first job with a small downstate Illinois newspaper. In 1966, he moved to the *Globe*, where he specialized in exposing public corruption and the abuses of the giant Teamsters Union Central States Pension Fund. When he came to Phoenix, he brought with him two huge suitcases containing all his Teamsters files. A stickler for documentation, his expertise was in the researching of public records. For the first couple of days in Phoenix he happily immersed himself in the mountain of files already gathered by the team. He was so enthralled by the records that he stayed up past 2:00 A.M. one morning, until a sleepy-eyed Greene literally kicked him out of the IRE office. On his way to his room, Teuscher bumped into Koziol, who had been down in the hotel bar with some of the other reporters. Teuscher went on and on about the story possibilities apropos the many schemes and swindles already suggested by the files. He brought Koziol into his room to show him the personal files he had brought from St. Louis, inviting Koziol to go through them.

Koziol hated records. Over the past few days Koziol had read enough files to last him the rest of his career. He politely refused the offer and went next door to his own room. Teuscher was still turning the pages of his files in the adjoining room.

On Tuesday, November 9, Greene paired Koziol and Teuscher as partners. He handed them a thick file marked "Hobo Joe's— Southwestern Research." It was filled with real estate records, financial statements, and corporation documents. Koziol needed more files like he needed a hangover. Teuscher eagerly opened the folder and began thumbing through the legal-sized papers.

Hobo Joe's was the name of a restaurant chain, Greene explained. It was owned by Barry Goldwater's brother, Robert; Robert's longtime partner, Joseph F. Martori; and a third man, Herbert Applegate. All three men were of interest to IRE. Robert Goldwater and Martori had been investigated previously in connection with the Goldmar Corporation and Arrowhead Ranch, continued Greene.

Koziol and Teuscher nodded. They had read the files on the history of the ranch and were familiar with the people involved in its operation. They also knew about Wendland's and Drehsler's adventures there the month before when they had gone out to document the illegal alien situation. Applegate, however, was a new name.

A native Detroiter, Applegate was a restaurateur who had moved his family to Arizona in 1964. For a few years, he had tried his hand at managing a couple of marginal restaurants, with just moderate success. But in the late 1960s, he hooked up with Goldwater and Martori. From their partnership, Hobo Joe's was born. Nine outlets were in operation by the late 1960s, with a number of others in the planning stages. A statue of a hobo with an old cutaway coat and a handkerchief on a stick stood out in front of each spot. They were small, family-type restaurants, each featuring the same decor and menu, including the special "Hoboburger."

A second chain, the Humpty-Dumpty Coffeeshops, developed from this three-way partnership. Applegate also built a large, more luxurious, gourmet restaurant, which he named after himself. And for a brief period of time, he even took over the management of the restaurant of the Adams Hotel.

In 1968, Goldwater, Martori, and Applegate took in a fourth partner, a corporation known as Southwestern Research. The reason was simple. They needed cash. In exchange for guaranteeing a $3 million loan, Southwestern was made a partner. It was this move that prompted the IRE interest. According to the files, the loan which Southwestern guaranteed was to be used only for construction of new restaurants. Yet in the preliminary analysis of the Hobo Joe's corporate records, it looked like most of the money had simply vanished or been diverted in a number of questionable areas.

"I'm really not sure what the hell we've got here," Greene told Koziol and Teuscher. "But it looks like there was a $3 million scam."

"What do you want us to do?" asked Koziol.

"You guys are pros..I want you to go out and find out how it was done."

The reporters began to dig into the file. It didn't seem to help much. The financial transactions were complicated. They learned that Applegate had died of a heart attack in 1974. And the Hobo Joe's chain had since been bought by another firm, unconnected with Goldwater or Martori. It seemed as if everyone who had had a hand in the partnership had faded from the scene. Even Southwestern Research had left Phoenix, after apparently getting stuck for the $3 million loan. They were now based in southern California.

From the index cards, which noted every name and business listed in the main files, Teuscher found a previous listing for Herbert Applegate. It was in the file on Peter "Horseface" Licavoli, the former boss of Detroit's old Purple Gang, now a resident of Tucson.

The notation was brief. A couple of paragraphs in a 1972 Republic story by Don Bolles mentioned that one of Licavoli's Phoenix friends was restaurateur Herbert Applegate. Interesting, thought Teuscher. Applegate was quoted as saying that he knew Pete Licavoli, Sr., from his old days in Detroit, when both had owned stock in a small coffee company. Applegate denied any business dealings with the mobster and said he had only seen him a couple of times since coming to Arizona.

The files also cited some sort of proxy fight between Southwestern and Hobo Joe's. Koziol figured that a disgruntled partner might be willing to talk. The Southwestern man who had been involved in the partnership was F. M. "Pat" McCown. Koziol checked telephone information operators in Los Angeles and several suburbs with no luck. He much preferred contacting McCown at home. Hating to tip his mitt, he dialed the main number for Southwestern and asked where he could reach McCown. "Why he's here, sir," an operator volunteered. In a moment, a pleasant but all-business voice was on the other end of the line.

Koziol introduced himself and told McCown that he was interested in learning the details of Southwestern's involvement in Hobo Joe's. "All I can say is that I really got screwed by those Arizona slickers," McCown said sarcastically.

"What happened?"

"It's a long story. But let me tell you this. If you have any money, don't ever go to Arizona, because when you leave, you'll leave without it."

Koziol explained the IRE task force and the Bolles bombing. He told the executive about their wide-ranging investigation and how they came to be interested in Herb Applegate, Robert Goldwater, and Joe Martori. "We went through all the corporate records we could get our hands on," he concluded. "And while we don't know how, it sure looks to us like the three million you guys brought into Hobo Joe's was sucked up in some scam."

McCown was silent for a moment. "You sure got that right."

"Then how was it done?"

Again a silence. "How do I know you really are who you say you are?"

It was a good question. Koziol carefully gave him the spelling of his name, his telephone number in Phoenix, and the city desk number of the *Chicago Tribune*. "Look, we'd really like to talk to you about this. You just tell us where."

"If I do agree to talk to you, it won't be in Phoenix. I won't ever set foot in Arizona again. You don't know the people you're dealing with."

Koziol felt the familiar tension that overcomes all reporters when they've just discovered something big. He hadn't really learned a thing from McCown. But he knew that if he could persuade the man to talk, he soon would. "No problem. We'll come out to California or anywhere you want. I can be there in the morning if you want."

"No. I'm still not convinced you're a reporter. I have to check you out first."

"Fine. Please do. I can't blame you for being cautious. I just want your promise to meet with us after you see that I am who I say I am."

"If you are, I'll talk with you. But I'll tell you this, there are some pretty powerful and ruthless people out there that you'll be looking into. You can get your heads blown off if you go too far."

Koziol told McCown that they needed to meet as soon as possible. But McCown would not set a time until he was sure of Koziol. He promised to phone the reporter back.

"I hope you understand my alarm. It's just that I've dealt with that Arizona bunch before. There have been threats. I'm afraid of a setup. I just don't want to take any chances." McCown hung up.

There was nothing Koziol could do but hope that he indeed would call back.

Meanwhile, Greene had plans for the IRE reporters.

"I want you guys to do more bar-hopping at night," he announced just before dinner.

The reporters glanced at each other quizzically. News people are not particularly known for their aversion to alcohol. On most any given night the downstairs hotel bar appeared to have been taken over by a convention of thirsty war correspondents.

"No, don't get me wrong. It's not that you haven't been drinking," Greene laughed, recalling the bloodshot eyes he saw in the troops each morning. "No, what I'm saying is that if you're going to have a couple to unwind each night, why not have them someplace where you can work at the same time?"

Again, there was puzzlement.

"What I've done," said Greene, who had been nicknamed, behind his back, "the Buddha," owing to his shape and commanding position, "is to prepare a list for you guys. We made this up with some sources in law enforcement. On it, you'll find every major hoodlum hangout in and around Phoenix. I want you guys to visit them all. Keep your eyes and ears open. Find out who the big shooters are. Figure out the scams. It's just good, basic backgrounding for us. Maybe none of the bar stuff will ever make the stories we'll be doing, but we're bound to understand the local scene a hell of a lot better."

The list contained the names of forty-seven bars, taverns, disco spots, and cocktail lounges. He gave the reporters a copy of it. "Have fun."

That night, Drehsler, Koziol, John Rawlinson, George Weisz, and Dick Levitan, the Boston reporter for CBS radio station WEEI, went out to check a few of the spots Greene had recommended.

Levitan, the only broadcast media representative of the team, had also acquired a nickname. He was called "Blackjack Levitan." Back in Boston, Levitan covered the city's infamous "Jungle" district of sleazy honky-tonks and trick houses. He had been threatened many times for his exposés on prostitution and organized crime activities. He carried a gun, a blackjack, and a can of Mace.

"I wanted to bring my piece out here," he told the reporters shortly after his arrival, "but I checked with the local cops before leaving and it would have been too much of a hassle to get a concealed weapons permit. So instead, I brought these." In his back pocket was a neat, fold-over blackjack. In his shirt pocket was a tear-gas pen. Levitan, forty-three years old and engaged to a motorcycle policewoman, never went anywhere without both. One night, following Drehsler on a tour of Phoenix nightspots, he had difficulty distinguishing the IRE car in traffic. So he got out of his car at the first stop and smashed the right rear taillight of Drehsler's car with his sap. Then he followed the car with the busted light. Levitan, who bore an uncanny resemblance to the actor Robert Blake of television's "Baretta" program, did not drink alcohol. Instead, he sipped Cokes.

The touring reporters stopped at a couple of places on Greene's bar list. But it was a Tuesday night and they were mostly empty. In suburban Scottsdale, they ordered drinks at a hole-in-the-wall joint whose chief drawing card was a bunch of aging strippers. Koziol counted six other nondescript patrons in the place. The biggest excitement came when Rawlinson returned from the restroom with a prophylactic he had bought from a vending machine attached to the wall over a urinal. The rubber, however, was not the standard kind. This one was for the tongue—"For safe, enjoyable oral sex," touted its foil packet. The reporters broke up. The place was a dump. They left without bothering to watch the dancer, a fortyish dyed redhead, finish stripping out of her dirty white nightgown.

The next stop was the Foxe au-Disco. Levitan almost overreacted there. It was his first visit to the place. So when Joey came over to Drehsler and playfully put his hands around Alex's throat in a mock strangulation greeting, Levitan thought it was the real thing. He reacted quickly, pulling the sap from his pocket. Fortunately, before Levitan could apply it, Koziol and Weisz pulled him off. Joey thought it was hilarious and ordered a round of drinks for the reporters. Then he motioned Koziol aside. "Meet me outside, around the corner, in five minutes," he whispered.

Koziol expected Joey to ask about his drive home the other night with Mandy. Instead, Joey had something else to talk about.

"Listen," he began, looking over his shoulder to make sure he wasn't followed. "I told you I had something for you. Okay, here it is. This is one hundred percent solid. The cops are barking up the wrong tree with Adamson.''

"How's that?'' asked Koziol.

"Adamson wasn't the guy that did it. The guy who rigged the bomb is a guy named Suitcase Willie. Check it out.'' Joey started to go back.

"Wait a minute, now. How the hell do you propose I do that?''

"You're the reporter. All I know is that this Suitcase was spending money like a drunken sailor after the bombing. He was spreading it all over town, including this place. And he was in the army, where he handled explosives.''

"What's this Suitcase Willie's real name?''

"That's it. I don't know his last name. They call him Suitcase because he's always carrying one.''

This was ridiculous. "Okay, Joey, we'll get right on it. Thanks.'' These guys were crazy, thought Koziol. First the woman the other night, now Joey was trying to send him off on a wild-goose chase.

Back in the bar, Jack Duggan, the other owner, came by. He shot the breeze with the reporters for a while, volunteering that he knew Adamson and ''He's no killer. He's being framed.''

The night had been a waste of time. But the next morning, things started to pick up. McCown called back from California. He had verified Koziol's identity and agreed to a meeting. It was arranged for the next day at the airport in Ontario, not far from Los Angeles.

At seven o'clock the morning of November 12, Koziol and Teuscher were on an Air West flight to Ontario. McCown, a tall, distinguished-looking man in his early fifties, was waiting for them at the airport. He carefully examined the reporters' press cards. They drove in McCown's car to a nearby Holiday Inn and went into the coffee shop. McCown sat down across from the two reporters, who could barely squeeze into a single booth seat.

"I don't know where to start,'' he grinned.

"Let's try from the beginning,'' said Teuscher.

"Okay. But I want you to know that everything I'm going to say can be proven. I've got canceled checks from Hobo Joe's, witnesses and everything. If I can't document a certain point, I can lead you to someone who can.'' McCown couldn't have said anything more promising to the reporters.

His investment company, Southwestern Research, was formed back in the mid-1960s. At the time it became involved in Hobo Joe's, its assets were only about six million dollars, consisting mostly of various holdings in unimproved land it hoped eventually to sell at a profit. Southwestern was a relatively small concern built on anticipated growth rather than performance. And it was in need of cash. So when the opportunity came in 1968 to buy into what appeared to be a dynamic chain of restaurants, it jumped at the chance. Under the terms of the deal, Southwestern became a fourth partner. Applegate didn't sell any of his stock, thus retaining major ownership and remaining Hobo Joe's president. But Goldwater and Martori each sold off about a third of their stock holdings, giving Southwestern a 27½ percent share of the chain's ownership. In exchange, Southwestern paid $275,109 in cash and guaranteed a $3 million loan agreement between Hobo Joe's and the Valley National Bank of Phoenix.

The idea, explained McCown, was that Southwestern would never have to repay the loan. Indeed, three million dollars was too much for the small firm. Instead, the three million was pegged to finance construction of a string of new Hobo Joe's outlets whose profits would make the loan payments.

Teuscher had been mystified by the loan guarantee. Valley National Bank certainly did not need Southwestern as guarantor. Robert Goldwater's connection with Hobo Joe's alone would surely have been enough to push through the loan. Besides being one of the city's most prominent businessmen, Goldwater was also a director of Valley National. That led the reporter to a single question: If Hobo Joe's didn't really need Southwestern to guarantee the loan, why did it get them to do so? One possible answer came immediately to mind. Perhaps somebody at Hobo Joe's knew all along that the loan would never be repaid and wanted to make sure that when the bank started hollering, somebody else would be stuck with the obligation.

"Anyway, we got suckered, pure and simple," McCown was saying. "Two years after we bought in, the three million was gone, the bank was pressuring us to pay the loan or completely buy out Applegate and the others. We were had. We were in a real crisis. They stuck it to us royally."

"The big question is, where did the money go?" Koziol asked.

"It was all diverted. Who knows exactly where? We could only account for a million and a half. That, we know, went to Applegate. In all, my guess is that closer to eight million was skimmed. I can't tell you for sure whether Goldwater and Martori got any. But they didn't lose anything, that's for sure. The bottom line is that a prosperous chain of restaurants in 1968, that should have been making money and growing by leaps and bounds over the next two years, instead went more than three million dollars in the red.''

"What did Applegate do with the million and a half?" Teuscher wanted to know.

"For starters, he built himself a home worth about $350,000. Then he built a little corporate party house which he staffed with former Playboy bunnies. He threw all sorts of wild orgies there. He made payoffs to the Mafia, he———''

"Hold it a minute. One thing at a time," said Koziol. "What about the house?"

"Sorry. Okay. Well, Applegate, you have to understand, fancied himself quite the swinger. I mean he always dressed in expensive clothes, carried huge bankrolls around, smoked Cuban cigars, you get the picture. Anyway, he built himself a house out of diverted funds. I'll give you the name of the contractor."

"Let's get one thing straight," interjected Teuscher. "All this was going on after you guys bought in?"

McCown nodded. "Right, we were supposed to be partners. I was sent to Phoenix to help run the chain."

"Then how did this all go on without you getting wise?"

"Fair question. Under the terms of the loan arrangement with the bank, none of the three million was to be disbursed unless there were two signatures. One from Hobo Joe's and one from Southwestern. What I found out, much too late to make any difference, was that some of the payout papers had no signature at all. Most had just Applegate's. But never was there a signature from Southwestern."

"Okay. Go on."

"Well, anyway, one of the legitimate things some of the loan money was to go for was to build a central commissary, a main supply center for all the restaurants. It was budgeted at $400,000. In the end, it cost $800,000. Well it was the extra $400,000 that built Applegate's house and the corporate party house."

"The what?" said Koziol.

"You heard me right. It was a duplex, out in Mesa just outside of Phoenix. Applegate put two or three broads in there. They were ex-bunnies or dancers I think. One of the girls was Applegate's mistress. Sandra Peterson was her name. Anyway, this place was used strictly for sex parties. And it was decorated like something out of a wet dream.''

''What's this you said a minute ago about the Mafia?'' asked Teuscher.

''Ever hear of Pete Licavoli, Sr.? Hell, I'm sure you have. Anyway, he was a close pal of Applegate's. So close that Applegate was paying him twenty-five hundred a month.''

''Out of his own pocket?''

''Hell, no. Out of the company funds. The deal was that Licavoli was supplying paintings. He owns an art studio or something down in Tucson. Anyway, once each month, he'd bring a load of them up to Applegate, collect the twenty-five hundred, and leave. Now I know something about art. And they were garbage. They looked like cheap reproductions. I found out about it one day when I was in the office. Applegate had a mild heart attack or something and was off for a few days. So this one day his secretary comes in and says that there's a Mr. Licavoli outside with a new shipment of paintings. I asked, 'What shipment?' I wasn't expecting any shipment. She looked real worried and said it was the usual delivery. I looked around. There was no purchase order, no delivery slip, no invoice. Nothing. And the whole place is full of pictures. I was up to my ass in paintings. They were laying on the floors, on the walls, on tables, all over. So I told her to go tell Licavoli that I didn't want any more paintings. She got more worried and told me that if she were me, she'd give him the usual check. I said no and she started to cry. Can you imagine that? So I got on the phone and called Applegate at home. He says to give Licavoli the money and not to ask questions. Well, I refused. The next day, I found out that he got the money anyway from somebody else in the company. Then, to top it all off, I'm driving home two nights later. All of a sudden, two cars come up from behind and force me over to the curb. These two goons get out of one of the cars and come over to me, and one of them says that if I value my life, I'll stop nosing around in the internal affairs of the company. That's what I'm talking about. That's what I mean by Mafia.''

''Can you prove any of this? Earlier, you said you had documentation,'' Teuscher reminded.

''I told you, I've got checks, canceled checks which document the payoffs to Licavoli.''

The reporters exchanged glances. McCown was giving them an incredible story.

But he wasn't finished yet. "They were stealing every way you can imagine. One day I got a phone call from this hysterical woman, who just had to see me. She came to my office terrified. She said she was threatened to keep quiet. But what she said was that every store manager placed a double order when ordering food supplies from the Hobo Joe's commissary. And when the stuff was delivered at night, it was always in two batches. One went into the restaurant food locker. The other was left just inside the back door. Soon after the commissary truck dropped it off, a second truck came by for the extra order. The woman asked the second driver one time where the extra order went. He said Tucson. Guess who lives in Tucson? Pete Licavoli, Sr.''

McCown said that he guessed a quarter of a million dollars worth of food went out the back doors of Hobo Joe's restaurants during a five-month period.

There was still more. A killing, the shooting death of a private detective sent by Applegate to Les Vegas to reclaim the clothes and automobile he had bought for another of his girlfriends, had been covered up, said McCown, most probably with Hobo Joe's funds.

"The girl's name was Dianna Willis," said McCown, spelling the name for the reporters. "It was in January 1969. She had dumped Applegate for another guy, a swimming pool attendant or something up there, and he was furious. So he sent this private eye and another guy. When they tried to force their way in, boom, the girl's new lover opened fire. The private eye died."

McCown said he knew of $7000 that was suddenly withdrawn from Hobo Joe's bank account after the killing. "I know Robert Goldwater was extremely upset by the whole thing. I mean he was Applegate's business partner. Anyway, the girl got some of the money. The rest was spread around up in Vegas to buy off any official investigation. You'll have to prove that one yourself. All I know is that the killing occurred, Applegate sent the private detective up there and his name was never connected to the incident in the Phoenix papers. It was a hell of a scandal at the time. The detective was the son of a justice of the peace. His brother was a real respected officer in the state Department of Public Safety. But Goldwater and his pals saw to it that the *Republic* and *Gazette* kept Applegate's name out." McCown gave the reporters the name of the dead private detective and a few other details which would help them later try to unravel the incident.

The reporters changed the subject for a few minutes, talking about McCown's background, his family, California weather, and a number of other things that gave them a chance to evaluate him. He was obviously bitter and vindictive over his Arizona experiences but, concluded Koziol and Teuscher, not without justification. The Hobo Joe's debacle had forced him to quit Southwestern and struggle among a number of poorly paying jobs to support his family. Finally, Southwestern got out of Hobo Joe's and returned to California in 1971 with its meager assets decimated. A couple of years later, McCown was asked to return to Southwestern, then run by an entirely new board of directors. At the time, he explained, the firm's payroll was $40,000 a month; it had just $1,200 in the bank and zero cash flow. But business had improved dramatically by 1976, and it appeared that the firm was on solid ground again, though not nearly as well off as it would have been had they stayed out of Arizona.

They had been talking for two hours. A thin band of perspiration shone across McCown's forehead. As he drove the reporters back to the airport, he seemed to relax for the first time. As they walked into the bustling little airport, McCown promised to get back to the reporters soon and arrange another meeting, at which he would turn over the canceled checks.

"There's another guy I want you two to meet," he said. "He was as deeply into the Hobo Joe's thing as I was. Maybe more so. He was the chief financial officer. He can verify a lot of what I've said and he saw a lot of things that I didn't. I don't want to give you his name right now because he's sort of in hiding out here, but I think I can persuade him to talk to you."

They shook hands and McCown walked back outside.

Two hours after Koziol and Teuscher had returned to Phoenix and were briefing Greene and the others on the California meeting, McCown called back. He was true to his word. "It's set for Tuesday at 10:00 A.M. Same place," he said. "Get a room there. I'll bring the things we discussed, including the other guy I mentioned. He's scared but he'll talk." Koziol thanked him and hung up. It was falling into place beautifully. There were four days until the next meeting with McCown. Meanwhile, they had more than enough leads to start running down.

On the morning of Friday, November 12, Koziol and Teuscher located an accountant named Tom Wilson, whom McCown had named as one of several people called in by Southwestern to help straighten out the confusing financial records of the Hobo Joe's chain. They found him in the telephone book under certified public accountants and went to see him. Wilson was a congenial man and a close friend of McCown's. He was also a native Texan and proud to point out to the reporters that he was not part of the Arizona power structure. Wilson said he had had major problems with Hobo Joe's books.

"For one thing," he said, "there was evidence of criminal fraud and misappropriation." No law enforcement agency had ever investigated the situation, he said. Two of the owners of Hobo Joe's— Goldwater and Martori—did not want an official probe. However, he had heard that they had hired a private detective to see whether Applegate was stealing. Wilson had also heard plenty of stories about Applegate's corporate party house, though he stressed that he had never been there. "It was out in Mesa somewhere," he recalled.

Did he know the contractor for Applegate's home? The reporters had been told by McCown that the same man who built the home had remodeled the partyhouse. Yes, Wilson did know who it was. His name was Ernest Byke. He lived in Scottsdale.

Next, the reporters drove over to the headquarters of the state Department of Public Safety, Arizona's equivalent of the state police. Teuscher had earlier telephoned the father of the private detective killed in Las Vegas while trying to retrieve the automobile and clothing of one of Applegate's fickle mistresses. The dead man was Bill Kimball. The father had referred the reporters to another son, Lt. Stan Kimball. The lieutenant, a trim fifty-year-old, ran the records section of DPS. He was waiting for them.

"My father told me to be expecting you," he said with a smile and an offer of coffee. "Sit down."

The reporters explained that they were interested in learning more about his brother's death seven years ago.

"Well, I'm the only one who can tell you," he said. "There are absolutely no more records on this. The Las Vegas authorities destroyed them all."

"They what?" Koziol had covered police news for years. Cops do not throw away homicide records. As a young reporter in Chicago, he used to while away boring hours reading the thirty-year-old reports of street shootings during Al Capone's heyday. He found it hard to believe that the Las Vegas police would not still have the original reports on the case.

"They don't. Go check and see. They were destroyed. A lot of powerful people were involved in this. There was one hell of a cover-up. Applegate never was exposed. His pal Goldwater was really concerned that they would all be embarrassed."

Lieutenant Kimball then turned around and pulled a thick blue notebook from a filing cabinet. "Here, take this and make copies or do what you want. It's the complete police report. It's the only copy remaining. I got it right after the case was closed from a friendly source up there. But this has everything, everybody's statements, all the lies, the police reports, the whole ball of wax."

The reporters thanked him.

"No, it's me who has the thanks," said Kimball, walking them out of his office. "Not just because you're interested in my brother's case. But for coming to Arizona. It's something this state has needed for a long time. Maybe something will be done now." On the way back to the hotel, Teuscher, the records man, started reading.

The report began with news clippings from the *Republic*. "Wound Fatal to Private Eye," read a headline from the January 14, 1969, paper which detailed how Bill Kimball, twenty-seven, "scion of a prominent Arizona family of lawmen," died from a single gunshot wound to the head the night before "when he and a friend, Phoenix restaurant operator Frank Casciola, were reported to have attempted to force their way into the apartment of a swimming pool attendant." In another clipping, the name of the restaurant Casciola operated was identified as "the Hobo Joe's coffee shop at 1601 E. Camelback."

Teuscher scanned all the clips. There was absolutely no mention of Herb Applegate. The closest was in a January 19, 1969, story by *Republic* reporter Paul Dean, headlined "Reasons for Kimball Death Remain Mystery." Dean told his readers that Kimball and Casciola had been dispatched to Las Vegas to repossess the automobile and personal effects of a "casino girl," who had recently soured a "sugar daddy romance with a married, wealthy, Scottsdale businessman." Dean quoted a source close to the Las Vegas investigation as saying that "a lot of heat was applied to Nevada authorities, reportedly from persons anxious to quell full investigation and to block all the circumstances and names surrounding the killing." While police placed no blame on the swimming pool attendant, Dean noted that further investigation could result in "technical charges" being filed against Casciola or against the businessman for forced entry or conspiracy.

On January 30, 1969, the *Republic* reported "Shooting Death of

Private Eye Is A 'Closed Case.' '' No inquest would be held and all investigation had stopped. The story quoted Clark County (Nevada) assistant district attorney Raymond Jeffers as saying that lies and inconsistencies were found in statements given investigators: ''But lying or no, there's nothing to file upon . . . no evidence of criminal responsibility on anyone's part . . . we're through with it.'' But according to the police reports and the statements of those involved, the lies and inconsistencies that Jeffers spoke of emanated from one basic source: Herb Applegate.

The facts of the shooting itself were fairly easy to discern. On January 12, 1969, at approximately 5:30 A.M., Kimball and Casciola, after several earlier attempts had failed to find anyone home, went to the apartment of Billy Ray Underwood, 28, a swimming pool attendant at Caesar's Palace and the new boyfriend of Dianna Willis. Miss Willis was at the time in Acapulco, Mexico, staying at a hotel owned by a friend of hers. But since the previous October, after breaking up with Applegate, with whom she had had an affair for some two years, she had been living with Underwood. When Kimball and Casciola, both wearing trench coats and hats, returned to the apartment, they found the lights out, indicating that Underwood was home. They knocked on the door, roused him from sleep, and told him they had been hired by Miss Willis to remove her clothes.

Underwood said the pair had forced their way into his apartment in a threatening manner. Casciola denied that any entry had been made. But armed with a .32 caliber revolver and claiming fear of his life, Underwood fired one shot. It struck Kimball in the face. Casciola fled.

An autopsy and subsequent police investigation backed up Underwood's claim. Kimball, at least, had indeed entered the apartment. The coroner ruled that it would have been impossible for him to move after suffering the wound. And the first police officers on the scene, who arrived minutes after the shooting, found Kimball's body two-thirds inside the apartment. Neighbors awakened by the ruckus caused when Kimball and Casciola knocked on the door verified that Underwood had not moved the body. So Underwood was in the clear. The killing appeared to be self defense.

The case became very confusing when police tried to figure out who had hired Kimball and why. Casciola, a boyhood friend of the dead man's who often assisted him on cases, said that Herb Applegate, Casciola's boss, had hired them on behalf of a third man, Jack

Morton, the Acapulco hotel owner with whom Miss Willis was then visiting. Casciola was told that it was Miss Willis's wish to remove her items from Underwood's. Applegate, who at first refused to return police calls and finally talked only when investigators flew to Phoenix, insisted he was just a middleman, that it was Morton who had requested help from him. He claimed his relationship to Miss Willis was "like a father."

Morton denied the whole thing. It was Applegate who hired the detectives, he told investigators during an interview. He knew nothing about it.

But the main problems came when police talked to Dianna Willis, who voiced outrage that Applegate or Morton or anyone else claimed she wanted to leave Underwood. She loved Underwood, she said, and was planning on marrying him in the spring. She had no intention of moving out on him. They had gone to Acapulco together the week before. The only reason she was there alone was that he had to get back to work. She was planning to rejoin him after the weekend of the killing. Applegate was lying. He was angry and dejected about being dumped for the young, muscular Underwood, she said. Applegate had given her a company car, a 1968 Mercury Cougar, and provided her with a gasoline credit card and a telephone credit card. But Applegate had kept a set of the car keys, she said. "That's the way he gave presents," Miss Willis told police. "As long as you're my friend, I'll let you drive the car. I'll keep the other set of keys so that if you're not my friend any longer, I'll come get the car." It was typical of Applegate to hire strong-arm types to come take his gifts back. "I have heard him talk about protecting his friends and that he had friends that will break somebody's legs and would take care of them," she told authorities.

She summed it up quite well. "It's stupid, you know. It's such a bunch of shit. A man's dead for no reason."

On November 13, a Saturday, Koziol and Teuscher located Ernest Byke, the Hobo Joe's contractor. It was a scenic drive to Byke's comfortable home in the foothills outside Scottsdale, about twenty-five miles out of Phoenix. Byke, a mild-mannered sort, was happy to tell the reporters what he knew about Hobo Joe's.

"Everybody in the firm was a swinger," he recalled. "I felt like a fifth wheel because they would never include me in the parties."

The reporters asked him what he knew about the Mesa house.

"Well, I knew they had a place there," he said. "The guys talked about it in the office after the parties. It had mirrors on the ceilings of the bedrooms and secret passageways in the closets in case of a raid.''

But it was not Byke who remodeled the Mesa house, it was an interior decorator named Dave Stevens, an old friend of Applegate's. Byke built Applegate's plush Camelback Mountain home, which was worth about $350,000, he said, and later hired on with Applegate as Hobo Joe's main contractor. He also said he was the man who finished work on the Hobo Joe's commissary. Byke confirmed that the commissary cost $400,000.

The contractor wasn't very happy with his experience with Hobo Joe's. ''Applegate was always too busy to spend time going over construction details,'' he said. ''With the constant flow of women going in and out of his office, I don't know how he got anything done.''

Byke, too, had seen Pete Licavoli, Sr., with Applegate. ''He'd come in about once a month with five or six paintings under his arm,'' he said. ''Applegate once told me that Licavoli painted the paintings himself, but they looked pretty cheap to me, like they were mass-produced.'' He said there were hundreds of them lying all over Applegate's offices.

What Byke most wanted to talk about were the women and the constant partying Applegate and his friends carried on at the Mesa house. ''You wouldn't believe the stories I used to hear them all tell,'' he chuckled. ''I guess I missed out. I was too straight.''

Sandra Peterson was the main Applegate mistress, the one who actually lived in the Mesa house. ''She had all sorts of friends, lady friends, who were always entertaining over there.''

Byke also knew Dianna Willis. ''She was his Las Vegas mistress; Sandy was his Phoenix mistress,'' he said. ''That guy sure liked his women.''

Before leaving, the reporters got the name of another contractor who had worked on the Hobo Joe's commissary. Byke walked them to the door and shook hands. ''You know,'' he said, ''I really enjoyed this conversation.''

The next day was Sunday. Koziol had been going for ten straight days. He slept till almost noon, had a long lunch of Bloody Marys, and tried to unwind. Teuscher went over the growing Hobo Joe's file.

On Monday, November 15, the morning radio news was announcing an impending strike by Air West, the only airline that flew to Ontario, California, where their all-important meeting with McCown was to take place the next morning. The strike was to begin at midnight. But the reporters had too much to do to leave early. All they could do was hope things would work out.

They went to see Rich Morganson, who had supervised construction of the Hobo Joe's commissary with Byke. Morganson said the commissary could have been built for $200,000, but that Applegate kept coming back with changes. It ended up costing $400,000, he said. One day shortly after the building was finished, he said Applegate came to him. "He wanted me to verify on a note that the commissary cost $500,000 so he could get the money from the bank." Morganson said he refused. "Applegate wanted me to do the remodeling on the Mesa party house but I wouldn't have anything to do with it," he said. "I had a pretty good idea what it was going to be used for. I understand it was laid out pretty elaborately." He, too, identified interior designer Dave Stevens as the man who handled the decorating.

That afternoon, Teuscher tried to reach Stevens. He was out of town, his secretary said. He would return next week. Could she ask what this was in regards to? For a moment, Teuscher thought of telling her. He decided that the fun of hearing her gasp would only tip their hand. He said he would call back for an appointment next week.

The threatened Air West strike was settled at the last minute, and early Tuesday morning Koziol and Teuscher were on the plane to California. Again, McCown was waiting at the airport. With him was another man, younger, in his late thirties. He looked nervous. The man was Paul Router, introduced McCown. And, during the period that the Hobo Joe's stealing was going on, Router had been Applegate's chief financial officer. They went to the same Holiday Inn they had met in the week before. This time, the reporters had reserved a room. Koziol called room service and ordered a large pot of coffee. But before getting to new matters, they had a question for McCown.

Tom Wilson, the CPA who had said he found criminal evidence of fraud in the Hobo Joe's books, had told the reporters that Goldwater and Martori had hired a private detective at one time to look into Applegate's wheeling and dealing. The IRE team had located the private detective, Steve Fortinos, who confirmed the investigation. Fortinos said he had uncovered obvious signs of embezzlement, as well as Licavoli's involvement with Applegate. He was positive that he had reported those facts to Goldwater.

"That kind of cheating can't be overlooked," Fortinos had told IRE.

McCown was asked whether he knew of Fortino's findings.

He nodded.

"Then why didn't you try to get Applegate out of there, to move against him?" Koziol asked.

"Nothing would have pleased me more," he answered. "But we couldn't do it. We were the minority stockholders. The firm was controlled by Goldwater, Martori, and Applegate."

"They wouldn't do it?"

"No. Herb was their boy."

"Okay," said Koziol. "Let's see that proof you say you have."

McCown handed over a batch of papers. They were photostatic copies of canceled checks, hundreds of them. Router estimated that they represented perhaps ten percent of the total issued by Hobo Joe's during the time period under investigation. The rest of the checks were missing, McCown explained. "So were the company books that would make more sense of them." Even so, the checks proved many of the kickbacks Applegate had engineered, including the payment to Licavoli.

Router verified most everything McCown had told the reporters the week before. He too, had been threatened when he balked at making a payment to Licavoli. "They took me outside to his car, where two oversized gentlemen were sitting," he said. "They told me that they don't like to be disappointed. I paid." But, said Router, just to make sure that he got the message, a couple of days later he received a telephone threat that if he wanted to stay healthy, he shouldn't make waves at Hobo Joe's.

Router knew all about the Mesa party house. He had actually been there. It contained a sunken Grecian bathtub with a built-in whirl massage. "The Greek gods didn't have one as nice as that," he said. All the towel hooks and doorknobs in the place were in the shape of an erect penis. There was a secret room which contained two-way mirrors, one looking out on the main bedroom's large, circular bed, the other facing the living room. Also inside the hidden room was expensive movie-making equipment. "I can't prove it, but I think they were secretly taking pictures and then bribing people. You wouldn't believe who some of their guests were. There were judges, lawyers, businessmen, and some pretty prominent politicians."

But Router could not recall the exact address although he remembered that it was within a mile radius of Country Club and Main in Mesa. It had been purchased in 1968 or 1969, he said. Three $500 Hobo Joe's payroll checks were issued to one of Applegate's woman friends, who used them as the down payment. The original cost was around $20,000, but its remodeled value was closer to $70,000. Sandra Peterson, Applegate's Phoenix mistress and the woman who lived in the house, drove a car leased for her by Applegate and paid for by Hobo Joe's. She also had a MasterCharge credit card, again in Hobo Joe's name, which racked up several thousand dollars in bills in a six-month period.

Router told the reporters that he was with Applegate the afternoon following the shooting of Kimball. He said that Applegate told him to write out a $7,000 check for Robert Goldwater, so Goldwater could settle the "Vegas thing." Applegate didn't want the check in Goldwater's name. Router was told to issue it on Applegate's private account. "I don't know what happened to it, but I know it was issued." Router said that Goldwater also knew Dianna Willis.

They talked for a couple of hours, mostly going over old ground. The reporters tried to trip McCown, to get him to change his original story. He stuck to it like glue, verified on many counts by Router.

The reporters ordered a drink after McCown and Router left. With the exception of the party house, virtually every major allegation was on the verge of being documented. "God damn," complained Koziol. "Everybody knows all about the place, but nobody can tell us exactly where it is." They had to find Sandra Peterson and the party house. Koziol decided to head back for Phoenix and start work. Teuscher would stay overnight in California, analyzing and categorizing the checks.

Dale Randles was a very close friend of Applegate's. He had been taken in by the flashy restaurateur at the age of fourteen to wash dishes in one of Applegate's Michigan restaurants. Later, he followed Applegate to Arizona, where he worked for a time at Hobo Joe's. The California informants had given Randles's name as a possible source of information on the party house. The day after his return from Ontario, Koziol and Boston reporter Dick Levitan drove to the Safari Hotel in Scottsdale where Randles's ex-wife worked. The former Mrs. Randles was cooperative but curious. The reporters were tight-lipped, saying only that they needed to get in touch with her husband. With a shrug, she gave them a telephone number in Florida, where he had opened another restaurant. They thanked her and left.

But on the way out of the hotel, Levitan, the weapons freak, spotted a display in the lobby advertising "Protection Against

Intruders—Tear Gas Flashlights—Sold on Second Floor.'' Levitan
dashed to the small gift shop. Elated at his discovery, he paid ten
dollars for a long, four-cell flashlight that doubled as a secret tear gas
gun. It was just the thing for his car, he told Koziol.

That night, Koziol reached Randles on the telephone. He was glad
to talk. He was particularly upset that he had been left out of Applegate's will. ''I was one of the only people who cried at his funeral,''
he said. ''Herb was like a father to me. He took me in when I was
orphaned as a child. Sometimes, I even called him dad. It was one
hell of a shock to find out I was left out of the will. I blame all those
moneygrubbers around him. Those no-good bastards pushed me right
out of the picture. All those assholes got what they wanted and I got
shit.''

Koziol, as he had been many times before, was amazed at the
things some people would tell complete strangers over the telephone.
He asked Randles about the party house.

''Yeah, sure. I remember it,'' said Randles. ''Sandra Peterson
lived there. Nice girl. Nice place.''

Did he recall its address?

''Gosh, no, I don't. But let's see. It was on a street to the right of
Country Club Lane, as you drive towards Scottsdale from Mesa. And
it was painted blue. That's right, blue.''

Randles then volunteered that about two months after Applegate
died, his widow, Mae, came to him and wanted to know about all of
Herb's girlfriends. ''I wouldn't tell her,'' he said. ''I told her it was
best she didn't know. But the old man, he sure lived it up pretty
good.''

By this time, virtually all the reporters in the office were caught up
in the search for the Mesa house, which they dubbed ''The Great
Love Nest Hunt.'' Despite phone directory checks going back for ten
years and dozens of interviews, nobody could find it.

''Damn it, we've got a half-dozen of the best investigative reporters in the country and not one of them can find a house we're told was
visited by half of Phoenix at one time or another,'' groused Greene
one night.

On November 18, with Teuscher back from California, Koziol got
the name of a former Playboy bunny who at one time worked with
Sandra Peterson. They drove out to the address they had jotted down
from the phone book only to find a vacant lot. Koziol made a call from
a phone booth to the IRE office, had someone look up the address

again, and found he had transposed a couple of numbers. They set off again, this time coming to the right address. It was about 10:00 P.M. Koziol knocked on the door. A female voice inside asked who it was. The two reporters identified themselves. "Just wait a minute, I've got to get dressed." Koziol winked at Teuscher. A moment later, the front door opened a crack. But the woman left the protective chain latched. Koziol took his press card out of his wallet and held it up for the woman to see.

"Now let's see the other guy's," she said.

But Teuscher, fumbling through dozens of papers, cards, and pictures, couldn't find his. Thirty seconds passed. Then a minute. Finally, Teuscher, with a sheepish grin, said he couldn't find it.

"See," Koziol told the woman behind the door, "it's not exactly like in the movies, is it?"

The woman, wearing a pair of tight-fitting jeans and a red bathrobe, laughed and removed the chain, inviting them in.

Yes, she knew Sandra Peterson. But Sandy had gotten married and changed her name. As far as the woman knew, Sandy was still in the Phoenix area. She, too, had been to the Mesa party house.

The woman's name was Georgia Yanke, and, for a couple of years in the late sixties, she had worked as a bunny at the Phoenix Playboy Club. That's where she had met Sandy. "I was only out there to the Mesa place once, with a couple of other bunnies. I don't even remember where it was, except it was hard to find. It was a gaudy place. I remember purple furniture and blue carpeting and walls. There was a huge mirror built into the living room wall. And there was a sort of hidden passageway. I remember one of the girls that lived there demonstrated it. She just disappeared into space, it seemed like. I mean the whole wall just opened up."

Miss Yanke said that Sandy once told her that she was going with a very successful businessman.

What was his name?

"Oh, let's see. He had a restaurant. A bunch of restaurants. Herb, that's it, Herb was his name. Sandy said she was getting fifteen hundred a month from him." Miss Yanke had an old telephone number for Miss Peterson. She jotted it down on a piece of paper and gave it to the reporters as they left.

Teuscher and Koziol felt they were getting close. The next day, they made a series of telephone calls and personal interviews, running down some of the other information they had picked up from the

California sources. From a former Hobo Joe's store manager, they confirmed that double orders of food were frequently delivered, one for the store and one which was mysteriously carted away by truck for Tucson. Another former employee told of excessive shrimp orders placed by Applegate. "He was buying mountains of shrimp from Mexico, enough to last for years, way more than we needed," said the ex-employee. The shrimp was brokered through Pete Licavoli, Sr., he said. Similarly, Licavoli and Applegate made a deal for shoestring potatoes, thousands of pounds worth, said another Hobo Joe's source. The potatoes were poor in quality and did not cook well, he added, but Applegate kept buying them because "he didn't want to get Licavoli mad at him."

On November 22, a Monday, they found the party house.

Koziol and Teuscher had tried just about every source they could locate who was involved in the operation of Applegate's firm. Everybody had heard of the Mesa love nest, many had been there, but no one could recall its exact location. The reporters expected a similar response when they went to the small office of Ed Pileto, an electrical contractor in Mesa who had done some minor work for Applegate during the construction of the Hobo Joe's commissary.

Dressed in tan work clothes, Pileto confirmed that he had done work for Applegate over the years.

"What we are interested in finding out is whether you know of another place Applegate was working on about the same time the commissary was being built. It would have been a remodeling job on a duplex," Koziol asked.

"Sure. You must mean the place over on Sixth Avenue."

Koziol and Teuscher felt their hearts skip a beat. "You know where it is?"

"Sure. Herb hired me to put in an air conditioner and a small electric fireplace. I know right where it is. It was a real fancy place."

Pileto didn't know the address, but he could take them there. Excited, the reporters persuaded him to get in their car and direct them. It was a short trip, just six blocks away. When they found the house and Teuscher noticed its address, he began cursing.

Over a week before, while searching records in the county building, he had come across a bill for a love seat and sofa, bought on a sales contract by Applegate, that were to be delivered to the very house they were now parked in front of. Teuscher had driven out and looked over the building, then scratched it from his list because it was neither blue nor a duplex. But the stucco building had been repainted. It was now green. And instead of sitting crosswise on the lot, it was built lengthwise, making it appear from the street to be a single residence.

The reporters thanked Pileto, took him back to his office, and returned to the duplex.

A man named Ed Yurgel occupied the front portion of the house. He was happy to show the reporters the inside. Off a kitchen broom closet, they located the secret passageway which connected the two apartments. It had since been boarded up.

Next door, a woman named Mitzi opened the door. She too, told the reporters to look around. Like hungry animals, they split up, going from room to room, frantically searching for something which would indicate the building's former use.

But a lot of time had passed since Applegate's romps. The only thing unusual was that the bedroom doors all had special locks that locked automatically whenever the door closed, similar to those on hotel-room doors.

They got the name of the building owner and contacted him. He had purchased the duplex in 1971, from one of Sandra Peterson's relatives. He admitted, however, that the elaborate furnishings had been removed by them.

"I was really pissed off about the mirrors," said the new owner. "When I bought it there were mirrors all over the place. But they took 'em out when they left. The only thing I found was two large vibrators in the front room and a picture of some broad in a bunny costume." So the Applegate love nest really did exist.

The next day, they found Sandra Peterson herself through the old telephone number. She lived in Scottsdale in a modest house. After several knocks Ms. Peterson answered the door. She was an attractive, well-built blonde woman of thirty and obviously nervous at seeing two strange men standing out front. But she invited the reporters inside and did not disappoint them.

"I never kept track of the money I got," she said. "Herb just paid the bills. It was a good life while it lasted." She also had a leased Hobo Joe's car and a credit card. She had been Applegate's mistress for about five years.

"Herb made a lot of promises to me," she said with a sigh, glancing about the cluttered living room and absent-mindedly smoothing her hair. "He told me he was going to get a divorce and marry me. But I soon realized that wasn't the case. I wanted to marry Herb. I loved him.''

She also found out about Applegate's other mistress, Dianna Willis, in Las Vegas. When she confronted him with it, Applegate vowed that he would never see the other woman again. ''He was such a good liar. I almost believed him,'' she said.

She broke up with him in late 1972, met another man, quickly got pregnant, and married. ''He knows about Herb and I,'' she said. ''But please don't use my married name in the papers. I've got a kid now. I've tried to put it all behind me.'' She confirmed that the party house was paid for by Applegate and that it was wildly decorated. ''You should have seen my bedroom, it was painted pink and red.'' But she said she would be surprised if movies had been made at the parties. ''They could be embarrassing, you know?''

She also knew Pete Licavoli, Sr. She had driven with Applegate to Tucson, where they had stayed overnight as Licavoli's house guests at his Grace Ranch. She said that Applegate had told her that ''Pete used to be involved in the Mafia but was clean now.'' There had been other trips, once to Vegas, once to Los Angeles, San Francisco, a vacation together in Mexico, she couldn't remember them all.

The interview lasted less than an hour. She talked with resignation, as though she had expected someone to come to her eventually. All she asked in return was to avoid publicly identifying her husband. She had done nothing criminal. All she wanted now was to bury the past. The reporters left, feeling slightly depressed.

There was just one more interview to do—David Stevens, the interior designer who had remodeled the Mesa party house. Stevens, a prosperous businessman in his mid-forties, was not hesitant in talking. ''My instructions in remodeling the Mesa place were to make it look like a million dollars for $10,000,'' he said. ''And it was really something, like a vision from a fantasy nightmare, all in hot pink. There was even a secret passageway connecting the two units. It was in case somebody knocked on Sandy's apartment. That way Herb could slip out through the back apartment.''

Stevens said that Applegate used to carry around newspaper clippings of Kimball's death in Las Vegas and that he used to brag about how his name was never publicly connected. ''But I'll tell you, Applegate didn't have the juice to keep his name out of the newspapers. That power could only have come through Bob Goldwater or old man Martori.'' He, too, knew all about the payoffs to Licavoli. ''The paintings Herb got from him were really junk. After Applegate died and Hobo Joe's changed hands, I got stuck with them for a while. They were cluttering up my garage. So one day, I loaded them all up and drove them to Tucson and gave them all back to Licavoli.''

Stevens had one conclusion he wanted to share with the reporters.

''I'll tell you,'' he said. ''There was a lot of money that changed hands during those days. Okay, Herb is dead now. So he's going to take all the heat 'cause he's not here anymore. Just remember though, Herb wasn't the only partner in that firm.''

The Hobo Joe's fiasco was just one more piece in the increasingly intelligible jigsaw portrait of Robert William Goldwater, Jr., being assembled by IRE.

Known in and around Phoenix as an amiable and shrewd businessman, the sixty-six-year-old Goldwater, one year brother Barry's junior, was also a man whose connections with persons of more unsavory background had never been examined. By the end of November, IRE had documented the terrible exploitation of illegal aliens at his citrus ranch, his involvement in a company apparently being shaken down by a notorious hoodlum, and his friendships with at least three major underworld figures—Moe Dalitz, convicted stock swindler Allard Roen, and Lou ''The Tailor'' Rosanova.

Back in the early fifties, Barry was said to have told brother Bob something to this effect: ''You manage the money, I'll handle the other end. Then, when it's all over someday, we'll combine what we've learned and we'll do what no Goldwater has ever done—we'll make a fortune.''

In 1976, Bob Goldwater, a suntanned, soft-spoken man who once won the amateur golfing championship of Arizona and the Southwest, was indeed a millionaire. Although he and Barry had long since sold their interest in the family business, a chain of department stores which still bear the Goldwater name, Bob appeared to be a self-made man as the chairman of the huge Goldmar firm and co-owner of a number of other investment and real estate companies.

Given the degree of prominence attained by the Goldwater brothers, one of whom, after all, had been nominated by the Republican Party for the presidency of the United States, the series of associations and dealings involving the Goldwaters and the mob uncovered by IRE reporters should have raised a lot of eyebrows.

In Arizona, eyebrows don't raise easily.

9 | Border Traffic

The cactus blossom is Arizona's state flower. A more appropriate symbol is the poppy. For the Cactus Blossom State is a doper's delight. The IRE reporters discovered that Arizona had become the major narcotics corridor in the country. Contributing factors are a sparse population, plenty of rugged country for cover, over two thousand clandestine landing strips for airplanes, and U.S. 19, Arizona's main north-south expressway, which connects with the Pan American Highway just inside Nogales, Sonora. After the 1972 ban on opium poppies in Turkey, Mexico had become the United States' main heroin source. From isolated mountain regions in southern Sonora and the adjoining Mexican state of Sinaloa, opium harvested from huge poppy fields was refined into the distinctively brown-colored heroin called "Mexican Mud." In the late 1960s it was almost impossible to find anything except the white heroin of the Near East on U.S. streets, but by 1976 over 92 percent of all the heroin recovered by American police was a product of Mexico.

And it was pouring across the Arizona border by the ton, smuggled in by truck, car, light airplanes, and even mule trains. From the modern jet airports in Tucson and Phoenix, smugglers had direct access to every major American city. IRE reporters surveyed federal, state, and local authorities in each of Arizona's fourteen counties, finding that there were no more than 180 narcotics agents available to stem the narcotics flow across the state's 113,909 square miles. Conversely, reporters had come up with estimates that as many as 800 pilots made a full-time living flying drugs out of Mexico into Arizona. They had identified 23 major smuggling rings operating through the corridor, made up of some 2,000 persons. At least five of the drug organizations were wholly or partially controlled by U.S. Mafia families—one of which was the Joseph Bonanno syndicate from Tucson, according to officials. Before leaving New York, Bonanno's family had set up the original French Connection for Turkish heroin. IRE reporters now had police intelligence reports detailing a meeting in Mexico between Bonanno and several of Mexico's leading suppliers.

139

There were other documented ties between Mexican smugglers and U.S. Mafia figures. On December 29, 1971, a fifty-five-year-old New York man arrived in the dusty cowtown of Douglas, Arizona, a hundred miles east of Tucson and directly across the border from Agua Prieta, Sonora. He was traveling under the name Pete Patterson, but his real name was Antonio Gambino, and he was the brother of the recently departed New York mob chieftain Carlo Gambino. In a secret meeting with a man who turned out to be a U.S. customs informant, Gambino said he had been sent to find a new source of supply for the East Coast, which was then feeling the pinch of the combined U.S.-Turkish crackdown on Near-Eastern opium. To show his good faith, Gambino flashed $60,000, which he was carrying in his briefcase. Four days later, Gambino hired one of the state's top drug-smuggling pilots, who introduced him to a Mexican narcotics source. By April the next year, the ring was fully operational. Somehow the snitch was discovered, and one night the customs informant was taken by four Gambino associates to a desert area outside of Tucson and shot twice in the chest.

The hard facts of the story had been gathered, written in memoranda, and placed in the IRE files. But a closer look was in order. And the only way to do that was to go into Mexico. Wendland and Drehsler were selected for the trip. Neither was particularly anxious to head south of the border. They would be totally isolated from the rest of the team. It would not be safe to use telephones in most of the places they were going. The files noted that the Mexican smuggling rings were a paranoid group, known to tap hotel telephones routinely. The Mexican police in the border towns were often corrupt and could not be counted on for help. The reporters ran the risk of being mistaken for U.S. undercover drug agents, on whom several Mexican drug dealers had allegedly issued an open murder contract of $1,000.

"You've got to understand that the places you are going to are totally and completely controlled by the dopers," they were warned by a U.S. Drug Enforcement Administration agent shortly before they left Phoenix. "Not even the army gets in there. Every damned villager from the little kids to the grandmothers are involved. The whole area is dependent on the drug business. Remember, in these areas you're dealing with Mexicans who don't go anywhere without a gun and a knife. These are dangerous, dangerous dudes."

On Friday, November 12, Wendland and Drehsler headed south.

The sixty-five miles between Tucson and the border on U.S. 19 was a scenic route. To the east rose Mount Lemon, showing the winter's first signs of snow at its crest. Below, just past the mountain's gently sloping foothills, flowed the underground Santa Cruz River, the main water supply for Tucson. The river flowed straight south to Mexico, before turning back to the States, almost parallel to the highway. Its path was marked by a lush but narrow green belt of paloverde trees. To the west, the highway passed barren desert land, occasionally broken by a stately Saguaro cactus. A dead coyote lay on the shoulder of the road as a pair of turkey buzzards made lazy circles in the sky waiting for a break in the traffic that would allow them to partake of the waiting feast below. The reporters passed the beautifully preserved San Xavier del Bac mission, founded in the late seventeenth century by Spanish Jesuits dispatched to convert the Indians, and, as they neared Nogales, Arizona, the deep gorges and colorful rises of the Red Rock Mountains.

They reached the American city of Nogales about noon, checking into a downtown motel just a few hundred yards from the ten-foot-high wire fence that separates Nogales, Sonora, from Arizona. After a quick lunch, they drove around the city of fifteen thousand for a couple of hours, identifying various spots that looked like clandestine border crossings, such as a confusing network of sewage canals that began a block from the border and ended just outside of town. The file memos had noted that the canal was heavily used by smugglers, who knew full well that American customs or border patrol agents would never follow them there.

They saw no point in going across to Nogales, Sonora, until after dark. The people they would be looking for were probably still asleep. So they killed the rest of the afternoon back at the motel, reading a local newspaper and watching Mexican soap operas on television. About six o'clock, it began to rain. Just after dark with the rain still falling they crossed into Mexico. Nogales, Sonora, was in another world, a boom town gone wild, crowded with over 120,000 residents, swelling each day with hundreds of new arrivals. As in most border towns, there was virtually unlimited access for U.S. tourists, who were simply waved through by a bored guard. Even in the rain the narrow streets were crowded. The last of the tourists were making their way back towards the border as Mexican shopkeepers and downtown office workers waited on street corners for buses. By eight o'clock, the rain had chased all the tourists away for the night and a new type of people emerged. Groups of young, gaunt-looking men stood in the doorways of closed tourist shops. Occasionally, a taxi would pull up and an American, usually young and long-haired, would get out to converse with one of the Mexicans. It looked to Wendland like John R. and Brush Streets back in Detroit, where narcotics deals go on around the clock.

Since parking the car, they had already been approached a half-dozen times by peddlers hawking joints of marijuana, pills, and, from a parked cabdriver who proudly opened his glove compartment to display his wares, small, foil-wrapped packages of heroin. But the reporters weren't interested in street dealers. The only thing unusual about the street scene compared to the slums of any large American city was that all the action transpired under the noses of Mexican police officers, who seemed to be on every corner nonchalantly passing the time of day with the dope dealers.

The reporters walked east of the main downtown tourist district to Calle Ruiz Cortinas, a narrow brick street of mostly warehouses and old, decaying office buildings. Both were getting wet. They were looking for La Posta restaurant, one of several nightspots identified as places where major deals were regularly made. A taxi driver, spotting the lone pair of Americans, pulled to the curb.

"Taxi?" asked the short, greasy-haired driver.

The reporters shook their heads and continued walking.

He ran after them. "Eh, *uno momento, por favor*. It's a very bad night, hey? Listen, I know a nice place with nice ladies, you know? I take you there. It is not far. You like ladies? They got nice ladies in this place. They got Americano ladies. Mexican ladies with big chi-chi's. Even black nigger lady. You come with me, hey?"

Drehsler mumbled something in Spanish, and the driver, looking surprised, turned and went back to his cab.

"What'd you say?" asked Wendland.

"I told him to fuck off. You can't be polite to those dudes. They think you're a tourist and they won't stop. This way, he doesn't know who we are, but he knows we speak the language and we aren't interested in getting hustled."

They found the restaurant they were looking for in the next block. From the outside, it appeared to be just a hole in the wall. But inside, it was a carbon copy of any expensive stateside restaurant. Neat, candlelit tables, doting waiters in red coats, and expensive-looking art work gave the restaurant a mildly chic atmosphere. They went to the bar and ordered a couple of Carta Blanca beers, telling the maitre d' that they would have dinner later.

The place was much bigger than the reporters had expected. As their eyes adjusted to the light, they saw that it occupied both sides of the block. A second entrance connected to the next street over. In the back of the main dining area, a carpeted stairway wound its way up to a second floor. The restaurant was owned by Hector Miller, one of Mexico's top narcotics wholesalers.

There were fewer than a dozen people in La Posta. Though it was nearly nine o'clock, it was still early for dinner by Mexican standards. The reporters sipped their beer and watched a couple of waiters running back and forth between the main floor and the upstairs area. It was up there where the deals went down, they figured.

"We'd like to eat upstairs," Drehsler told the maitre d' after they finished the beer.

"I'm sorry, señor," he replied, carefully looking the two reporters over, "but that is a private area."

Instead, he ushered them to a rear table on the main floor. "Enjoy your dinner," he smiled as he walked away. Instead of returning to his station, the maitre d' went up the stairs. He was back down in about two minutes.

"My guess is that we'll soon see if we're right about what's going on up there," said Wendland, pouring a second beer. Drehsler nodded. It didn't take long. Two men, both Mexicans in dark suits, came down the stairway. They quickly walked into the bar and then, trying to look casual, strolled back towards the headwaiter. As they pretended to be talking with him, they carefully scrutinized the two gringos at the back of the restaurant before returning upstairs.

"They don't know who we are," said Drehsler. "They probably think we're either a couple of dudes looking to make a score or a couple of drug agents. For our sake, let's hope it's the first." For American undercover drug agents are given no legal authority or protection in Mexico. They are not even allowed to carry their own weapons.

The restaurant was heavy on steak "done to the perfect degree of doneness." Neither piece of meat ordered by the reporters was particularly good, though the steaks were certainly done, so well-done they were dried out.

There was a shuffle of feet on the second-floor landing above. The reporters looked up. The same two men who had checked them out before came down the steps. Both had their hands in their right coat pockets. They were followed by two other men, one a tall, balding Mexican of about forty-five, the other a young, well-dressed American. The bodyguards followed the two through the bar and out the second door.

"What the hell do you make of that?" asked Drehsler.

Wendland shrugged. "Something went down up there, that's for sure." Wendland was about to get up and go to the door, to see if he could spot what kind of car the men had. But the maitre d' was carefully watching him. He sat back down and finished his dinner. "No sense in spooking him now," he said.

The bill came to just over eleven dollars. They left the waiter a five-dollar tip. "That way, they'll know we aren't cops," laughed Drehsler. The maitre d' was solicitous and hoped they had enjoyed their meal. They had, they assured him. "Say, has Hector Miller been around tonight?" Wendland asked.

The maitre d's eyes narrowed. "He just left, señor. Not five minutes ago."

That's what the reporters thought.

They went out by the other door, onto a street called Calle Elias, and walked north. It was still raining. The odor of burning kerosene filled the air, coming from the ramshackle homes that began to scale the slope of a mountain that loomed at the end of a side street off to their left. Garbage was strewn across the sidewalk in many places, its sickly sweet smell mixing in the wet night air with the odor of the fuel oil.

But a few blocks further up, they abruptly came to La Rocha, Nogales's best restaurant. Literally carved into the side of a small mountain, complete with a courtyard and fountain illuminated by discreet electric bulbs and flickering torches, its opulence mocked the poverty surrounding it. The dining area was reached by a narrow stone stairway. Inside, the restaurant was empty except for a small group of well-dressed Mexican men being entertained by a twelve-piece mariachi band and served by a retinue of uniformed waiters. A huge mesquite log burned fragrantly in the stone fireplace.

The reporters ordered a drink. The elegance of the place was overwhelming, the equal of anything the reporters had ever seen. Soft lights brought a rainbow of unseen color from the stone walls and filled the room with an atmosphere of intimate charm. Wendland

counted sixteen employees, who, with the exception of the four who
were waiting on the single dinner table, looked like statues formed
from the mountain itself.

Wendland and Drehsler nursed their drinks. There was nothing of
interest to observe. The band played softly. Both reporters missed
their wives. The restaurant was an incredibly romantic place. It
would have been nice to have had their women with them. They had
been away from home a long time.

It was almost eleven. They had two more places to check out. But
neither would be anything like the two restaurants they had just taken
in. The new places were on the other side of the proverbial tracks, in
what local people called *la zona de tolerancia* or *la zona roja*—the
red-light district.

Prostitution is legal in Mexico. And it is a traditional part of many a
Mexican man's lifestyle. In tourist towns like Nogales, the red-light
districts used to line up almost on the border fence. No more. Forced
by awakening community values, they have been moved back to the
outskirts of town. But they are still prospering. Nogales's
whorehouses are clustered on a dirt path called Canal Street, which
backs up against the first slopes of the Pajarito Mountains.

The windshield wipers of the IRE car had trouble, even at full
speed, in clearing the sheets of driving rain. Traffic was light. It was a
terrible night. Drehsler, who had been in Nogales many times before,
had no trouble finding Canal Street. But instead of stopping, he drove
to the end and made an abrupt right-hand turn on a side street.

"Don't think I'm getting paranoid," he said, "but I think we're
being followed."

Wendland turned around. Back about a hundred yards, a pair of
headlights turned the corner they had just taken. "Who do you think it
is? The police?"

"I don't know. But let's find out." Quickly, he made another
right, then a left. A dirt trail wound its way to a small parking area
behind a warehouse, and he took that, dousing the car lights.

The other vehicle wasn't far behind. Slowly, it cruised down the
street they had just turned off from. It missed the dirt turnoff and
continued past. But from their hiding place, the reporters made it out
to be a silver Mercedes, with two occupants.

"Well, we know they aren't the cops," said Wendland.

They waited five minutes but the car did not return. Drehsler pulled
out of the parking lot and headed for the Club Mexico. Out front, a

running stream of water cascaded over the pockmarked sandy street. Dodging puddles and the rain, the reporters raced out of the car and up a short staircase leading to the club's main entrance.

A small mariachi band played for a dozen customers in the dining area. Eight hookers, all plumpish Mexican women stuffed into hot pants, platform shoes, and low-cut, frilly white blouses, sat around a single table. Three more prostitutes were seated at various tables with the male clientele.

Wendland and Drehsler went directly to the bar and ordered beer. To their right sat an American couple in their late thirties. The reporters could hear the man trying to converse with one of the hookers. "My name's Don," he slurred. Obviously he'd been drinking for a while. "And this here's my wife, Mary Anne. We're from America. Been married six months. I thought I'd bring Mary Anne down here to show her what I've been missing." The wife looked mortified. The hooker, standing between them with her arms around their shoulders, didn't understand a word of English.

"Don, I don't like it here. Let's go back."

"Now, just hush up," he shot back out of the corner of his mouth. "You don't want to insult these people." With that, he gave the whore a big grin and reached up to squeeze one of her breasts.

"You're insulting me, Don. Please."

"Oh, shit, Mary Anne. You're no goddamn fun at all." He got up and, handing the hooker a dollar bill, grabbed his wife's elbow and steered her out of the bar. "I was just having a little fun." The whore shrugged and walked away, stuffing the dollar into a side pocket on her shorts.

The reporters shook their heads. "Jesus, no wonder Americans got such a crappy reputation," said Wendland. Suddenly, two of the hookers were all over the reporters. Caressing their shoulders, arms, thighs, and backs. Wendland started to push one of the women away.

"Don't," smiled Drehsler. "They're frisking us for guns."

"What?"

"Standard procedure. They're just making sure we're not carrying heat."

Satisfied, the women sat down on either side of the reporters. "Buy us drink?" one of them asked. Wendland motioned for the bartender, who poured the women some sort of an orange concoction.

"Ah, *mi amor*, I love you, I love you, let's go fuck," said the girl on Wendland's right.

He laughed. "She certainly has a way with words," he said to Drehsler.

"You like my chi-chi's?" she said, cupping her breasts. "I love you. I have hot pussy. You like hot pussy?" Her hand began to creep up his leg.

Wendland grabbed it. "Hold it. No. You understand? No."

She smiled, taking her hand back with a mock pout. "You no like Flora?" she asked. "Flora likes you. I fuck you for twenty dollars."

Wendland had been hustled before, but never so aggressively. Remembering the way Drehsler had dealt with the cabbie earlier, he summoned up a severe look.

"No. I don't want you, Flora. Leave me alone. I'm here to drink. That's all."

It made no difference. Her hand went back to his knee.

"Goddamn it, no." His voice was louder than he expected. The whore hesitated for a moment, then started to reach again. Wendland didn't want to make more of a scene, but it was getting ridiculous. He grabbed her chin and forced her hand back.

"Now listen, bitch. I said no. And I mean no. You do that again and I'm going to break your arm."

She understood. "Okay, okay. Shit, I am just trying to make a living." Her English, though heavily accented, was obviously a lot more fluent than she wanted her customers to know. "Who are you gringos?"

Drehsler, who had similar problems with the girl on his left, had cooled her advances by talking to her in Spanish. He was now deep in conversation with her.

"Never mind who we are," said Wendland, continuing the bravado. "We're just here to do a little business. But not with you. We're here to meet somebody."

"Ah, sí. You mafioso."

In Mexico, drug dealers and smugglers are referred to as mafia, with the lowercase m.

"Never mind."

"You're here to see Jesus, hey? Well, he is not here. He is away on business. He will not be here tonight."

Wendland had no idea who this Jesus was. But he grunted what he hoped was a suitably depressed acknowledgment of his disappointment at not finding Jesus present.

"When will he be back?"

"Who knows these things? Ask Pancho." She pointed to the bartender. "So long, gringo." She went back to the table of waiting women, taking her orange juice with her.

Drehsler was still talking to his whore. Wendland looked around the bar. They were the only two Americans. No one seemed to be paying any attention to them.

"*Uno más?*" asked Pancho the bartender, pointing to Wendland's half-empty beer.

He shook his head. "*Habla inglés?*"

"*No, señor.*"

In English, Wendland asked the bartender where Jesus was. He looked up from pouring the beer. "Culiacán. He will be back tomorrow. Maybe Sunday." He walked away.

Drehsler's girl was leaving. She smiled at Wendland too, as if he were an old friend. Alex finished his beer and the reporters left. Outside, he filled in his partner on what the girl had told him. She also thought they were mafiosos come to see Jesus. She said that Jesus, who used the place as a sort of narcotics brokering office, was in Culiacán, the capital of Sinaloa, the state just south of Sonora where most of Mexico's clandestine heroin labs are located. She suggested, however, that they return later on that night. "Jesus has a friend, Miguel, who sometimes helps people like you," the girl told Drehsler.

They drove around Nogales for half an hour, finally locating the Matador Club, a sleazy bar identified as a hangout for Johnny Grant, one of Mexico's top narcotics dealers. Also known as "El Negro Johnny," Grant, the son of a Mexican woman and a Cuban black, had been deported from the U.S. in the early 1960s, only to settle in Nogales. With Hector Miller he established a heroin smuggling operation that was estimated by U.S. Drug Enforcement Administration agents to gross nearly seven million dollars a year at its peak. Grant, who sported a diamond for a front tooth after the real one was knocked out in a barroom brawl, had recently been released from prison and was supposed to be rebuilding his smuggling operation.

The Club Matador was practically deserted. Wendland and Drehsler took a rickety table near the bar and ordered another round of beer. This time, the waiter brought a shaker of salt, a plate of lime wedges, and a bottle of hot sauce with their drinks. Drehsler showed his gringo friend how to use the garnishments. "First you squeeze lime juice around the top of the can," he demonstrated. "Then shake out a couple of drops of the hot sauce. Add a little salt and take a sip.'' It wasn't bad.

The only other patrons were at the rear where a table of three Mexican men were drinking whiskey out of an open bottle. Wendland watched a cockroach wiggle its way across the bar. The aproned waiter, who had absent-mindedly been shaking dice in a cup, also spotted it. Slowly, he walked over to the cockroach, made an over-done display of raising his right hand, and, making sure the reporters were watching, brought his thumb down to squash the cockroach. He then turned to glare at the gringos before resuming his original station with the dice.

''I don't think that dude particularly likes us,'' said Drehsler.

They finished their beer and left. An hour had passed. They'd try the Club Mexico again, to see if Miguel had shown up.

But outside the Mexico, standing on the porch, were the same two bodyguards the reporters had seen earlier in La Posta, the restaurant owned by Hector Miller. Their backs were to the street, and they were talking to the whore who had told Drehsler to come back later. Parked in front was a silver Mercedes.

The reporters turned off Canal Street without being spotted.

''How about that?'' said Wendland. ''I'll give you two guesses what those two are talking about.''

''Yeah, you and me.''

The reporters figured they had blown it. They had asked too many questions at La Posta. Whatever the two bodyguards wanted with them, they decided, wouldn't be worth finding out. They needed a better way to get close to the smugglers. They only spooked the dealers by going in cold and asking questions. They needed a plan.

They decided to return to the border. The IRE files had detailed the ease with which smugglers could cross the border. While there is a checkpoint through which all pedestrian and vehicular traffic must pass, the reporters were breezed through with only one question asked—what their nationality was. Wendland found it easier to cross from Mexico into Arizona than to cross into Detroit from Canada. Still, some random automobile searches were conducted. They scanned the darkened hillsides on both sides of the border checkpoint. The IRE sources had reported that dope smugglers often stationed a lookout on the American side with a pair of binoculars to determine what pattern the guards were using to search cars. By sending signals with a flashlight, the lookout lets the actual smuggler on the Mexican side know that, for example, every third car is being searched, allowing the smuggler to ease his car into the line in such a way as to avoid the pattern. The night's rain and the lateness of the hour had reduced border crossing traffic to a trickle. And the reporters saw no sign of a lookout. But the checkpoint was not the only place where smugglers crossed. Indeed, the really large dealers seldom used it. There were plenty of easier crossings.

On a previous visit to Nogales with Lupe Sanchez, Wendland had found a spot on the border fence a quarter-mile west of the checkpoint that was particularly active. In a fifteen-minute period, he and Lupe had counted seven Mexicans climbing the fence. And that was in broad daylight. When he had stopped to photograph the scene, he had been driven back to the car by a barrage of rocks tossed by a group of Mexicans on the other side. That was during a reconnaisance visit two weeks before. Now was time for another look.

The reporters drove the short street which parallels the fence for a half-mile. It was quiet. At the end, they stopped the car and got out to inspect the fence, leaving the lights on. The Border Patrol was supposed to patrol the fence around the clock. In addition, special sensors, of the type used by the army in Vietnam, had been installed at various locations along the border to alert authorities to illegal border crossings. Wendland walked to the fence and shook it. Footprints were all around on both sides. Drehsler pointed to the top of the ten-foot-high fence where the three strands of barbed wire had been cut in several spots to allow a fence climber to roll across the top without snags. Further down, they found a small section of fence that had been cut at ground level.

They had spent ten minutes at the border with the car, engine running and lights on, conspicuously parked in the middle of the street. But there was no sign of the Border Patrol.

They drove to the east side of the border, where a narrow series of almost vertical streets climbed a small mountain. Winding their way up and towards the fence, they came to a deeply rutted dirt road that dead-ended in a tangle of underbrush. As Drehsler tried to maneuver the car so it could be turned around, Wendland grabbed his arm.

"Hold it, I think I saw something. Shine the lights off to the left."

It was the border fence. But what had attracted Wendland's interest was a movement of some sort. He thought he had seen someone. With the lights still on, they got out of the car and walked east along the fence a few hundred feet. There, they discovered that an entire section had been knocked down. The hole was at least ten feet wide, enough to drive a truck through. And in the thick mud caused by the rain was a fresh set of footprints, heading north. It looked like the big hole in the fence had been there for months. A virtual footpath had been worn down the middle of it.

"You saw somebody crossing?" asked Drehsler.

"I think so. It was just a flash of something moving."

"Incredible. Look at the size of this hole."

Wendland stood at the missing section of fence, one foot in the U.S., one in Mexico. They would want to photograph the scene in daylight.

"I wonder how many people use this place every day," mused Drehsler.

"If we can drive up here bold as hell in the middle of the night, just think how easy it is for the guy on foot."

They returned down the winding little roads to Morley Avenue, the city's main street. As they stopped at a traffic signal on the way towards their motel, a green Border Patrol car pulled alongside.

"Well, what do you know, these guys really work after all," said Drehsler.

The reporters were sure they were about to be pulled over. It was nearly 3:00 A.M. on a rainy night. Their car was splattered with mud, and they had just come off a road that led to the fence. But when the traffic light changed, the Border Patrol car drove off without a second look at the reporters.

The next morning, the reporters set out to learn more about the problems facing Nogales, Sonora. They were considerable. In just four years, between 1970 and 1974, the population had nearly doubled in size, swelling from 53,000 to just over 100,000. No one knew the exact population for 1976, though estimates ran as high as 150,000. On the American side, Nogales, Arizona's population remained a steady 15,000. The population explosion had caught the Mexican city totally unprepared. There were severe shortages of water, housing, transportation, and medical facilities. Over a quarter of the population was without running water, and outhouse latrines were common sights as the reporters drove around during the daylight. Most of the immigrants were from dirt poor villages from the south, drawn to the border and its legendary higher wages. But in the fall of 1976, the reporters found that the average hourly wage, for those peasants lucky enough to find work in the city's few industries, amounted to sixty-eight cents American.

There were three neighborhoods the reporters wanted to visit. The first was the place many of the new arrivals settled in. The *colonia*, or neighborhood, was called "Without End." Located on the southern outskirts of the city, it housed several thousand new residents. It resembled a refugee camp. All around were cardboard shacks and crude shelters that reminded the reporters of the illegal workers they had encountered at the Arrowhead Ranch back in Phoenix. There was no water, no electricity or plumbing. Garbage and open latrines surrounded the ramshackle little homes clinging precariously to mounds of worn dirt.

Drehsler talked in Spanish to one weather-beaten woman who looked to be near sixty but, she said, had just turned thirty-five the previous month. Her family—twenty persons, including nine children, grandsons, nieces, and cousins—had come from a small village near Guadalajara. Her husband had looked for work in the manufacturing plants without success. He was now a gardener. His weekly salary averaged thirty-two dollars. When Drehsler asked her about narcotics smuggling, a panic-stricken look came over her. She wheeled around, mumbling "mafioso," and ran off.

Closer downtown and almost resembling a modest suburban U.S. subdivision was the neighborhood of Buenos Aires. The homes were small, prefabricated, ranch-style buildings. Various sources back in Phoenix had cautioned the reporters not to leave their car while visiting the neighborhood. And they were told never to go there at night. For Buenos Aires was mafioso territory, where the up and coming young smuggler lived. Gunfire was often heard there. Strangers were unwelcome. Even the Nogales police refused to patrol there at night. On seeing a strange car with two Americans, little children abandoned their play to run to the porch and summon their parents, who stared coldly at the passing car. And outside one house, three men stood in apparent guard duty around a small, wooden hut. A rifle leaned conspicuously against its door.

Nogales's newest and smallest neighborhood was Colonia Kennedy, whose large homes, elaborate brick buildings heavy with wrought iron and stained glass, reflected the status of their owners. There were Cadillacs and Lincoln Continentals parked in the drives. Law enforcement sources referred to the neighborhood of two dozen mansion-like homes as "Dopers' Row," for this was where the narcotics kingpins lived.

The federal prosecutor for the state of Sonora and the man charged with keeping the dopers in line was Jorge O. Villalobos, whose downtown Nogales office was stark by U.S. standards, the furnishings consisting of a battered desk, a couple of file cabinets, a transistor radio which blared Mexican music, and a black telephone that the prosecutor answered himself. There was also a loaded semiautomatic rifle propped up in a corner. Villalobos was a short, slightly built man with a limp handshake. He did not fit the image of a macho Mexican law enforcer. But the reporters' sources in Phoenix had told them that he was indeed a rare breed. He refused to take the *mordida*, or payoff money, from the dopers. And he was also an endangered species. There was, he said in matter-of-fact tones, a mafia assassin looking for him at that particular moment. Such things were not unusual in Mexico, he explained with a shrug. His counterpart in the adjoining state of Sinaloa, Antonio Coppola, had recently been shot down in a burst of machine-gun fire.

"I walk to work every morning clutching my revolver inside my coat pocket," Villalobos told Drehsler in Spanish. "If they want to kill me badly enough, they will do it, despite every precaution."

Villalobos was uneasy with reporters. He was asked whether the Nogales police department cooperated with him in cracking down on narcotics smugglers. He shook his head. The local police, he felt, were apathetic, even though the mafiosos were all about the city. For example, Villalobos described the recent arrest of a major drug smuggler. The guy had pulled out a gun and Villalobos had shot him. "Although he was seriously wounded, he still tried to kill me," Villalobos explained. "We wrestled on the ground as I tried to get his gun away from him. I saw a local policeman standing nearby. He was just calmly watching us struggle. I yelled out for him to come over and give me his handcuffs. It took a long time, but finally he did."

Villalobos's assertion had to be checked out with local police. Rafael Torres was police chief for the city of Nogales. Drehsler asked him whether city police handled drug investigations. "Drug trafficking is a federal crime and the city police do not investigate federal violations," replied Torres.

So much for the Mexican side.

The reporters drove to the American side, left the car there, and walked to the Mexican side for some shopping. There was a welcoming party waiting for them when they returned. The Border Patrol had found the reporters' car, parked on a side street about six blocks from the border, and had surrounded it. A patrol car with emergency lights flashing was parked directly behind it. A jeep was parked in the street right next to it. A U.S. Border Patrol agent named R. G. Ramos and three other agents were leaning against a jeep waiting. Earlier, the reporters had encountered Ramos in downtown Nogales. They had introduced themselves and asked a few questions. He had refused to answer and, instead, insisted on searching the trunk of the IRE car. The reporters had complied but were convinced that the search was simply a means of harassing them. Ramos obviously didn't like their snooping around. He told the reporters that if they intended to stay in the area asking questions, they had better "clear" their activities with his superiors because his agency didn't want to be portrayed in a bad light. The reporters told him they had no intention of "clearing" their questions with anyone. Ramos stalked off, looking angry. And now he was waiting at the IRE car. He looked like he meant business.

"You looking for us?" Drehsler asked as they approached the agents.

"Yeah," answered Ramos. "Open your trunk."

"Again? We've already gone this route today," said Wendland. "Just open it."

"What's this all about?"

"We have reason to believe that you have illegal contraband," replied Ramos. "We had a tip that when you went back up to the hole in the fence, someone from the other side tossed you a sack."

"That's pure bullshit," said Wendland. "You're making the story up just to hassle us."

"I'm not going to ask you again. Open that trunk."

It was ridiculous arguing with them. Drehsler found the key and popped the trunk. Ramos went through everything, opening suitcases, searching the tire wells, looking through the pockets of the reporters' clothing. Finding nothing, he went to the inside of the car and began a similar search of the glove compartment, the seats, even under the vinyl carpeting. Wendland pulled out his camera and focused on Ramos.

"Hold it," warned another agent. "You can't do that."

"The hell I can't," said Wendland, turning to also photograph the other agent, who quickly displayed his backside.

Ramos spent nearly fifteen minutes going over the car. He found nothing. He didn't say a word when he finished. Instead, he got back in his car and drove off, followed by the other agents in the jeep.

"What the hell do you make of that?" Wendland asked his partner. The incident unnerved them, not because there was any chance the agents would have found anything but because the search had given them an opportunity to plant something on the reporters' car which would conveniently be "found" by another crew of agents. The reporters spent ten minutes checking each area Ramos had examined, making sure that the agent hadn't left anything behind.

It was three o'clock, time to make a telephone call.

Drehsler's wife was from the Mexican town of Agua Prieta, one of several Arizona border cities used as major smuggling centers. Before leaving Phoenix, Drehsler had called his wife's brother, tactfully explaining their need to meet and talk with a couple of narcotics smugglers. The brother had agreed to help, though he could not guarantee anything on such sensitive matters. Drehsler was to call back to see what could be arranged.

Three hours later, after a meeting had been arranged for seven o'clock that night, they were in the small cowboy town of Douglas, crossing over the Mexican border into Agua Prieta, a smaller and much neater version of Nogales. The reporters arrived at the restaurant-cantina designated as the meeting place ten minutes early. They ordered Mexican beer and soup and had to wait less than five minutes.

Alex's brother-in-law, a tall, slim man of about thirty, came in. He was alone and greeted Alex in Spanish. They talked for a few minutes about family before getting to the matter at hand. The brother-in-law had found two men, brothers, who would help the reporters out. The brothers were top smugglers, using a small resale business they ran as a cover for traveling throughout Mexico and the southwestern United States. There were conditions to the interview. The reporters were not to directly identify them in print and, if possible, were to obscure their descriptions so that authorities reading about them in the States would not be able to identify them from the newspaper accounts. The reporters were free to ask the brothers anything they wanted. If the smugglers didn't answer, the question was to be dropped.

"I tell you this," said Drehsler's relative. "These are good, proud men. They are friends of mine. They will help you because I asked them to help you. But you must understand that this is their business. Their families survive by their work. You will be their guests tonight. They will be friendly to you. But they expect you to be friendly to them as well. Do not do them harm. That is all I ask of you."

The relative left, giving Alex an address, not far away, where the brothers were waiting for them.

The reporters immediately decided to give the smugglers different names in the story they would eventually write. They would call the eldest brother Pancho. The other brother would be referred to as Fernando, named after a pop song they had been hearing on the car radio for the last several days.

Pancho, a short, stocky man with neatly combed hair, welcomed the reporters warmly in the office of his resale shop. On the way in, Wendland noted that the main area of the small shop was crowded with inexpensive looking art work, a couple of young workers, and a shiny green pickup truck. The office itself was spartan, containing only an old wooden desk, a pair of folding chairs, and a small radio. Pancho shut the door between the office and the main area.

"I understand that you want to know of our business," he said in Spanish, sitting down behind the desk.

The reporters nodded. Wendland, using the little Spanish he had learned in school and what he had picked up from Drehsler, told Pancho that he did not speak the language well.

"Then I will speak in English. But before we talk, I want you to listen to me for a little while. You understand that this is, for my brother and me, a somewhat delicate discussion?" The reporters nodded again. "Good. Then you should also understand that here in Mexico, what we do is not a bad thing. What we sell is a crop, grown on farms. What your people in the United States do with our crop is another matter. For our people here, there is no other way to make a living. Mexico's economy is ruined. The value of the peso is half what it used to be only a year ago. Today, the average wage here is twenty-two dollars American a week. So we do this to survive. It is a business, that is all."

The smuggling business Pancho and Fernando ran began in the fall of 1975, he said, just a year before. Now, it employed some fourteen persons who supported nearly fifty dependents in all, located in Agua Prieta and a couple of villages to the south. "We are not the largest," said Fernando. "To be really successful, one must be mafioso, or organized." He described the mafioso as the elite of the smuggling world. "They are what you would call gangs, many different gangs, all separate but all together. They have one big boss, who collects from everyone."

Pancho readily admitted smuggling marijuana, which he said

"grows everywhere here, like trees in a forest." He was vague about what other drugs were handled, though he implied that heroin and, more recently, cocaine were starting to be hauled north across the border in the fleet of five pickup trucks he and his brother owned. Their primary sales area was the Southwest, with most of their business being based in Tucson and Phoenix. "We have been to California and one time, even to Chicago." His customers were Anglos. "They are wealthy people in Arizona" was all he would say.

The reporters wondered how he got his drugs across without problems. He rubbed the thumb and first two fingers of his right hand together. "Everyone thinks the *mordida* just happens in Mexico," he smiled. "But it works on both sides." Sometimes, depending on the cargo, his trucks moved across the border at checkpoint stations. At other times, "there are many places to cross. Between Agua Prieta and Nogales, the border is unguarded. The fence is broken everywhere."

But it was a rough business. "There are *banditos*, who try to steal from us. There is the mafioso, which wants us to join them." He and his brother were always armed, as were their "mules," the people they employed to haul the drugs across. Then there was the expense of his trucks, all of which were specially outfitted with false bottoms, heavy duty shocks and springs, and four-wheel drive.

What about police?

"They are our friends. Everyone here in Agua Prieta is involved. It is all there is for us." There were occasional problems with the Mexican army but nothing that could not be handled by *mordida*.

They were interrupted by a knock on the door. It was Fernando, the younger brother. He shook hands with the reporters and, from a paper sack he carried, handed them each a can of beer. He looked to be in his late twenties, slim of build with long hair and a scraggly beard.

"So you are the two reporters who want to get killed?" he laughed. "This is a dangerous business. It is not wise to ask too many questions."

Where Pancho was the office manager and chief accountant of the family business, Fernando was the foreman, the one who was out in the field handling the day-to-day mechanics.

"You see this?" he asked, brushing his black hair off his forehead to reveal an ugly red scar that extended from just over the left eyebrow to the hairline. "From a bullet. Not two months ago. The mafiosos they think that maybe we are getting too big."

Pancho interrupted. "It was a small problem. It is resolved now." The look he gave Fernando indicated the subject was closed.

"I am sorry but there are matters I must attend to," said Pancho. "My brother will talk to you now. You will see our town."

They got into the reporters' car, leaving the elder brother. Fernando was in the back seat.

"Fernando, I have a question," said Wendland. "You and your brother have a good small business. You said all your employees are Mexican. But what about Anglos? Are they partners with you?"

"But of course. They are our good friends. When Pancho and I began, they lent us the money to buy our vehicles."

"Where are these Anglos from?" asked Drehsler.

"Ah, that I cannot say. They are very powerful men. They have friends in many places in Mexico and your country."

"But they are U.S. citizens?"

"But of course. But, please, I can say no more. They would not want me to say even these things."

"We understand," said Wendland. "But it is important for us to know how powerful these Anglos are."

"They are very strong. We are not their only friends here. They have airplanes that they use. And they have partners like us in other places in Mexico."

"Are they mafiosos?" asked Drehsler.

"You must understand. These are things I cannot talk about."

"Did they give you that bullet scar?"

"Oh, no. This was from the Mexican mafiosos. You see, there are Mexican mafiosos and American mafiosos. The Mexican mafiosos want to have all businesses like my brother's and mine with them, so they can deal from a position of strength with the American mafiosos. Sometimes, there are difficulties. We are partners with some Americans. The Mexican mafiosos want us to be partners with them, so that the Americans do not get so much money. And there are different Mexican mafiosos. And they fight between themselves. It is very difficult to explain."

"What about you and your brother? Who are you with?" asked Wendland.

"We are alone. We are still small. Sometimes, we have problems. But we work them out, you understand? Right now, the different mafiosos are too busy fighting among themselves to bother with us."

"Why were you shot, then?"

"It was because I would not go along with them."

"How did you settle it?"

"Please, you are asking too much from me. In Mexico, there are ways these things are settled. A man cannot back down. That is all. Such things must be settled."

The reporters decided to drop it. But without knowing it, Fernando had told them a lot. His brush with the mafiosos had been settled, the reporters suspected, with blood. And the smuggling operation the two brothers ran was obviously much more organized than Fernando and Pancho wanted them to realize.

There was one more thing the reporters wanted to do before leaving Agua Prieta. Next morning, they asked Fernando to show them some of the routes used to smuggle narcotics across the border. He was waiting for them outside the resale shop used as the headquarters for the smuggling operation, sunning himself on the stoop and reading a Mexican comic book. His brother Pancho closed the shop and joined them.

Three miles south of Agua Prieta, on the only real road leading out of the town, was a Mexican government checkpoint. Armed guards were stationed at the checkpoint, charged with restricting passage into Mexico's interior only to nationals and tourists with proper visas. Wendland and Drehsler had no such tourist cards.

"Where are you going?" asked a checkpoint guard in a wrinkled brown uniform.

"Nine miles down the road," replied Pancho.

The car was waved through with no further questioning.

"You see how easy it is?" grinned Fernando. "You are two Americans in a very dirty car. You are not asked for the proper identification. There is no reason for you to be going nine miles down this road. The nearest village is fifty miles away. There is nothing between here and there. Nine miles will take us to nowhere."

The unmarked but paved two-lane road dipped south of Agua Prieta a few miles and then wound its way to the northwest to Naco, a border village forty-eight miles from Agua Prieta. It was, explained Pancho and Fernando, one of their favorite smuggling routes. The brothers pointed out numerous dirt roads and trails leading north from the highway to the border. The trails were deeply rutted with many tracks.

To the south were mountains and small peasant farms. "It is there where our crops grow," said Pancho. "Look about you. You see few cattle, no corn or tomatoes. Up there are poppies. In the foothills grows the marijuana."

Heroin was referred to as *chiva*, meaning nanny goat, or *carga*, which roughly translates to load, he explained. A kilo of heroin cost about $15,000 in the mountains around Agua Prieta. Across the border, cut five or six times, the same kilo brought $600,000. Marijuana sold for about $10 a kilo in Agua Prieta, wholesaling in Phoenix for $125.

They passed a couple of pickup trucks heading in the opposite direction. Heavy tarpaulins covered the cargo area. "They are full of marijuana," said Fernando. "See how some of it falls out? Those seeds will sprout next season. All along the shoulder of this highway marijuana grows. You plant trees and cactus to decorate your roads in the United States. In Mexico, we plant marijuana."

They reached the small village of Naco shortly after one o'clock. There was little to see. Pancho pointed out a body shop that specialized in making false bottoms for the trucks used by smugglers. "This is a smugglers' town," said Fernando. "See all the new trucks."

Unlike Nogales or Agua Prieta, Naco was a border town without a sister city on the U.S. side. At the American Customs checkpoint, an elderly guard waved the two Americans and two Mexicans through without a single question. They returned Pancho and Fernando to Agua Prieta by the American side. On the way back, the brothers pointed out dirt trails leading south, which connected at the border with the roads they had seen on the other side. "You see, if we had been loaded with a cargo, we could have crossed many places," said Pancho. "It is very easy. We have encountered no authorities from Mexico or the United States. It is always like this."

The reporters dropped the brothers off at their resale shop, thanking them for their help. The brothers had enjoyed it, they said, inviting the reporters to spend Sunday night with their families. But the reporters had to move on. Maybe they could return someday. They said goodbye.

Monday morning, after their best sleep in days, the reporters were off to survey the border between Sierra Vista and Nogales, identified by U.S. law enforcement sources as one of the drug smugglers' most heavily used stretches of land.

It was the most incredibly beautiful but rugged country the reporters had yet seen. Nogales was fifty-six miles to the west. And there was nothing but mountains and deep gorges between the two cities. The border was totally unguarded, marked only by a six-foot wire fence. Much of the land on the American side was in the Coronado National Forest. At the Patagonia ranger station about ten miles south and west of Sierra Vista, the reporters pulled in to look at a map of the area. Paul Thompson, the forest service ranger, seemed pleased to have company. The reporters identified themselves and told him why they were there.

"I suggest that if you're going to drive between here and Nogales, you be extremely careful," said Thompson. "There are a lot of narcotics smugglers who use this country and they don't like having strangers around." Thompson said that his rangers had recently asked for authorization to carry side arms when patrolling the area. "They've occasionally stumbled across a smuggler and the smuggler opened up," he said. "So far, none of our people have been hurt. We've been lucky. My advice to you guys is to go ahead and drive through, but stay on the main road. And if you see something unusual, don't stop to look."

The road they were on narrowly wound its way to the peak of Montezuma's Pass, elevation 6,575 feet. At a turn-off overview, the reporters got out of the car for a look. The wind howled as they stared down the mountain slope to Mexico, just two miles to the south. From their vantage point they could see nearly fifty miles of border. It was wide-open country. As they got back in the car, they spotted a coati-mundi, a slinky little black animal that looked like a cross between a beaver and a fox, watching them from the other side of the road. A mile or so down the mountain to the west, a herd of ten scruffy javelinas crossed the road in front of them. It was beautifully desolate country.

"Hold it, stop the car," said Wendland a few minutes later. "Down there, look." They were nearly down the mountain. A half-mile away, not far from the border, was a tan automobile. Two men were by it. Wendland pulled out a pair of binoculars. The trunk of the car was open, and one of the men appeared to be loading something into it. The other man was squatting on the ground, next to a pile of what looked like bricks. Leaning against the car was a long stick. Or was it a gun? It was too far to say for sure. Wendland handed the binoculars to Drehsler. "What do you think?"

"I don't know. It sure as hell looks suspicious."

They watched the men for about five minutes. The pile of bricks was transferred into the trunk of the car, which was then closed. The men then sat down around a campfire. It looked like they were eating something. There was no way to know what was in the trunk without inspecting it. And there was no way to know whether the stick was a gun without going closer. Neither solution seemed particularly wise to the reporters, who drove off, headed toward Nogales.

Twenty minutes later range land gradually began to replace the rugged gorges and mountains. They passed a signpost and backed up. Facing south, the weathered metal sign warned vehicles entering the U.S. to report immediately to the nearest U.S. Customs office. A two-wheeled, deeply rutted trail led away from the sign towards Mexico. The reporters bounced along the trail for a quarter-mile. It ended at the border fence.

There were truck tracks, horse tracks, and footprints all over the ground on both sides of the fence. It was obviously a heavily used illegal crossing point. After photographing the scene, they got back in the car. Drehsler put it in reverse gear. But nothing happened. "Oh-oh," he said, getting out and looking under the car. "You'd better take a look at this." Oil was pouring out from the undercarriage.

"We got a big problem," Drehsler understated. "We're in the middle of nowhere."

They got back in the car and again tried reverse. Something was obviously jammed. It refused to engage. They tried the drive gear and sighed with relief. At least they could go forward. Drehsler made a sweeping turn and, creeping along, maneuvered the car down the trail back to the main road. Nogales was still nearly forty miles away. It took nearly two hours but they made it. At one point, Drehsler missed a turn on the main road and had to drive an extra fifteen miles down a bumpy dirt fire-trail until there was a spot wide enough to turn the car around in the forward gear.

In Nogales, they found a gasoline service station and dropped the car off for repair.

They had lunch and made a telephone call. One of their federal sources in Phoenix had given them the name of an undercover drug agent who worked in Nogales. The agent would talk to the reporters strictly on a background basis, and at no time were they to reveal his name. Drehsler called the source. He would meet the reporters at seven that night in the bar of the El Dorado Motel.

The gasoline mechanic had repaired the oil leak. The rough roads had poked a hole in the oil pan and a rock had been jammed in the transmission. He charged them twenty-five dollars and filled the car with gas.

The source showed up a few minutes past seven, just after "The Captain and Tennille" show began blaring out of the bar's television set. He didn't want to talk in the bar, so he took the reporters outside to his car. They began driving around the city.

He had a lot of things to say.

"If they took dope out of here, the whole town would collapse. Everyone is involved in it in one way or another. And that's here, on the American side. It's even worse across the fence. There's a war going on over there. Three and four people a week are either disappearing or being gunned·down." He told the reporters of several known U.S. organized crime figures who had been observed in Nogales, Sonora, including mobster Moe Dalitz, a friend of Phoenix's Robert Goldwater.

"Two years ago, Dalitz is spotted entering the U.S. from Mexico. He's in a big motor home, accompanied by a man and woman, neither of whom we'd ever heard of before. We ask him what he was doing there. He says he was on a little vacation, that he was going to visit the interior but was turned back because he didn't have the right identification. He didn't have a tourist card."

"So what's wrong with that?" asked Drehsler.

"The whole story stinks," said the agent. "For one thing, Dalitz is a very, very wealthy man. He doesn't vacation in motor homes. He goes in style, Learjet all the way. For another, he's not stupid. Everyone knows you need a tourist card to go to the interior. And a tourist card is easy as hell to get. So he doesn't have one? All he has to do is ask and he would get one."

The source gave the reporters a list of major narcotics traffickers on both sides of the border which they could verify after returning to Phoenix. He drove them past a palatial home just a few blocks north of the border. "It belongs to one of the big dealers. He just had the place remodeled. Spent one million dollars doing it. He even brought in workmen from Italy to do the stone work."

Finally, he had two incidents to relate, both of which involved Joseph Montoya, the senior U.S. senator from New Mexico for the past twelve years. He showed the reporters government files documenting them both.

The first incident occurred on April 9, 1971, at Tucson International Airport. "The feds got a tip from a very reliable informant about a twin-engine airplane coming out of Mexico. It's supposed to be carrying drugs. So Customs sets up and hits on it at the Tucson airport. On board the plane is Senator Montoya. Customs wants to search the plane, but Montoya blows up. He's furious, and refuses to let the agent search. Instead, Montoya goes to a telephone and gets on the horn to Washington. He calls the head of the whole Customs department, Myles Ambrose. Okay, now the agent gets on. He talks to one of Ambrose's assistants. He's told that Montoya is a very powerful man and that it could cost him his job. So the plane isn't searched."

The next incident took place on November 14, 1973, and involved the transport of an old red, white, and blue forty-one-foot pleasure boat from Guaymas, Mexico, through Nogales on to Albuquerque, New Mexico. "Again, there was a tip to the feds about this boat," explained the agent. "It was supposed to be carrying fifty kilos of heroin. Anyway, one day, just as the tip had it, the boat shows up, being towed across the border. Customs conducts a stem-to-stern search of the whole boat. I mean they go over every inch. Nothing. Then they realize they haven't checked the boat's engine. It's a big operation, pulling an engine and searching it, so they go to the phone for permission. Now, here's where Montoya comes in. While they're waiting for authorization to pull the engine, the agents get to talking with this guy named Joe Cruz. This Cruz fellow is the guy in charge of hauling the boat across. He tells the agents that when the boat got to Hermosillo, Mexico, it gets pulled over by Mexican police, who say that it can't go any further because it doesn't have a highway permit. So Cruz says he calls Senator Montoya for help. He says he was given Montoya's name by the junkyard owner in New Mexico who hired him. After that, Montoya is supposed to have gotten on the phone and called the Mexican authorities. Bingo, just like that, their problems are over. They even get a police escort from Hermosillo to Nogales."

"Then what happened?" asked Wendland.

"Meantime, word from the Customs brass comes back. Agents are not authorized to pull the boat's engine. They said it would cost too much. So the boat is released. Well, we decide to watch it. We follow it all the way to Albuquerque. It's taken to a junkyard there. And guess what the first thing is that happens to it as soon as it arrives? They pull the goddamn engine and scrap the rest of the boat. Interesting, huh?''

The reports the agent had produced verified his story. Later, when IRE reporters telephoned Montoya, who had lost his senate seat in the 1976 election, they were rebuffed in trying to find out more. ''You guys distort everything,'' Montoya said. ''I'm not even going to talk to you. You don't have any business talking to me.'' Ambrose also was contacted about the airplane incident. He could not recall such a telephone call from Montoya.

Drehsler and Wendland wanted to know what Customs, the Drug Enforcement Administration, and the Border Patrol were doing to combat the flow of narcotics through Nogales.

The source chuckled. ''That's part of our problem. Some of the investigators are being paid off. My personal work has convinced me that at least a half-dozen are turning their backs.''

He mentioned one U.S. government official in Nogales who was under active investigation for taking narcotics payoffs the year before. ''This guy made a salary of something like $12,000 a year,'' explained the agent. ''Well, we were able to find $17,000 in a safe-deposit box under his name. We started to put the pressure on him and he cracked. He implicated three others. Then one night, I get a call at home. The guy's dead, he supposedly shot himself in the head. We rush over and sure enough, he's dead. The case was handled by local cops. And it was botched up bad. I looked at the photographs they took of the death scene, and, in five of the six pictures, something had been moved. The gun he supposedly used was jammed or something. So, instead of sending it to a crime lab, they dismantled it with a screwdriver. Can you imagine, a screwdriver? But that's not the worst. Two hours after its discovery, the local cops release the body to the undertaker and it's embalmed. All the evidence was destroyed. Our whole case just went down the drain.''

The agent dropped the reporters back at the motel.

''Good luck,'' he said. ''I hate to wash our dirty linen like this. But maybe you guys can do something about it. These things just get covered up. This whole state is like that. I hope you guys do some good.'' He drove off, leaving the reporters standing in the darkness outside their motel rooms.

They stood there like that for five minutes. Then, not saying anything, they went into their rooms.

Both reporters had trouble falling asleep. They now realized just how hopeless the American government's much-touted effort to curtail the flow of narcotics into Arizona really was. The rugged terrain along the border and the lackadaisical, corrupt officials in America and Mexico spelled a dismal story. Like so many other criminal aspects of Arizona, the drug problem was totally out of hand. And no one, anywhere, appeared to be doing anything about it.

10 | Mafia West

There has always been something about Arizona that has attracted the outlaw. Bank robbers, claim jumpers, hired gunfighters, and such famous badmen as the Hole in the Wall Gang and Butch Cassidy are synonymous with the Old West and Arizona's history. In the early days, it was the state's proximity to Mexico and its wide-open, rugged terrain that attracted the old-style hoodlums. The state had room to hide in and a foreign border to flee to should legal pursuit be too intense.

In the twentieth century, crime and criminals are more sophisticated. Yet Arizona, which somehow has remained a step or two behind the rest of the country, remains equally appealing to the criminal. Mexico is no longer a sanctuary: today it is almost like a business partner for the American hoodlum, a place where the raw material—opium—comes from for the mob's main business—narcotics. And the state's wide-open spaces, while still plentiful, are more aesthetic than protective. Instead, Arizona's chief appeal to the criminal lies in the cumulative effect of the outlaw's heritage, the attitudes and actions accepted through centuries of apathy. For the criminal, Arizona is a good place to do business. It is a state where the outlaw has always flourished. Indeed, even today, in such tourist attractions as Tombstone and Old Tucson, the outlaw is celebrated with twice-daily mock shoot-outs by actors and stunt men.

The crudeness is not as blatant as it was in the old days. Phoenix and Tucson both abound in cultural activities. There are excellent local theatres, symphony orchestras, art museums. But just beneath the surface, much more obvious than in most Eastern cities, is a macho-like respect for the maverick, the man who makes his own rules, lives by his own law.

The Old West is not very old in Arizona.

It was that element of Arizona society that the IRE team would investigate next. What the reporters would find was that, like the old-fashioned outlaw who drifted West from back East, Arizona's new hoodlums were immigrants from elsewhere. And, like the narcotics pouring across the Arizona border, the state was being inundated with them.

167

Wendland and Drehsler returned from Mexico to find a surprising number of new team members. The suite was crowded and the telephones so busy that it was often all but impossible to find working space. Doug Kramer, a young reporter from the *Elyria Chronicle* in Elyria, Ohio, had arrived for a couple of weeks' work. Jerry Uhr-hammer, a forty-three-year-old, mild-mannered writer for the *Eugene Register-Guard* in Oregon, was there for an indefinite stay. So were Steven Wick and David Freed from the *Colorado Springs Sun*. Ed Rooney, a grizzled old police reporter from the *Chicago Daily News*, had given up ten days of his vacation to come work on the Arizona project. He also paid his own expenses.

Ross Becker, a tall, gangly, bearded young reporter who joined the project in mid-November, was an anomaly among team members. He had next to no substantive journalism experience and, instead of being recruited, talked his way onto the team by simply pestering Greene. But he would be a full-time member, with the project until its completion.

At twenty-four, Becker had been working out of a trailer on the 642-square-mile Zuñi Indian reservation in New Mexico, covering Indian news for the *Gallup* (New Mexico) *Independent* when he heard about the IRE team and decided that he wanted to enlist. He tracked down Greene and began calling the IRE office almost daily, begging for a chance. But Greene was concerned about Becker's background. The kid had just over a year's experience in newspaper-ing, almost all of it with small papers in remote parts of the South-west. The Arizona project, Greene felt, would be over Becker's head. But instead of flat-out telling the persistent young reporter to get lost, Greene kept stalling him, hoping he'd get the hint. But Becker continued calling each day. Finally, after Greene began refusing his calls, Becker got up one morning at five-thirty, borrowed a girlfriend's car, and spent six hours on the road, reaching Phoenix shortly before noon. From the lobby of the Adams, he phoned the IRE office. Marge Cashel, the secretary, routinely told him Greene was tied up in a meeting and would call Becker back.

"The hell he will," said Becker. "I'm downstairs and coming up to see him."

They met in Greene's connecting bedroom to the IRE suite. Becker told Greene he realized his background was less than complete but vowed to make up for it by enthusiasm. He said he'd do anything, even the dirty work and errand running, he just wanted in. Each time Greene started to protest, Becker cut him short. It was a chance of a lifetime, he told Greene, and he wouldn't rest until Greene let him join. It took fifteen minutes of face-to-face badgering, but finally Greene, the tough, veteran investigative reporter from Long Island, gave in to the young, inexperienced cub from the Indian reservation.

"You did it, kid," said Greene, slapping Becker on the back. "You wore me down. You're in."

Becker virtually floated back to New Mexico. In mid-November, after quitting his job with the *Independent*, selling his own car, and taking out a $500 bank loan, he arrived at the Adams for good. He had no idea what he'd do after the project ended, and all he could do was hope that the $800 he had to live on would last. But he was in.

When Becker volunteered to do the dirty work, he didn't realize that he would be taken so literally. The day Wendland and Drehsler returned from the border, they ran into a stranger on the third floor of the Adams parking garage, sorting through a huge pile of garbage that had been dumped on the floor. "Hey, there's this kid down in the garage with a pile of trash," an incredulous Drehsler told the office as they came through the door.

"Yeah, that's Becker," said John Rawlinson. "He's a new reporter. He didn't have anything to do, so Greene sent him out to steal Bob Goldwater's trash and see what goodies it contained."

A few minutes later, Becker, smelling of coffee grounds, came in waving Goldwater's bill for $300 from the Phoenix Country Club. All it established was that Goldwater liked to play golf and eat well. Still, it went in the Goldwater file.

Meanwhile, Greene was swamped in paperwork. He spent eighteen-hour days behind his corner desk reading the reporters' memos, marking them for various files, and spotting holes that needed to be filled. Each afternoon, he would slowly nod off to sleep. One day he was rudely awakened when his hair caught fire from a cigarette he had forgotten to extinguish before resting his head in his right hand.

The Buddha was the closest thing the reporters had seen to a human computer. His ability to read long, complicated financial statements and memoranda and then file them away in his memory for near total recall weeks later was amazing. He was like a master juggler, keeping the various story projects going in a dozen different directions, while always looking around for new angles. If he had one fault, the reporters felt, it was that he sometimes worked too closely with law enforcement officials.

Public officials, of course, have always been major news sources.

Owing to the similarities between their jobs, police and reporters often overlap on certain investigations. Confidential trade-offs sometimes occur, e.g., police provide information they have developed in exchange for some of a reporter's. It is seldom discussed, but every reporter has done it at various times. In most cases, the cooperation works to everyone's benefit. But on sensitive matters, it can become a major moral dilemma for a newsman. A reporter is only as good as his word, and many times a news source will talk only with the promise of anonymity. Often, an investigative reporter's sources are the very persons police are trying to make a case on. So trading information with the police must be weighed carefully.

And Greene had been giving a lot of it away.

One night in mid-November, Arizona Attorney General Bruce Babbitt came into the IRE office with a district attorney from Alaska. From conversations with Greene, Babbitt knew that the IRE team had documented several ties to Alaska by members of the Licavoli and Bonanno organized crime families in Tucson. Among other things, IRE had established Arizona mob interests in Alaskan prostitution and narcotics trafficking. Babbitt suggested that Greene share the team's intelligence with the Alaskan prosecutor.

Nina Bondarook, one of the ASU student workers, was asked by Greene to Xerox the entire file on the Alaska-Arizona connection for the Alaskan prosecutor. She was going over the files when she saw that one of the team's sources was named. John Rawlinson, who had worked on the Alaskan end of the investigation, was sitting nearby. Bondarook called him over and told him what Greene intended to do.

"You're shitting me," he said. Rawlinson had dealt with the source on a confidential basis. He couldn't believe that Greene would simply turn it over to Alaskan authorities without clearing it first. Rather than confronting Greene in front of Babbitt and the Alaskan prosecutor, Rawlinson put through a call to his Alaskan source, who allowed him to reveal his identity.

The incident disturbed most of the reporters. Greene had been dealing closely with local and state police officials all along. Indeed, his relationships had saved reporters days of work and provided major breaks in their investigation. But along with the police assistance, each reporter had developed his own sources, some of whom would be extremely upset to know that their names were being bandied about in front of lawmen. While their memos seldom identified sensitive sources by name (a special code was used consisting of the initial of the reporter's last name followed by the letter *S* for source and an identifying number), the source's real name often could be easily divined by someone familiar with the subject. And Greene knew the names of many confidential sources since he usually assigned the reporter to contact the source in the first place.

There was another annoying problem: the *Arizona Republic*. Wendland's Henny Youngman source, the ex-real-estate salesman and private eye who had earned his name by spouting off a dozen news leads in one-liner fashion, kept insisting that somebody at the *Republic* was out to sabotage the IRE investigation.

"You still don't believe me," said the source one afternoon shortly after Wendland's return from Mexico.

Wendland shook his head. "Give me something specific, something I can check out. So far, all you've done is claim the *Republic* is double-dealing us."

"I wish I could be more specific. But they're suckering you guys. They are not about to print what you come up with."

Republic city editor Bob Early and reporter John Winters, the staffer assigned to work on the team, certainly gave no indication of that, Wendland thought. Indeed, Early had been up in the office several times late at night and, after going through some of the files, had had high praise for the team's work, even to the point of saying how eager he was to see it in print.

"Well, all I can tell you is that I'd be damn careful of what I let them see," said Henny. "I mean, if certain people are tipped off to what you guys are looking into, they can cover certain things up before you can get to them, right? I mean look at Harry Rosenzweig. He's a very big man in this state, close to the Goldwaters and all that. And he's nervous as hell about what you guys got on Bob Goldwater and that Herb Applegate."

"Go on."

"That's all I know. Something about a killing up in Las Vegas."

Wendland tensed. The Applegate investigation was one of the team's most closely guarded secrets. "What are you talking about?" he asked, trying to sound bored and irritated.

"Something about a girlfriend of Applegate's and a private eye that got killed. I don't know anything more about it except that Rosenzweig's been told that you guys got the goods on Applegate and Goldwater."

"I don't know what the hell you're talking about. Who told Rosenzweig what?"

"The *Republic*. The *Republic* tipped him. He's worried about a bunch of personal stuff coming out about Goldwater's company, you know, sex orgies and all that."

"Where the hell are you hearing all this? You're not making sense."

The source shrugged. "I told you, I can't say how I know this. I just do, that's all. Okay, so maybe I'm all wet about Rosenzweig. But you've got to believe me about the *Republic*."

Henny Youngman couldn't provide any more details. After he left, Wendland wondered. The guy was persistent as hell. Why? Was he a plant, sent to get the various reporters on the team suspicious of each other and thus divert their energies, or was he for real, just a local guy who had seen how corrupt the state was and wanted to get even with those who had screwed him? Wendland didn't know. While he still met with the source once or twice a week, he had not yet gotten anything concrete from him. Or had he?

That night, Wendland and Koziol went down to the hotel bar for a couple of drinks before turning in. Wendland told him what the informant had said about Rosenzweig's being tipped off about the Hobo Joe's investigation. They went over all the bases. Koziol and Teuscher had asked a lot of questions of a lot of people. Rosenzweig could just as easily have learned of the reporters' investigation from someone other than the *Republic*.

But Koziol, too, had questions about the *Republic*'s way of handling certain stories. One of his first assignments after arriving in Phoenix had been to interview Jack Karie, a former *Republic* reporter. It was Karie who, in the early fifties, discovered extortionist and ex-pimp Willie Bioff living in Phoenix under an assumed name and socializing with the city's elite. But when he wrote a story which exposed Bioff, the *Republic* killed it. The reason: Bioff had gone to his friend, Harry Rosenzweig, who in turn used his clout with Gene Pulliam, the *Republic*'s owner. It was because of this favor that Bioff made a $5,000 campaign contribution to Barry Goldwater's first senate campaign, directed by Rosenzweig. The favor did Bioff little good. In 1955, he was blown apart in a bomb blast.

Koziol found Karie, who had quit newspapering in 1963, in a makeshift gymnasium in Scottsdale where the ex-reporter taught boxing to youngsters for the suburb's recreation department. A solidly built, white-haired man of about five feet, eight inches, Karie was familiar with the IRE team and was glad to help out. Koziol asked him to talk about the Willie Bioff story.

"Sure, I remember it well. A guy came up to me one day at the bar in the Arizona Club and told me that this guy we all knew as Bill Nelson was really this hood named Bioff," Karie recalled. "I went right out and started nosing around. It didn't take much to verify. So I shot a couple of pictures of his house and wrote the story. It was a damn good one, too. So I'm waiting a couple of days for the story to come out. This one afternoon I stop by a liquor store and who do I run into but this Nelson-Bioff guy. He's acting like a real smart-ass. He tells me he knows all about the story I wrote and says he's taken care of it, that it won't run. Then he threatens me, says he has a lot of powerful friends and I'd better stay off his ass or else. Well, I really got pissed off. I went storming into the office. I couldn't figure out how Bioff knew about the story. Sure enough, the editors are real wishy-washy when I start bitching. I finally am told that it was killed on orders of old man Pulliam."

Karie said he went out and had a few drinks. Then he remembered seeing Rosenzweig in the office the day before, talking to Gene Pulliam. "See, you got to understand, Rosenzwieg ran that newspaper, probably still does." But Karie still thought he had a good story. And rather than let it die, he went to Tucson and called syndicated columnist Westbrook Pegler. "I gave the whole thing to Pegler and he used it," Karie bragged.

The ex-reporter had lots of criticism for the *Republic*. "They tried to break me after that. They took me off the street, tried to keep me away from my sources. I finally got so fed up that I left. You had to fight your own people."

As Koziol left, Karie remembered one thing. "Hey, you know what my last assignment was before I got out?"

Koziol shook his head.

"I was the guy who broke in Don Bolles."

Gene Pulliam, the *Republic*'s crusty old publisher, was dead in 1976, though the paper was still controlled by editors who shared his friendships and philosophy. Koziol and Wendland had each come into contact with many of Don Bolles's closest friends. As they sipped their drinks in the Adams bar, they wondered about the *Republic*'s integrity. For everyone who knew Bolles had said he was a disillusioned man in the months before his death. He, like Karie, had often complained about wishy-washy editors. A certain amount of griping is standard in the newspaper business, a traditional city-room cynicism that is as much a part of newspapering as printer's ink.

But wherever the IRE reporters went, they heard few good things about the *Republic*.

Despite the pledges of cooperation from Early and Winters, there had been a few incidents. Most recently, IRE members had been refused access to news clippings in the *Republic* library by managing editor Harold Milks.

Wendland finished his drink. "Shit, we're worrying about shadows. We've got enough work to do. Let's not let this get us down."

Koziol agreed. They said good night and went up to their rooms.

In mid-November, after miles of "deep 'n dirty" traveling about the state, Tom Renner finally showed up. The team's mystery man turned out to be a short, slightly balding fellow with an ulcer and an engaging smile. Renner had been on the road full-time since the project began, and he was beat. But he was also very pleased. He had brought in piles of information that spelled out the current activities of Joe Bonanno and Pete Licavoli, Sr. It showed that the mob was slowly but surely moving in on the Southwest, building a tightly run operation rivaling the power of the long-established New York mob.

Actually, the Mafia had been in Arizona for thirty years, though Renner's files noted that it had only just begun to consolidate its strength. Joe Bonanno had come to Tucson in 1943, for the health of his eldest son, Salvatore, known as Bill, who had an ear mastoid. The best treatment for the boy was to sit in the sun and let the ear drain, said Bonanno's New York doctors. So Bonanno came west and settled into a comfortable house on Tucson's East Elm Street. The next year, he was joined by an old friend, Detroit mobster Pete Licavoli, Sr., who purchased a sprawling ranch outside of town.

This westward migration did not put an end to either mobster's crime activities. Bonanno continued to run his New York family. Licavoli, taking advantage of the then-emerging gambling in Las Vegas, set up his own gambling wire for horse and dog results.

Bonanno, of course, found that his reputation had preceded him. But in the Western tradition, he was received by the Tucson citizenry openly and with no prejudice. Soon Bonanno was parlaying some of the profits from his New York earnings into large land holdings in Arizona, appearing at the right parties, keeping a low profile, and donating time and money to his church. Just how well established he had become was made evident in 1954 when federal officials tried to strip away his U.S. citizenship. At his deportation hearing, Bonanno lassoed a passel of Arizona pioneer family members as character witnesses, among them U.S. Representative Harold "Porque" Patten, Roman Catholic Bishop Francis J. Green of the Tucson diocese, and Evo DeConcini, a former state supreme court judge and a man of enormous political influence whose son, Dennis, was elected a U.S. senator in Arizona's 1976 elections.

His influence continued to grow. Augustus "Gus" Battaglia, a man without a criminal record but an old friend of Bonanno's from the New York days, moved to Arizona in the mid-fifties, building a giant cotton farm midway between Tucson and Phoenix and soon becoming a powerful figure in state politics, famous for hosting lavish parties. Renner obtained a guest list from one of those parties, held in 1959. Among those attending were the Arizona governor, the state's attorney general, the Pima County sheriff, two of the state's congressmen, the heads of most of Arizona's major regulatory agencies, and Joe Bonanno.

Bonanno, however, couldn't leave well enough alone. While forming new alliances and planting roots in Arizona, he was still very much active in the administration of the New York mob. In the early sixties, he began a series of moves aimed at consolidating his interests back east. His big mistake was in calling for the assassination of mob chieftain Carlo Gambino. Gambino's well-organized family nipped the plan in the bud, snatching Bonanno off a New York street during one of his frequent visits home. He was to be killed. But because the Bonanno kidnapping was drawing an incredible amount of newspaper coverage and police heat, the ten-member mob ruling council stepped in. If Bonanno were eliminated, a major gang war was sure to follow. And Bonanno was a native Mafia son, one of the original founders of the American Cosa Nostra. He was not simply a cocky street soldier or an informer. His life would be spared, but only if he would agree to "retire" back to Arizona and stay out of the New York mob's affairs.

From 1965 to the mid-1970s, Bonanno did just that. But then a number of lesser mob figures, realizing the enormous potential in Arizona, began moving into the state, carving off territories in prostitution, gambling, and loan-sharking. They began fighting among themselves. Sitting in Tucson, Bonanno knew opportunity when he saw it. He had promised the Mafia council to stay away from New York, a promise he had pretty much kept. But it was a different matter in his new home state. He began meeting with the other newcomers, expanding his influence and cementing working relationships.

Arizona was a jewel in the desert and Bonanno began polishing it. But with Arizona came other areas. Colorado, with a growing population and no real organized mob, was another plum waiting to be picked. Using the alias "Mr. Veccio," Bonanno made at least two trips to Colorado Springs in 1974 for organizational meetings with his new associates. Since his two sons, Bill and Joe Junior, were already established in Southern California, the old man began moving in there, too. Federal officials noted that after each Bonanno visit, his sons would fan out in meetings with local mobsters, passing the information they had received from the father. Carmine Galenti, who in the fall of 1976 was vying for control of the East Coast mob after the death of Bonanno's old nemesis Gambino, flew to California for a meeting with Bonanno, apparently giving East Coast approval to an organizing drive in the West.

Joe Junior, the old man's second son, had not escaped legal difficulties himself. In fact, a 1972 case against young Joe was probably one of the most bizarre examples of Arizona justice encountered by the IRE reporters. It was a conspiracy case. Joe Junior and a friend, Arthur Grande, Jr., were convicted in the Phoenix courtroom of U.S. District Judge Walter E. Craig of taking part in a murder-for-hire conspiracy. Five codefendants had previously pled guilty before Bonanno and his friend found a similar fate at the hands of a jury whose members unanimously agreed that the old mobster's son had tried to hire a hit man to kill a Phoenix hotel owner he was not getting along with.

The unusual aspect of the case came on June 19, some six weeks after the conviction, when Judge Craig suddenly reversed the jury's verdict. In a seventy-minute, early-afternoon hearing, the judge declared that he thought the jury had convicted because it believed Bonanno and Grande to be guilty of a shakedown attempt, which had come out in trial testimony, but not of the murder conspiracy.

It is highly unusual for a judge to toss out a jury verdict, especially more than a month after the verdict has been handed down. It is likewise virtually unprecedented for a judge to do so without first polling the jury as to why they convicted. But that was precisely what Judge Craig did. He simply assumed that he knew what the jury's thought process had been without talking to its members. Then he arbitrarily freed the defendants.

IRE reporters decided to go back and talk to some of the principals in the case. John Rawlinson, the *Tucson Daily Star* reporter, interviewed jury member Robert W. Clark. Four years later Clark was still furious about the judge's unexplained reversal. He had been so angry at the time that he had written letters of complaint to the U.S. Supreme Court, U.S. Attorney General Richard Kleindienst, and Senator Barry Goldwater, charging that Craig's conduct during the trial had been "anything but impartial."

"Just what do you mean by that?" Rawlinson asked.

"His reaction to various witnesses and their testimony left little doubt as to what he thought of them," said Clark. "When witnesses hostile to the defendants were on the stand, Craig would get these incredulous looks on his face. I remember he kept making noises, shaking his head and looking in disbelief every time somebody said something against Bonanno."

Clark said he had sat on a number of juries before and had never seen a judge behave like that.

Rawlinson had an exact copy of the judge's words in overturning the decision. Said the judge: "I think what may have happened to the jury in this case was that they, at least the majority of them, felt that they could not sustain a conviction on Count Eight [conspiring to hire a hit man] and that they ultimately compromised because they did not like what possibly has transpired in the two defendants getting away with $5,000 [from the shakedown]." Rawlinson asked whether the judge might have been right.

"No way. There was no such action on the part of the jury. We reached a very honest and unanimous decision. We believed that the evidence proved them guilty, and that judge's speculating as to how and why we reached the verdict was just not true."

The foreman of the jury was Jerry Boyd, a Phoenix gas station owner. Rawlinson asked him the reaction to Craig's sudden reversal of their guilty verdict. "We were flabbergasted," said Boyd. "I mean it was a real insult to us. How could he know what we were thinking? The whole jury was absolutely convinced of their guilt." Boyd said he had been told by several jurors that they had received threatening phone calls during the trial and that one of the male jurors had been followed home after court one day.

"Then something real peculiar happened," said Boyd. "The morning after we found the Bonanno kid guilty, I come into my gas station and I find that someone had shot a large hole in the front window. Now I've been in the same location for twenty years and never had vandalism problems. But that's not all. That very same morning, Valona Hughes—she was on the same jury with me—she comes into my station. Now normally, she'd just stay in the car while I filled the car. Well, fortunately, this time she gets out to go in for a pack of cigarettes or something. Anyway, seconds after she gets out of her car, this huge lumber truck comes careening into the station and smashes into her car. Well, all hell breaks loose. The driver of the truck says he's hurt and an ambulance suddenly shows up. Then the police come. A couple of days later, I find out from the cops that the truck was stolen and they were never able to find the driver or the ambulance.''

Boyd said he reported the incident to the FBI but that nothing ever happened. ''I'll tell you this much,'' he told Rawlinson. ''Those things were much too coincidental. They scared hell out of me. I figured they must have had something to do with the trial.''

Ann Bowen was the assistant U.S. attorney who prosecuted young Bonanno. A small, intense woman, she too was incensed by Craig's handling of the case. It was almost as if the judge deliberately attempted to scuttle the trial himself, she felt.

When she questioned witnesses, said Ms. Bowen, the judge buried his face in his hands. Often, at key moments in the middle of tough questioning, he would openly laugh. She remembered him mimicking one of her witnesses in a falsetto voice and ridiculing her by gesturing and rolling his eyes throughout her presentation. Like the jurors, Ms. Bowen tried to do something about Craig's actions. She wrote a lengthy memorandum, citing numerous examples of his judicial indiscretion. She asked her superiors to appeal the case. It never was.

The same day that Judge Craig announced his decision to toss out the jury's guilty verdict, another interesting development occurred in Tucson, a two-hour drive south from Phoenix. IRE had come up with some solid information from federal sources that sharply illustrated old man Bonanno's concern for his son's legal problems. The government had learned that a week or so after his son's conviction, the old man, who had showed up as a spectator each day of his son's trial, told a close associate that he needed to come up with a large sum of money to ''get my son off the hook.'' Bonanno said he needed cash that he would not have to account for later on and that it would have to come from someone else. Exactly what, if anything, was worked out that day was unclear. But on June 16, Bonanno's longtime friend Pete Licavoli, Sr., deposited $25,000 in his personal account at Southern

Arizona Bank in Tucson. And early on the morning of June 19, Licavoli went to a branch office of the bank and tried to write himself a check for $25,000 cash. But the bank didn't have that much money on hand so early in the morning. Licavoli then went to the main office downtown, where he was described by federal agents as nervous, sweating, and obviously in a hurry. He was given the $25,000 as requested, in $100 bills. Nobody knew where he went after rushing out of the bank.

Just after noon that day, Craig overturned the conviction against Joe Bonanno, Jr. In his previous interviews with IRE reporters, Craig denied any knowledge of the Tucson transactions.

That was in 1972. And in 1976, the old man, at seventy-two and still in excellent health, continued to be a very busy man. Renner had gone to Bonanno's new home in North Tucson one morning in November to watch the old man for himself. About ten, Bonanno stepped out the back door of his unpretentious brick house, situated on a well-landscaped, curving suburban street with a breathtaking view of Mount Lemon. His silver hair gleamed in the sun as Bonanno called over his Doberman, Greasy, who prowled the front and back yards during the night. Bonanno put the dog in the house and got into his brand-new silver Cadillac Fleetwood.

Renner was familiar with the routine. His sources told him that Bonanno would drive a half-dozen blocks to the Lucky Wishbone, a small, neat restaurant which specialized in takeout fried chicken. Bonanno seldom went into the restaurant. Instead, he carefully closed himself in a telephone booth out front, fished a handful of quarters from his pocket, and dropped one into the slot. Renner's sources had watched him make over a dozen calls. That was Joe Bonanno's office.

The reporter's law enforcement sources had told him that the phone booth routine occurred each day, though the old man changed booths every couple of weeks. Exactly what Bonanno said was usually known only to him and the person he was talking to. He spoke only in Sicilian. Renner looked at police surveillance reports indicating that Bonanno entertained a number of visitors in his home. Some were prominent and came in through the front door, as evangelist Billy Graham had a couple of years before. Others, however, were strictly backdoor visitors. Federal agents once watched Bonanno's longtime bodyguard, Peter Notaro, meet four well-known mobsters at Tucson's International Airport, place them in the back of a station wagon, cover them up with carpeting, and then drive them to Bonanno's house, where they quickly unloaded around the back.

That Joseph Bonanno—whose New York crime family designed the infamous "French Connection" for Turkish heroin—was now involved with Mexican drug dealers was well established by lawmen. Among the pilgrims to Bonanno's was Hector Mar Wong, a Chinese-born drug wholesaler who operated one of Mexico's biggest heroin smuggling rings. And on March 1, 1976, Bonanno was observed flying in a private plant to Culiacán, Mexico's main drug processing center, where he was met by Victor Savela, the brother of one of Mexico's top heroin suppliers. From the Culiacán airport, Savela drove Bonanno to the Camino Real Hotel in nearby Mazatlán, where he met with Demetri Alonzo, of Bogotá, Colombia, a major South American cocaine merchant. After a four-hour meeting, Bonanno returned to Tucson.

Bonanno had to be careful with Peter "Horseface" Licavoli, his old hoodlum friend from Detroit who had come to Arizona the year after he did. It did not look well for the two to be seen together too often. Their carefully nurtured images of "retired businessmen" would crumble were their real associations out in the open.

But Licavoli was still very much in business as well. At seventy-four, suffering from cancer, Licavoli was in big trouble with the law in the fall of 1976. He was scheduled to go on trial in December on federal charges of receiving a stolen painting and offering to sell it to an undercover FBI agent from the art gallery he ran from his eighty-acre Grace Ranch. Licavoli was later found guilty and sentenced to serve eighteen months in prison. But stolen paintings weren't Licavoli's only criminal activity. IRE reporters had obtained wiretaps and tape recordings which implicated Licavoli in the sale of stolen Israeli machine guns and counterfeit money.

The first tape was made two days after Christmas in 1973 by an undercover informant of the U.S. Treasury's Alcohol, Tobacco, and Firearms Division. Licavoli met the ATF informant, who was wearing a hidden body bug, near the American Airlines counter at Phoenix's Sky Harbor Airport and took him outside to an automobile. Inside the car, the gray-haired, ruddy-faced Licavoli produced nine forged twenty-dollar bills and a single fifty-dollar note. The bills were excellent counterfeits.

"I can get you up to twenty million dollars' worth of these bills," boasted Licavoli, who believed the informant was an organized crime

The power structure. Arizona's political king makers Harry Rosenzweig (*top left*) was chief mentor to Senator Barry Goldwater (*top right*). *At bottom* is the senator's brother Robert, who has maintained business and social ties to Rosenzweig and several organized crime figures.

The IRE's team headquarters at the Adams Hotel.

Above, Jerry Uhrhammer, Eugene (Oregon) Register-Guard, and Ray Schrick, Wenatchee (Wash.) World.

At left, Ross Becker, who quit his job with a small New Mexico newspaper to join the IRE team.

Assistant team
leader, Dick Cady,
Indianapolis Star.

Tom Renner,
Newsday.

Bob Greene,
Newsday reporter
who led the IRE
team.

Alex Drehsler
(*standing*) and John
Rawlinson (*at
typewriter*) of the
Arizona Daily Star,
and George Weisz
(*at right*), team
researcher.

The author, Mike Wendland of the *Detroit News,* with Ron Koziol, *Chicago Tribune.*

Dave Offer, *Milwaukee Journal.*

John Winters, *Arizona Republic* (Phoenix).

Dave Overton, KGUN-TV, Tucson.

Myrta Pulliam, *Indianapolis Star.*

Susan Irby, *Gulfport* (Miss.) *Daily Herald.*

Ross Becker (*left*), *Gallup* (New Mexico) *Independent;* Dick Lyneis (*center*), *Riverside* (Calif.) *Press;* Ken Matthews (*on phone at right*) *Idaho Statesman.*

Harry Jones, *Kansas City Star,* in the office with some of the file cards compiled by the team during the Arizona Project.

figure from the East. Licavoli would sell the counterfeit bills for twenty-five percent of their face value. The aging mobster also had other merchandise for sale, in particular, some 200 Uzzi machine guns, manufactured in Israel, available with or without silencers.

"Open the glove compartment," Licavoli instructed the informant.

Inside, there was a .22 caliber Baretta, equipped with an elaborate silencer, which Licavoli said was representative of the quality of the merchandise he was selling. It was Licavoli's own personal weapon, he said. The meeting ended with Licavoli promising to locate three telephone booths in Phoenix, which he would use to communicate with the informant as they conducted future negotiations.

Another meeting was held two weeks later. Again the informant was wired as Licavoli took him to Applegate's Olde English Pub in Phoenix, owned by restaurateur and longtime Licavoli pal Herb Applegate. Inside, there was a long line of luncheon customers. Licavoli was immediately recognized by the hostess and was ushered ahead of the waiting diners to a secluded table. During lunch, Licavoli again spoke proudly of his ability to provide the stolen machine guns, though the conversation was frequently interrupted as some twenty different persons—lawyers and prominent Phoenix businessmen—recognized the hoodlum and came over to his table to exchange greetings. Licavoli seemed proud of the attention and boasted to the informant about how well connected he was. He even said he had a "twist" on Senator Barry Goldwater through his association with Herb Applegate, the business partner of the senator's brother.

The tapes underscored facts already uncovered by IRE reporters Koziol and Teuscher in their investigation of Applegate's chain of Hobo Joe's restaurants, information which established $2,500-a-month payoffs to Licavoli.

In 1969, a widely traveled Arizona contractor, a man who served on the loan clearance board of a Phoenix bank, told the FBI that he had taken nine million dollars to the Bank of Tokyo and deposited it for Licavoli. IRE reporters had documented Licavoli's financial interest in an Arizona race track, millions of dollars in secret real estate holdings, and hidden ownership in a score of restaurants and parking lots. He was a very wealthy man.

And he had done it all. In the thirties, Licavoli had been the head of Detroit's so-called Down River Gang, a powerful branch of the

Motor City's old Purple Gang. He had been a suspect in a half-dozen murders, including the 1930 killing of Detroit radio newsman Gerald Buckley, and had served prison time for everything from bribing a Customs official to income tax evasion. But perhaps the most bizarre thing that Licavoli ever tried took place in the fifties. That's when he attempted to purchase an entire town.

Tom Renner had found a Tucson attorney, who confirmed the incident. The lawyer said he was approached by Martin Fenster, a known front man for Licavoli, who wanted him to form several corporations which would hide Licavoli's involvement. Then the corporations would completely buy the little border town of Lukeville.

Lukeville wasn't ever much of a town, situated on sixty-seven acres of barren desert land about fifty miles southwest of Tucson. Permanent residents had never totaled more than sixty, and there was nothing to the real estate but a cantina, a gas station, a trailer court, and a small motel. It was an extremely isolated spot where water had to be trucked in and normal amenities like electricity and telephones cost dearly. But Licavoli wanted it.

The one thing Lukeville had going for it was its location. It was the only border crossing along a barren 250-mile stretch of desert between Nogales on the east and San Luis Rio Colorado on the west. More than half a million tourists annually crossed at Lukeville, most of them headed for Mexico's Puerto Peñasco and the rich sport fishing waters of Cholla Bay. As such, Lukeville was a natural crossing point for drug smugglers as well.

The Tucson attorney said he had refused to go along with the secret maneuver to buy the town up for Licavoli and didn't know what the man had tried next.

Further research led Renner to one Stan Tanner, who quietly took title to the town in 1962. Tanner had been a friend of Licavoli's since the mid-1940s. Contacted by IRE reporters, he said he had no idea that his pal Licavoli was ever interested in Lukeville. "Isn't that something?" he said with a smile. In 1967, public records showed, Valley National Bank in Phoenix foreclosed on a loan to Tanner, and the town was sold to a man named Alfred Gay, a wealthy ex-con who owned an Alaskan flying service.

Meanwhile, reporters learned about other Licavoli associates, suspected by the U.S. Drug Enforcement Administration as up-and-coming smugglers who operated a prostitute, narcotics, and stolen goods ring between Mexico and Anchorage, Alaska. Interviews with law enforcement and underworld sources indicated that the old man was passing on the family business to the associates, who were frequently seen all over the Southwest in the company of known organized crime figures.

The team had established that the Mafia was very much present in Arizona, prospering and expanding like a conglomerate.

Over Thanksgiving, the office fell into a slump. The reporters were overwhelmed with work. As Phoenix went about decorating its downtown streets with papier-mâché Santa Clauses wearing Mexican sombreros, the reporters missed their families back East. Then Nina Bondarook, the ASU student volunteer, burst in Saturday afternoon with twenty-five dollars' worth of garland and tinsel and Christmas candy canes that she strung up all across the office. It was a bit too gaudy, but it cheered everyone up.

No sooner did one reporter leave than he was replaced by new recruits. Dave Overton, a tall, bearded newsman from KGUN-TV in Tucson, arrived the first week of December. So did David Offer, a thirty-five-year-old investigative specialist from the *Milwaukee Journal*. Both would be with the project through the end of January, when most of the reporting was expected to be wrapped up.

There was one more permanent addition. He was Dick Cady, a slightly built man in his early thirties who came from the *Indianapolis Star*. Cady would be Greene's assistant, assigned to play vulture with the files, to pick them apart for accuracy and to detail where more work needed to be done. He knew his job. Back home, Cady was head of the three-man investigative team whose probe into police corruption won a 1975 Pulitzer Prize. Along the way, however, Cady and another *Star* reporter had been indicted in a police setup aimed at discrediting the newspaper's investigation. The charges of attempting to bribe a police officer were dismissed after Cady's team continued its work, unintimidated by the pressure. Besides the Pulitzer, journalism's most coveted award, the *Star* team also won the Drew Pearson Award for Investigative Reporting.

It took Cady more than three weeks of sixteen-hour-a-day reading just to get through the massive files already compiled by the team. When he did so, he was asked what he thought.

"Fantastic," he grinned.

His opinion was shared by Tony Ansolia, a managing editor of

Newsday, who flew out in early December for a week's reading. Ansolia was one of the most skilled editors in the business. He would spend the entire month of February in Phoenix, editing the dozens of stories which would finally be written. Originally, Greene had expected no more than eight to ten stories to emerge from the project. The whole investigation was not expected to stretch beyond the end of December. Now, it looked like the earliest the team could finish would be the end of February. Ansolia, Cady, and Greene saw over fifty individual news stories that could be written from the files.

Bob Weaver, a short, quiet, forty-one-year-old reporter from the *San Jose Mercury* in California spent two weeks in early December working on the team. His paper paid for one week, the other week was his vacation. He took the bus to Phoenix to save expenses and, despite chronic high blood pressure and a slight heart condition, Weaver worked fifteen-hour-a-day stints, mostly in the office, where he did eye-straining record research into the giant Goldmar and Del Webb Corporations. This labor was bound to catch up with him. One night, ten days after his arrival, he began to feel dizzy. He figured it was because he had been neglecting the long walks prescribed by his doctor back in San Jose. About eight o'clock, he left the office and headed for the street. He was sure he'd feel better if he could walk around in the fresh air. He had gotten no further than the downstairs lobby when the dizziness, now accompanied by chest pains, overcame him. He made it to the house phone and called upstairs. Jerry Uhrhammer rushed down to help his stricken colleague, whose face had turned a pasty white.

Weaver thought he was having a heart attack. The other reporters put him in his room and tried to locate a doctor. The Adams had no house physician, and a Phoenix medical referral service had no one on call. Meanwhile, Weaver thought he was feeling better. He tried to sit up in bed, but the chest pains returned again. He attempted to hide the discomfort, but his appearance convinced his friends that he needed immediate medical attention. Wendland rushed downstairs to get a car out of the hotel garage while Dick Cady, Uhrhammer, and Carol Jackson, a student volunteer, helped an unsteady Weaver out of his room and into the elevator. Wendland picked the group up in front of the hotel and drove to St. Luke's Hospital, which specializes in coronary care.

It took about two hours to run a battery of tests. Fortunately, Weaver had not suffered a heart attack. His problem was fatigue, brought on by overwork and stress, which had caused an imbalance in the various medicines he was taking for the high blood pressure. The emergency room doctor suggested a couple of days' rest and a return to his normal exercise. "The main thing is to take it easy," he said as Weaver was dressing to go. "You're exhausted. Get some rest."

The next day, Weaver was back in the office at noon. When his coworkers protested, he said he had slept in an extra two hours and was just fine. He had several more days to stay in Phoenix, and he didn't plan to spend them in bed. There was work to be done.

While Renner was documenting the activities of the Bonanno and Licavoli crime families, John Rawlinson and Norm Udevitz headed northwest to the Arizona-California border and the bustling desert spa of Lake Havasu City, an entirely new town built in 1963 on 14,000 acres of rocky and arid Mohave County wilderness by the giant McCulloch Corp. It had grown to quite a resort, permanently occupied by nearly 15,000 "snowbirds," or retired Midwesterners glad to exchange their frigid winters back home for Arizona's fabled climate, and thousands of tourists and would-be residents who came to partake of the community's golf courses, recreational amenities, and a tour of the London Bridge, which McCulloch purchased in the late sixties and had shipped to the desert as a promotion gimmick.

The reporters spent several days in Lake Havasu City, returning to Phoenix with still another example of the mob's presence in the state. For what they found was, in the words of Joe Chapin, an investigator for the Mohave County sheriff's department, "almost a complete transplant of the Rochester, New York, chapter of the Mafia."

"We're just a small sheriff's office," Chapin insisted. "We don't have the manpower or the equipment to know what the hell these people are up to. But we know they are here."

Mohave County was one of Arizona's least populated counties. All but 10,000 of its 25,000 residents lived in the brand-new city of Lake Havasu. It was an unincorporated city, with no police force of its own. The only lawmen for miles around came from the office of county sheriff David Rathbone, who talked with the steel-jawed cowboy twang made famous in the old Western movies.

"I'm no good on them eye-talian names," Rathbone drawled. "But we sure got us a lot of Mafia types around here."

One of the county's most prosperous businessmen was Edward Eugene Frederico, Jr., a darkly handsome forty-two-year-old who, among other things, owned the area's only asphalt and concrete plants, which held million-dollar subcontracts with the Lake Havasu Irrigation and Drainage District to build city streets. Frederico, who moved west in 1973, was a native of Rochester. In Lake Havasu, he was the head of the hundred-member Italian-American Antidefamation League.

"Just because I'm Italian and grew up with the Mafia back in Rochester and a lot of my friends are mobsters doesn't mean that I am," he told Rawlinson and Udevitz.

Frederico apparently did not hold membership in the mob against his friends. Among the incorporators, officers, and key employees of his two firms, Rawlinson and Udevitz found Quinto Leo Polidori, an enforcer for the Rochester mob convicted in 1975 of beating a delinquent loan-shark victim, and Joseph Vincent Sciolino, a soldier for the Rochester family convicted with Polidori in the 1975 incident as well as on a federal charge of dealing in stolen checks.

Two other once-prominent Rochester natives had also moved to the booming new Arizona resort. William Hamill, Rochester's former deputy police commissioner came out about the same time as Frederico. He left the city's police department under the cloud of a grand jury indictment accusing him of leaking evidence in a major gambling case against a notorious Rochester mobster. Hamill's background came to light when he applied for a job with the Mohave County sheriff's reserve. He did not get it.

The Rochester fire department was also represented in Lake Havasu. Joseph Nalore, formerly the fire chief of Rochester, emigrated to Arizona and tried to get a job with the Lake Havasu fire department. He, too, was turned down because of a grand jury indictment. Nalore was accused of arson, i.e., of showing certain Rochester mobsters how to make fires appear as accidents. He was also accused of torching seven Rochester buildings for insurance proceeds.

And the reporters had learned of a dozen more Mafiosi who kept popping up in town to soak up a little sun, visit old friends, and play some golf. It was an interesting place. The Rochester mob was loyal to Joe Bonanno. And its growing presence in Lake Havasu illustrated another phase in Bonanno's move to consolidate the Southwest into a single organized crime family.

11 | Arizona Justice

The State of Arizona continued having trouble with the prosecution of John Harvey Adamson. Originally scheduled for the first week of December, the trial was again delayed when the court agreed with Adamson's defense counsel that pretrial publicity in and around Phoenix had made it impossible to conduct a fair trial there. It was moved to Tucson, to the court of Superior Judge Ben C. Birdsall. Jury selection would not begin until after the first of the year.

Meanwhile, a new controversy briefly cropped up, this one involving Arizona Governor Raul Castro, who had removed the case from the Maricopa County Prosecutor's office in October and assigned it to the state attorney general.

Adamson's lawyers, in a motion filed with the change of venue request, noted that Castro's name had appeared in connection with Kemper Marley, the wealthy rancher whose close friend and business associate, Max Dunlap, had passed money to help finance Adamson's defense.

"One of Max Dunlap's closest friends is Kemper Marley, a person who, according to police reports, may also be suspected of not only aiding and abetting, but being a principal involved with the homicide," declared Adamson's attorneys. "Kemper Marley is reported to be a close friend of Governor Castro's and is reported to have contributed in the neighborhood of $19,000 to the election campaign of the governor." The defense motion went on to claim that because of Marley's relationship to Castro, the government "may have an obvious conflict of interest" in prosecuting anyone involved in the killing of newspaperman Don Bolles.

The development brought some news coverage and a denial of any impropriety from the governor's office. Defense attorneys, who lost in an effort to have Castro testify as to why he took control of the case from local authorities, said they intended to pursue it during the actual trial.

IRE itself was the subject of several media accounts. In the December 16 edition of the *Tucson Daily Citizen*, editorial page editor Asa Bushnell told his readers about a dinner party he attended over the weekend with ten of the IRE reporters. It was hosted by the Arizona Association of Industries, which had raised more than $20,000 to help finance the team's probe. Bushnell was clearly impressed by what he saw. His column called the reporters "cracker-jack probers" and was full of glowing adjectives about the team's work. "I liked what I saw and heard during the course of a stimulating evening," Bushnell wrote. "I ended up very confident that the net results will prove beneficial to Arizona. It made me glad I'm in the same business with those dedicated people."

It was a nice party. For the reporters, it was the first time their seven-day-a-week work routine had been interrupted by social contact with outsiders. Bushnell's laudatory column was like a belated western welcome to the reporters.

The column came on the heels of similar public friendliness voiced by *Republic* city editor Bob Early, who told *The Quill*, a journalism magazine printed by Sigma Delta Chi, that the reporters on the IRE team were some of the best in the world. "When people of that caliber can concentrate on specific topics for long periods of time, the chances of them [sic] accomplishing their goals are excellent. Since the results of their work will be made available to the *Arizona Republic*, the effect of the IRE team is to give our newspaper more manpower in an area in which we really need it."

Early went on, praising the project's motives: "This is a unique effort in journalism. It points out a solidarity in the newspaper business. It lets the criminals of this world know that they cannot attack a reporter without massive, effective countermeasures from the press nationally. And that message to the criminal element of our society, I believe, will have an effect in putting an end to such attacks in the future." These comments temporarily eased the concern of some of the reporters that the *Republic* was not dealing with them in good faith.

On December 17, the *New York Times* also mentioned the IRE team. In a fairly detailed piece on the delays in the Adamson trial, the *Times* quoted "sources familiar with their findings" as saying that the team had documented a wide variety of illegal activities. "It's amazing what they have uncovered," the *Times*'s source said. "They are going to shake up this state like it's never been shaken before."

One paragraph in the story made some team members nervous. It noted that "the reporters are said to have implicated the brother of one of Arizona's best-known political leaders, as well as a powerful

Phoenix businessman and Republican leader, in a number of criminal activities, in some cases in collusion with Mafia associates.'' IRE reporters thought the *Times* story had gone too far. Not that it was inaccurate, for they had dug up plenty of questionable activities by Robert Goldwater and Harry Rosenzweig. Rather, it was felt that the *Times* had tipped IRE's hand. The time to announce the team's findings was after the work was completed, not while it was still underway. The source for the *Times* statement was Greene. Koziol, Wendland, and Weisz had overheard him giving the off-the-record quote to the *Times* reporter.

Most of the reporters went home for Christmas. Greene was joined in Phoenix by his wife, Carolyn, and, on Christmas Eve, they drove up to the Grand Canyon, where he had rented a lodge not far from the South Rim. On Christmas Day, Drehsler, who had brought his wife up from Tucson for the day, sneaked into Greene's bedroom and stripped his bed, putting on the team leader's official Christmas gift from the team—a king-sized sheet emblazoned with the same ''Deep 'n Dirty'' emblem drawn up for the reporters' T-shirts.

Between Christmas and New Year's, there was a skeleton crew working in the Adams. The out-of-state reporters spent the time at home, catching up on sleep and calling long distance every day to see what was happening back in Phoenix. It was as if they had become addicted to the project.

''I'm glad you guys are back,'' Rawlinson said the day Wendland and Koziol returned. ''Now maybe the phones will stop ringing with calls from lonesome reporters and maybe we can get back to work.'' January would be the last month of reporting. Time was running out. There was much to do.

Koziol and Wendland were paired as partners for the month. Their first task was to examine the scales of justice in Arizona, which apparently tilted toward the mob. Their first interview would be with Walter E. Craig, the sixty-eight-year-old chief judge of the U.S. District Court in Phoenix, and a former president of the American Bar Association.

They spent several days preparing a detailed background report on a number of Craig's past decisions, which, like the case involving young Joe Bonanno, raised many an eyebrow. For Craig's handling of several important cases indicated a benign attitude towards hoodlum defendants and a marked leniency towards the local power structure.

Craig was an amiable man who wore horn-rimmed glasses, smoked a corncob pipe, and reminded the reporters of Jimmy Stewart's portrayal of the country lawyer in the old movie *Anatomy of a Murder*. As such, he slightly disarmed the reporters, who had been told to expect an arrogant, crusty old S.O.B.

"Gentlemen, gentlemen, please, sit down. It's always a pleasure to talk to the press," he said as he welcomed his visitors to his chambers.

Koziol and Wendland exchanged glances. A reporter from the *Republic* had told them that Craig usually refused to talk to reporters and that when he did, he spent more time attacking than answering questions.

They began the interview politely, talking about their mission in Arizona, the Bolles case, and, finally, organized crime.

"Well, let me say this," said Craig, using a golf tee to tamp down the tobacco in his pipe. "If there is in fact an overabundance of organized crime for our population, I'd say fine, let's clean it up. But I don't think there is. I know I've never seen any hard evidence—it's never been presented to me."

It was time to get to the point. "Okay, Judge. Don't you consider more than a dozen unsolved gangland murders evidence enough?" asked Wendland.

"Now sure, we've had some killings, sure. But who says they are connected with organized crime?"

"The police. The FBI. The media. It has been pretty obvious, Your Honor."

"Well now, how do they know? Anyway, I hear our murder rate is dropping. And that's certainly good news."

"Judge, besides the unsolved organized crime killings, police have identified over two hundred mobsters or key associates in Arizona. On a per capita basis, that gives this state probably more hoodlums than any place in the country."

"Well, are those two hundred still engaged in criminal pursuits? You know this is still the West. I mean we are tolerant of a person's past mistakes. But I don't know anything about that anyway. That's not my department."

The reporters began asking Craig about his handling of various cases. In particular, they were interested in the reasons why Craig had tossed out a case involving a well-known Phoenix gambler.

"You know, I just don't remember individual cases," he drawled over his pipe. "These cases go through here like money in a slot machine."

"How about Olen Leroy James?"

"I don't recall the case."

"It was a gambling case, Judge," reminded Wendland. "James was a well-known bookie. Phoenix police wiretapped 872 of his phone conversations. He was alleged to help run a five-million-dollar ring. There was an IRS lien on him. You tossed it out. The government said he owed a considerable amount in back taxes, $21,019 to be exact."

"I just don't recall any such case."

It was time to bluff. Neither reporter had talked to James, who worked out of a small downtown Phoenix bar. But they'd pretend.

"You say you don't recall him?" Koziol asked, setting up the bluff.

"No, I just don't remember it."

"That's funny," Wendland interjected. "We understand that you and Mr. James are longtime friends, that you were a customer of his." The tip had come from a couple of police sources. But the reporters wanted the judge to think they had talked to the gambler himself. "In fact, we're told you like to place a few bets yourself. Is that true, Your Honor?"

Craig paused for just a moment. His eyes narrowed. But then, he just shrugged. "No, no, I'm not a gambler, fellows. I don't even play cards."

"What about Leroy James?"

"Sure, I know him. Hell, I used to go in his place and buy hamburgs. I've known him since he was sixteen years old. But I can't believe Leroy ever had more than $5,000 to his name, ever."

"Then you do know him?" asked Koziol.

"Sure, I know him. You boys been talking to Leroy?"

The reporters avoided the question. "You say you know him and have known him since he was a child. You say you'd be surprised if he ever had more than $5,000 in his life," Wendland continued. "But then you tell us that you don't remember a case right out there in your courtroom where he stood right in front of you charged with avoiding over $21,000 in back taxes. Judge, that doesn't make sense. You expect us to really believe that?"

There was just the faintest change in his voice. His eyes did not reflect the smile that came when he shook his head and apologized, saying, "I'm sorry, but it's true. I just don't recall the case."

There were other cases: a notorious, organized-crime-connected con man with a lengthy record whom Craig sentenced to an amazingly light six-month prison term, even after the ex-con was caught red-handed with part of some $49 million in stolen securities; a land fraud associate of Ned Warren, Sr., freed without bond despite warnings by the prosecutor that he planned to flee the country; a 1976 appointment of a man convicted of tax fraud in Craig's courtroom several years before to the board of receivers of a bankrupt Phoenix savings and loan association; and delayed or extremely lax sentences imposed on the sons of several well-known Arizona families found guilty of narcotics trafficking.

To each question, the judge's answer was the same. "I don't remember."

"Okay, Judge, what about the case of young Joe Bonanno?" asked Wendland. "I suppose you don't remember that one either."

"Not in detail."

"Maybe you don't, Judge, but a lot of other people do," said Koziol, who pulled out a sheaf of papers. "I have here a great number of statements we've obtained from people connected with the case. And what they say is that you made facial gestures whenever testimony against the defendant occurred. They say you used unflattering words to the prosecutor and even went so far as to mimic one witness in a falsetto voice. Do you recall that?"

"I do not."

"Do you recall reversing the jury's verdict?" continued Koziol.

"Yes. It's my obligation to set aside a jury's verdict if I believe they made a mistake in the verdict. That's what happened in that case."

Koziol read the words Craig uttered in announcing the reversal. "Judge, why didn't you bother to poll the jurors before doing this?"

"I don't have to. If I believe they made a mistake, that's all that counts."

"What reason did you have to think they made a mistake?"

"I don't remember."

"What do you remember?"

"I remember young Bonanno being in here. I got the feeling he was being tried more for his father's name than his own," Craig said, measuring his words. "I believe the jury made a mistake. I corrected it."

Now it was Wendland's turn. He reached inside his briefcase and, from a folder marked "Craig-Bonanno Wiretap," took out several sheets of paper. The reporter made a big show of rustling through the papers, hoping to give the judge time to see the identification label on the folder. In truth, there was no wiretap at all. But the judge didn't necessarily know that. "Your Honor, I would like to summarize for you certain information we have relating to the same day you tossed out the Bonanno jury verdict." Wendland summarized the activities of Joe Bonanno, Sr., how he told an associate he needed a large sum of cash to get his son off the hook and how, on the morning of the reversal, Pete Licavoli withdrew $25,000 from a Tucson bank. In reading, Wendland used words like "subject" and "officers observed," trying to make Renner's memo sound like an official surveillance report. When it was over, he asked the judge whether he had ever heard about it.

Craig shook his head, his teeth clamped tightly around the pipe-stem.

"Do you know anything about this report?" Wendland asked again.

"No, I don't."

"Did you, just prior to reversing the jury verdict, meet with any of Mr. Bonanno's attorneys in chambers?" The reporters had received a report that such a meeting had occurred, though it had come from just one source. As a rule, such information was not used as an hypothesis for investigation unless it came from two sources. But there was no reason not to question the judge.

"I do not recall any meetings," Craig said.

They tried several more questions. Craig remembered nothing more about the case, he said, glancing at his watch impatiently. When the interview ended, he got in the last dig.

"Thank you for stopping by, gentlemen," he said as the reporters were leaving. "I'm glad I had the chance to be of assistance to you."

Still, it was a good interview. On two key points, Craig's answers taxed credibility. He said he knew Leroy James well but didn't recall the case. It is a legal tradition that a judge step down when he is asked to sit in judgment over someone he personally knows. Craig had not stepped down. Indeed, he had tossed the case out, freeing his friend.

On Joe Bonanno, Jr., he had said it was his impression that the son was being tried for his father's sins. Judges aren't supposed to have such biases or preconceived notions when trying a case. Craig had implied that he thought the son was being unjustly prosecuted even though a jury felt otherwise. It was a most interesting admission. For

Walter E. Craig was chief guardian of the quality of justice in Arizona. And, knowingly or otherwise, his decisions were one reason why organized crime was flourishing there.

But there were other judges whose friendships, associations, and personal behavior contributed to, or at least encouraged, Arizona's system of injustice.

One example of what is wrong with the Arizona judiciary occurred in 1967. That was the year Paul Laprade was running for Maricopa County Superior Court Judge, a position he won and continued to hold in 1976. On the night of August 8, 1967, the then forty-year-old Democrat was caught running around a swimming pool at the rear of a home on Phoenix's Valley Vista Drive. He was with a forty-year-old Scottsdale woman. And according to police reports found by IRE reporters, both of them were nude and creating a public nuisance. Laprade was arrested and charged with vagrancy and a sex offense because he "exposed his person in such a manner to be reasonably calculated to excite the sexual passion of the other." The loitering charge was lodged because he "loitered, prowled, or wandered around the private property of another in the nighttime without visible or lawful business with the owner." It was a rather sensational case. Laprade was well known, having served as an assistant state attorney general and deputy county attorney. And there he was, caught by police stark naked with a similarly unclad woman. In any other state, the arrest would have been enough to crush his political dreams. Not so in Arizona. Instead of contesting the charge, Laprade simply forfeited his $500 bond, which was, in effect, an admission of guilt, according to court officials. But the disgrace didn't bother his judicial campaign. He was known as "the virile candidate."

Then there was the case of J. Kelly Farris, a disbarred Oregon lawyer who was a business associate of land fraud czar Ned Warren, Sr., in the early seventies. Farris, in what looked like an obvious front for Warren, was able to breeze through the State Liquor Board and get a license for a small tavern backed by Warren. Farris got the license largely because of his personal references. They were James "Duke" Cameron, who just happened to be the chief justice of the Arizona Supreme Court, and Maricopa County Superior Court Judge Jerry Glenn, a veteran Arizona jurist.

Both judges were contacted by Wendland and Koziol. Both confirmed that they were friends of Farris's and had attended parties in his home. Though neither judge could recall the liquor license ence, both told reporters that they would probably have vouched for Farris at the time. Neither judge knew anything about Farris's disbarment or his associations with Ned Warren, Sr.

Finally, there was the case of Supreme Court Justice Jack Hays and his son-in-law. Jack Hays was perhaps, next to Barry Goldwater, the state's most beloved politician. Born in a Mormon ranching community in Nevada, he had come to Arizona in the forties and had done it all, from local GOP organizing in Maricopa County to serving as Arizona's U.S. attorney in the mid-fifties. He had also been a Maricopa County superior court judge, a Phoenix juvenile court judge, a perennially considered candidate for governor and the state legislature, and, since 1968, a justice of the Arizona Supreme Court. His son-in-law was a quiet, darkly handsome young lawyer named Joseph Abate, who moved to Arizona in 1973 after marrying the justice's daughter, Rhory.

Before moving west, young Abate had a fairly impressive employment history of his own. He had worked for New Jersey Governor William Cahill, Congressman Charles Sandman, and, during the 1972 election, Richard Nixon. It was while serving as a director of one of Nixon's young voter organizations in Washington that he met Hays's daugher, who was then in Washington working for Arizona Congressman Sam Steiger.

With the door to political success nudged open for him in Arizona by his famous father-in-law, young Abate had done well for himself since settling in Phoenix, working in the attorney general's office, the Arizona legislature, and the state's most prestigious law firm. He was in all the right civic and political agencies. Friends said young Abate would soon be a legislative candidate himself. And he was just thirty-one years old.

Apparently unknown to the majority of his Arizona friends, young Abate had another well-known relative besides Justice Hays.

His own father, back in Margate, New Jersey, was publicly known as Joseph Francis Abate, the coat-maker, the owner of the prosperous Atlantic City Coat Company. But in police files, he was also known as Giuseppe Abate, alias Joseph Pignati, alias Giuseppe Abater, alias Joseph Pernatto, and, on the day in 1923 when he entered the U.S. from his native Italy, alias Giuseppe Massei. He was arrested as an illegal alien in Chicago a few weeks after his entry. The address he gave was that of Al Capone's old headquarters. His associates were a couple of Capone hit men. He was immediately released on $2,000 bond which he defaulted on. Arrested two years later, Abate was again released on bond. Somehow, it wasn't until 1937, after two more arrests, that deportation proceedings were officially begun. But too much time had passed. A Chicago judge ruled that the government had dragged its feet too long and dismissed the case. In 1940, he did a one-year prison sentence for a liquor violation. Then he showed up in New Jersey.

In 1977, Abate, Sr., had become a full-fledged U.S. citizen. But, according to law enforcement officials, he was also a *capo*, or boss, of the Atlantic City, New Jersey mob. In 1973, young Joe Abate applied for a job with the U.S. attorney's office in New Jersey. He didn't get it, IRE reporters learned, because of his family background. It was after this rejection that he moved to Arizona.

Whether public knowledge of Abate's parentage would have adversely affected his rapid success in Arizona is impossible to discern. For no one bothered to check. Instead, without any investigation of his background, Abate was almost immediately appointed an assistant attorney general in Arizona's law enforcement organization and, later, as a special counsel to the state legislature. Those who knew him had only praise for him. What intrigued reporters was the lack of background checking before he was given authority in sensitive governmental positions.

So Koziol and Wendland went to his father-in-law, Jack Hays, a distinguished, gray-haired man who wore a bolo tie held in place by a large chunk of turquoise carved in the shape of Arizona. Tactfully, the reporters asked whether the justice had recommended his son-in-law for any of his jobs. "I'm sure I have," replied the justice, who went on to cite several examples of how he had pulled strings and called on his governmental friends for young Abate.

Koziol then brought up the junior Abate's application with the Justice Department to become an assistant U.S. attorney back East. Hays said he was aware that young Joe had applied. "He was never given an appointment. He was rather concerned that he wasn't. But he never told me why." Hays seemed puzzled by the question.

Wendland asked the justice what he knew of the background of young Abate's father.

Hays shrugged, and conceded that he didn't know much, only that he owned a clothing company and was a terrific cook. He related to the reporters with a grin how the elder Abate had once prepared for him a delicious Italian dinner, completely from scratch. The reporters then carefully read from the information they had gathered on the elder Abate, including his aliases and past associations with the Al Capone gang. They concluded by telling the justice that old man Abate was still considered by police to be an active mob boss.

Sometimes, asking tough questions is the most enjoyable part of interviewing. Weeks of researching come to a climax when the reporter finally faces a news source, looks him straight in the eye, and, letting him know how much the reporter knows, unloads the big question. Most of the time, it's the best part of reporting. It wasn't this day.

For Justice Jack Hays did not know his son-in-law's family background. He had never been told. And the news hit him hard. The reporters could see it in his eyes. He was sincerely shocked. "My reaction is that I find it almost unbelievable," said Hays, who seemed hurt and confused. "I'm sure that if the Justice Department was aware of what you just told me, and I have no reason to doubt you, that would be why he didn't get the job."

Hays was in an embarrassing situation. He had been with the father on several occasions. Once he had even been the elder Abate's houseguest in New Jersey. "I had never been aware that he had a criminal record," he told the reporters. Now, Hays realized how bad it looked. He was one of Arizona's most powerful jurists, who not only made but interpreted the law. And there he suddenly was, related by marriage to an alleged mobster, a man he had socialized with, whose son Hays had helped enter the state's most influential agencies. And the justice's son-in-law had never once told him. That may have hurt the most. The reporters believed Justice Hays, and, as they left his comfortable office in the state capitol complex, they felt sorry for him. He had been taken.

Yet, the ease with which Hays had been put in a potentially compromising situation was amazing. It typified another Arizona ill. It was a state where few people asked questions about strangers. The Old West was still very much alive.

It was time to talk to Joe Abate, Jr. But he would have nothing to do with reporters. "What do you want to talk about," he hedged when contacted by Koziol on the telephone.

"I think this is something that should be handled face-to-face," replied Koziol. "It has to do with your father and some serious questions that his background raises." There was no need to go into the questions. Young Abate already knew that reporters were asking about him. Before seeing Justice Hays, Koziol and Wendland had talked to several legislators and former coworkers of young Abate's in the attorney general's office. He had already been tipped.

"The accusations you guys are spreading around seem like a bunch of crap to me," the young lawyer snapped. "It's a lot of maligning and a bunch of garbage. My dad is a wonderful person and I can't conceive anything else about him. Obviously, I didn't know anything about these accusations. Further, they're simply not true."

"Look, if the information we have is wrong, then just tell us. Tell me, Joe, was your father born in Italy?"

"I told you I don't want to talk about it. It's not true and that's all I can say. I've got nothing to hide. I'm a respectable man and so is my father, I think."

"You think?"

"Look, this is a very emotional thing for me. You guys are going around asking questions, and I just don't want to talk about this now. Period. I have your number. If I change my mind, I'll call you back." With that, he hung up.

Finally, Koziol put through a phone call to the old man himself. He was reached at his Atlantic City coat factory and, in heavily accented English, echoed his son.

"I got nothing to say. I know what you people been talking about. I got a list of what you been talking and everything else. I mind my own business. I don't belong to anything or anyone. I don't do anything under the law. I can't talk to you." He, too, hung up.

The Abates, junior and senior, were stonewalling it. It made little difference. The reporters' information on the father's background was solid. Koziol and Wendland wrote their memo on the various interviews they had done in tracing Abate junior's job history.

Time was at a premium at the IRE office in the Adams. There were a half-dozen major projects yet to be undertaken, and they all had to be finished by the end of January. Because of the need to work efficiently, the reporters and Greene agreed upon a rule. The day would begin promptly at eight-thirty every morning, when the door to the office would be locked. An informal staff meeting would be held; the various reporters would fill in their comrades on what they were working on and where they would be that day. Since most of the investigations touched on each other, more often than not the entire staff was interested and could usually offer a couple of leads. Early on in the investigation, reporters had purchased a roll of plain brown butcher's wrapping paper and thumbtacked four long strips on the wall behind Greene's desk. With a felt-tip marker, they broke the investigation down into four areas: Power, The Mob, Land Fraud, and Power Movers. Beneath each main title were subtitles such as narcotics, political corruption, and business fronts. Beneath the titles and subtitles were the names of over sixty people. Many of the names, those that most frequently came up in the various investigations, appeared beneath more than one title. Originally, the butcher paper was put up so that the reporters would come to recognize instantly those targeted for investigation. By January, the team could spell each name backwards and the paper was taken down, primarily because the office was being visited by politicians and police and the team didn't want its priorities telegraphed.

Instead of the butcher-paper wall decoration, a new sign went up. This one bore the figure of the IRE T-shirt's "Deep 'n Dirty" trench coat-clad reporter and the Latin phrase: "Noli Permittere Illegitimi Carborundum," which roughly translated to "Don't Let the Bastards Grind You Down." A similar motto hung in the Washington, D.C., office of Senator Barry Goldwater.

The eight-thirty staff meeting was not difficult to keep for the reporters staying in the hotel. Most rolled out of bed at a quarter past eight, staggered to the shower, got dressed, and simply walked across the hall to the office. Myrta Pulliam, the *Indianapolis Star* reporter, should make the morning coffee, the male reporters jokingly contended one morning. An avid, some charged rabid, feminist, Pulliam, whose vocabulary of four-letter words was impressive, adamantly refused. It became a standard office joke until the morning that Myrta finally made the coffee. She was never asked to do so again. The thick, foul-tasting mud she brewed convinced her fellow team members to order coffee from the hotel's room service and wait for Marge Cashel, the secretary, to come in at nine and brew the first of the daily ten pots.

The locked door rule for the eight-thirty meeting was more symbolic than serious. The only team members who had difficulty making it were the Tucson reporters. Although Drehsler and Rawlinson had shared a nineteenth-floor room just down the hallway from the IRE office for the first two months, the expenses were considerable, averaging $1,500 per month. At the end of December, their paper had them move out of the hotel into a $275-a-month apartment in north central Phoenix, about eight miles from the Adams. They shared the two-bedroom apartment with Dave Overton, the Tucson television reporter who had joined the team in December, and occasionally got stuck in heavy traffic and missed the morning staff meeting. They would stand red-faced in the hallway, loudly pounding on the locked door for fifteen minutes. Then, properly humbled, they would be allowed in to start work.

Koziol, however, figured a way around the rule. He would roll out of bed at 8:29 A.M., attend the fifteen-minute meeting, and then, announcing that he was meeting a source for breakfast, sneak back into his room for an hour's clandestine sleep.

Again, there was a flood of new team members. Ken Matthews from the *Idaho Statesman* in Boise, Dick Lyneis from the *Riverside*, (California) *Press*, and Jack Wimer from Oklahoma's *Tulsa Tribune* all showed up for the final few weeks of reporting.

So did Susan Irby, a twenty-eight-year-old reporter from the *Daily Herald* in Gulfport, Mississippi. Susan had worked in Gulfport for six years, covering mostly police and consumer affairs news. She had driven her car the 1,600 miles from Mississippi to Phoenix, and, while her paper had agreed to pay her salary, she was absorbing all the expenses herself. What made her unusual was her size. Susan was a dwarf, just under four feet in height. But she was also a hell of a reporter, assigned by Greene to dig into Phoenix's flourishing massage parlor prostitution racket. By the time her three-week hitch was over, she had traced the complicated property ownership of more than three dozen of the storefront whorehouses, linking several prominent Phoenix businessmen and politicians to the seamy business. Her tape recorded interview with one of the massage parlor owners was a classic.

Arizona has no statutes against prostitution. The only state law dealing with it was written in the early 1800s. And all it did was prohibit a whorehouse from being located within 300 feet of a mining camp. Though a couple of municipalities like Phoenix and Tucson had passed antiprostitution ordinances, the rest of the state was fair game, including Maricopa County outside the city of Phoenix. Still, most of those who prospered from the state's booming vice business preferred to downplay their activities. Such was the case of one particularly overbearing massage parlor owner Irby interviewed.

"You're saying there is no prostitution in your place?" asked Irby, who knew full well it was going on after spending several days observing the man's various outlets from her compact car, specially outfitted with extended controls to accommodate her stature.

"Pardon?"

"I said, 'Are you saying there is no prostitution going on there?' "

"Did I say that?"

"That's what I'm asking, did you say that?"

"I didn't say that."

"Then it does go on?"

"I didn't say that."

"Well, does it or doesn't it?"

"I'm not saying."

There was still another case involving prostitution that illustrated the Arizona power structure's penchant for easy money and easy women. It involved Mark Harrison, a young, good-looking Phoenix attorney who, as an influential wheeler-dealer in Democratic politics and the president of the Arizona State Bar Association, should have been the paragon of virtue. The Harrison case began in 1972. The IRE team learned of it through several confidential law enforcement sources who were involved in the investigation into Harrison's activities. During the course of that probe, authorities had secretly tape-recorded attempts by Harrison to set up a prostitution ring catering to high-class businessmen and professionals. One of the team's sources was the electronics expert who supervised the recording.

Harrison had become the subject of police interest purely by chance, during an intensive investigation into the activities of a notorious local hoodlum named William Kaiser. In the course of their investigation, the police came across relationships between Kaiser, a number of other mobsters, a couple of public officials, and several prominent people. One of these was Mark Harrison, who had become closely associated with one of Kaiser's sidekicks, a minor hood and convicted pimp named Jerry Mandia.

On July 8, 1972, a well-known call girl and occasional police informer told police she had been called by Mandia and invited out for lunch to discuss a business proposition. Mandia told the woman that he and a friend were interested in starting a prostitution ring that would front as an escort service and cater to the well-heeled businessmen who gather in the plush suburban Phoenix resorts each winter during the booming convention season. According to the woman, Mandia wanted a "class operation," with the women screened and categorized as to appearance and sexual specialties. Their photographs would be shown discreetly to prospective clients in a sort of directory. The various prostitutes working for the service would be paid a percentage of the money they generated in tricks. After outlining the proposition, Mandia wanted to know if the woman would manage the operation.

She was interested. Fine, said Mandia, who then suggested that she contact his partner the following Monday to discuss the entire operation in detail. As the meeting ended, the woman said, Mandia told her not to worry; from that moment on she would have full legal protection. For his partner was a very powerful and influential man. He gave her the partner's name and telephone number. It was Mark Harrison.

About 8:00 P.M. on July 10, the woman arrived at Harrison's office. She told police that after introducing himself, Harrison stressed that he had to be extremely careful with whom he dealt because he had an excellent professional reputation. The woman then got down to business. She asked what Harrison expected of the girls she would recruit for the ring.

"He said he expected every girl to take as many tricks as she could," said the call girl. "I asked him if the girls would keep the money they got from the tricks."

"Hell, no," she said Harrison replied. "How can we make any money that way?" Harrison, said the prostitute, then went on to say how lucrative the business would be. He bragged that he could keep fifteen girls so busy at the annual bar association convention that they couldn't handle it all. There was no need for her to worry, the woman said she was told, because "I'm a big man in this town." In exchange for managing the operation, the woman said, she was promised twenty percent of the action, a leased car, a furnished apartment, and an expense account for gas and clothing.

A number of subsequent contacts between Harrison and the call girl were noted by police. IRE reporters were told by their sources that Harrison went into elaborate detail with the woman, discussing possible locations for the operation and an auxiliary business which, through some of Kaiser's associates, would have the more talented prostitutes pose for pornographic movies and photographs, which could then be sold to the customers and generate still more money.

Police documented most of the meetings and compiled a lurid and detailed series of tape recordings, which were reported back to the Arizona Crime Prevention Council, a jointly staffed state agency made up of several police departments, which had first targeted Kaiser, an associate of a top Illinois Mafia leader and the operator of an interstate stolen goods ring, as the subject of an investigation.

Shortly after the report had been sent in, one of the IRE police sources said he was called before Gary Nelson, then the Arizona state attorney general and a member of the council. Nelson was deeply concerned. He said he knew Harrison personally and simply could not believe the information police had uncovered. Nelson was convinced that the investigators were wrong. The IRE source then played some of the Harrison tape recordings. Nelson just buried his face in his hands.

Shortly after the session with Nelson, however, police noted a change in Harrison. With no warning, he suddenly stopped contacting the prostitute who had been their snitch. So did Kaiser and Mandia. They went cold, almost as if they had been tipped to the investigation.

The investigation was abruptly stopped. Two years later, in November 1974, the tape recordings were ordered destroyed by the brass at the Arizona Department of Public Safety. The police sources who worked the case smelled a whitewash.

IRE reporters were certain of their sources, who vowed that if push came to shove and Harrison filed a libel suit against the team, they would publicly testify as to the veracity of the information they had turned over to the team.

But there was a complication for the IRE reporters. Mark Harrison happened to be the personal attorney of Rosalie Bolles, the widow of the slain reporter who had brought them to Arizona in the first place. Greene had conducted several meetings with Mrs. Bolles. His heart ached for her. She and her three children had suffered enough. How would the Harrison revelations affect her?

Yet the team had come to Arizona to shed light on the state's ills, not to leave the doors closed. As reporters, they had to go ahead and follow the story where it led. On January 24, Myrta Pulliam and Dave Overton went to Harrison's law office. After small talk about Mrs. Bolles and Harrison's legal and political background, they got down to the questions.

Overton began, noting that Harrison, as bar association president, had often spoken about ethics in the legal profession. "We are also interested in that,'' he said, ''and we want to ask you why it was that you attempted to set up a prostitution ring in 1972.''

Harrison's face visibly paled. He was silent for a long ten seconds. Then, carefully measuring his words in a low voice, he shook his head.

''That is categorically untrue in the first place.'' But then, his face pained, he seemed to contradict himself. ''That is something that has been on my mind, the whole ridiculous episode. I'd like to talk to Bob Greene about it.''

The reporters explained that Greene knew they were there and why they had requested the interview. And they were talking to Harrison on behalf of the team leader.

Again, Harrison was silent. He got up and walked to his office window.

''Please,'' he said at last. ''Give me two minutes to think about it. I won't run away. I'm not going anyplace.'' With that, he walked out of the office.

Ten minutes went by. Just as the reporters figured Harrison had fled the building, he reappeared.

''I'd like to have my partner in here,'' he said.

The reporters had no objection. The partner was Bob Myers. ''Is he here as your legal representative?'' Overton asked.

''No, not really. But he does know all about this.'' Harrison sat back down. He was clearly shaken. For almost another ten minutes he was silent, occasionally getting up and walking over to the window. He sighed a lot.

He broke the silence by clearing his throat. ''Do you use tape recorders?''

Overton shook his head. ''Do you?''

''No, I'm not much on tape recorders.'' Again he was silent. Finally, the partner came into the room.

Myers wanted to know if the interview was on the record. It most assuredly was, the reporters said.

''Look, I think the best way for us to proceed is for Mark to tell the whole story. Then, I think the thing will make sense to you,'' said Myers.

Harrison began. ''As a preface to this, I'm not terribly clear when everything happened. I've tried to sublimate this as much as possible. But you must understand, this all happened during a difficult period in my life and marriage.''

Pulliam and Overton began taking notes.

"I knew a fellow who told me he knew a high-class prostitute who he thought I could have relations with." Again he paused, looking at his law partner for a moment before continuing. "I said something like, 'Well, I've strayed a few times in my marriage, but I've never paid any money,' and he said I should tell her I was interested in starting a call-girl service for winter visitors and I could score with her. I didn't have my head on straight and I acted on impulse. I called her up, I guess. I have no specific recollection. I talked to her on the phone three or four times and visited her probably two or three more times. Sure, I gave her some relatively meaningless types of things, like to start a thing like this in the county and not the city, things like that. But I never had any intention of doing anything illegal. It was a pure and simple con job on a pro to get some action. I saw her three times maximum. I haven't seen her since, never talked to her since. And I've never been involved in any illegal activity of any type in my life. If you are doing a thorough investigation of my life, as I'm sure you are, you won't find anything at all. If you want me to say it was idiotic and stupid, I will, I plead guilty. Look, has your investigation shown anything else?"

"We understand that you were making points with her, that you scored with her," said Overton.

"As I already told you, I probably scored with her three times. I was using some pretext, some line of baloney about setting her up in business. There was nothing of substance after the second or third time we met. It is my understanding that there was a tape."

"Didn't you, in fact, offer a woman twenty percent of the deal, of what she made from working the Johns at the big suburban hotels?" asked Pulliam.

"It was a con job, fun and games. I don't recall the specific things I said to her, but it was all baloney. Look at it realistically. I had a decent practice, I represent responsible clients, I was an officer in the bar association with a family and children. I wouldn't ever dream of committing a criminal activity."

"Do you know Bill Kaiser?" Pulliam wanted to know.

There again was a pause. "I met him at a coffee shop. Maybe I met him there on two or three occasions."

"Why?"

"That gets back to how this all started. I had never heard of him before that. When I was at another law firm, before we started this firm, I had a client who was sort of a Damon Runyon-type character. He was always talking about deals, and he came in and I represented him. He'd come in and out.''

"What's the name of this client?"

"That could be privileged. I don't know if I should give you that.''

"It most certainly is not," said Pulliam.

Myers interjected; his voice was sarcastic. "I'm glad you are that sure, Miss, but I've been an attorney for twenty years and I'm not as sure as you are. Nevertheless, we can ask that person's permission to give you the name.''

Harrison continued. "Anyway, it was this Damon Runyon character who introduced me to Mr. Kaiser.''

"Could this Damon Runyon character have been a man named Mandia?" asked Pulliam.

At the same time Myers said no, Harrison said yes.

"Mandia told me about this woman, that I could give her a line of baloney. And he was the man who introduced me to Kaiser. But I'm unclear about a lot of this. It's a chapter in my life that I'm trying to forget. I suspect that I used this Kaiser's name in a phone call to the girl. I don't recall exactly how he fit in. I suspect I saw him thereafter, at the time the affair was going on. Subsequently, after I'd seen her a couple of times, I must have asked Mandia about Kaiser and he told me some things that made me think Kaiser was a pretty bad guy and I got frightened. Kaiser subsequently called me here, maybe after this, to represent him, and I said no. It was a criminal charge. The whole thing began as a harmless thing. Then it got way out of my league.''

"In the meantime, you met with Kaiser two or three times; is this correct?" asked Overton.

"Yes.''

"And you never asked about him?''

"I may have. Mandia may have been saying that I should call the girl and maybe Kaiser was involved in setting up this thing. Then I found out Kaiser was charged with something to do with stolen vehicles.''

"Do you know why you were tape-recorded?''

"No, and the person who told me didn't know either.''

"Was it Gary Nelson who told you, the attorney general?" asked Pulliam.

"No.''

"Do you know Gary Nelson?''

"Sure, I know him. We were once partners in the same law firm."

"When did you find out about the investigation?" asked Overton.

"I don't know. Two years later. Maybe it was a year. It could have been a few months after the affair. It was closed in my mind."

"Did you ever talk to anyone about destroying the tapes?"

"Not specifically, certainly."

"You said 'not specifically,' then you did do something. What was it?" pressed Overton.

There was a long silence. Harrison turned to gaze out the window again.

"I'm trying to recall what, if anything, I did. I am sure that, it logically follows that whoever was attorney general at the time knows about it. And it could have been Nelson. I never asked him or anyone else about it."

"Could someone else have asked about destroying the tape on your behalf?"

"Absolutely not."

"But earlier you said 'not specifically.' "

"I'm trying to be as specific as I can. I may have had a conversation with Nelson. But I never suggested or hinted or asked that the tapes be destroyed."

"What prompted the conversation with Nelson?" asked Pulliam.

"My concern was about a tape that was devastating to me, personally. It was innocent but it looks sordid."

"What did you learn about the tapes?"

"I honestly don't recall."

"Did Nelson give you any indication of what he might do?"

"No. It was just my seeking to see if it did exist. I believe—I'm sure—that he did confirm it."

That was enough for the reporters. Gary Nelson, the state attorney general, had apparently tipped his old friend off to the investigation. And Harrison, who had served as special counsel to the attorney general, had admitted that he had plotted to set up a call-girl ring with the prostitute, a plan taken very seriously by the woman and the police. It made no difference that Harrison said he was just kidding. The facts were that police had cause to believe they had uncovered a conspiracy and that their investigation into it was suddenly dropped after Nelson had reviewed the evidence.

That night, Overton called Nelson at home. In 1974 Nelson had left the attorney general's office and, in 1977, was serving as a judge on the state Court of Appeals. Overton asked Nelson about the conversation Harrison had told them about.

"Assuming he was under investigation, it would be strictly confidential information, and I could not talk to you about that in any way, shape, or form," said Nelson.

Overton kept pressing. "But did you talk to Mr. Harrison about this matter?"

"If, in fact, there was an investigation, I certainly did not talk to Mr. Harrison until after it was concluded, if, in fact, there was one. I never would have talked to him during the investigation. Look, that's the best I can do. And that's probably too much. All my counselors say I tend to talk too much. But I always figure the truth is important."

So did the IRE reporters, Overton assured him. "Did you ever talk to someone regarding destruction of the tapes?"

"I don't remember, but if I did, it would be in terms of a general policy about destruction of non-useful wiretap evidence. That's a standard procedure in cases that are not going to be prosecuted."

Nelson refused to talk further about Mark Harrison. When Overton continued asking questions, Nelson turned churlish.

"What you reporters are doing is going out to kill someone as dead as Don Bolles," he snapped. "The only difference is he died by a bomb and you're using the pen. That's very dangerous and there's nothing that can be done to prevent those kinds of assassinations because the people who do that never get prosecuted. Hopefully, they go to hell."

Nelson hung up. He said he would have nothing more to say.

He had already said it all, thought Overton as he replaced the telephone receiver.

12 | Ned Warren, Sr., Talks

Halfway between Phoenix and Tucson, just outside the tiny desert town of Florence, stands the Arizona State Prison. Its cream-colored walls are patrolled by machine gun-toting guards in cowboy hats and mirrored sunglasses. The place is forbidding. Hopelessly overcrowded with nearly twice its twelve-hundred-inmate capacity, the prison has often been used by Hollywood film makers to set the mood for B movies on the horrors of prison life.

And indeed, the prison's sixty-nine-year history is filled with dozens of real-life examples of such horrors, not the least of which was an old Indian legend that proclaimed the early weeks of each year as "the months of blood," a time when the Indian war gods would demand the lives of the prison's most notorious stool pigeons. In the twenties and thirties, there had actually been a series of such killings. Six inmates were murdered under similar circumstances—a knife in the back, exactly as proclaimed in the legend. Although the tale no longer causes prison guards to go on alert each winter, other bloody incidents have occurred. Beatings, riots, breakouts, and random violence continue with regularity over the years, most often in the early weeks of the new year. While few of the inmates believe it, the Indian legend is still passed along on their grapevine. It is part of the prison's lore.

Tony Serra, a dark-haired forty-two-year-old con man serving an eight-year land fraud sentence, must have been well aware of the old story the morning of January 3, 1977. About 9:00 A.M., he mailed a letter to a Phoenix attorney who had been working with Richard Frost, one of the IRE team's land fraud sources. The letter was the third such note mailed or sneaked out of the prison over the last several weeks. The first two had gone to Frost. The third, on Frost's urgings, was sent to the attorney. All three letters had the same message. "They're going to get me," Serra warned. "I'm going to be killed. I know too much. Get me out of here."

Serra was the convict who had told Frost the previous summer that he knew where land fraud kingpin Ned Warren, Sr., had stashed a pile of incriminating documents. And Serra, once a close associate of

209

Warren's, had indicated to Frost that he just might be willing to start talking.

Ever since IRE team members had begun interviewing him on the land fraud industry, Frost had been harping on the Tony Serra case. Serra was in fear for his life, Frost had insisted to reporters. Unless he was removed from the state prison and transferred under another name to another prison, he was a marked man. The reporters had listened sympathetically to Frost. But they were powerless to do much about it. It was only Frost's word, though Phoenix detective Lonzo McCracken had voiced similar concerns over Serra's fate. McCracken, too, had told the reporters that not much could be done. Authorities needed something to go on besides fear.

In December, it looked like they had found that something else. Serra was hospitalized at the prison with a series of suspicious bruises and cuts. But prison officials had denied an assault on Serra. It was the result of a fall, a slight accident, McCracken was told.

Shortly after mailing his letter Monday, January 3, Serra reported for work in the prison's sign shop, a wide open area filled with some seventy-five inmates and large, noisy machines used to stamp out state highway signs. There was only one guard.

Serra was a nervous man that morning. He had stayed in his cell for the better part of a week, refusing to mix with the other inmates or show up for his job in the sign shop. When he reported for work a few minutes before ten, he was met by Robert Deardorff, the sign shop supervisor.

Deardorff was angry. Why had Serra skipped work? Did he want another job? Was he unhappy?

Serra was quiet. No, he would stay there. He hadn't been feeling well. But he'd be okay now.

Deardorff shrugged. Inmates were often like that, sullen and moody. He wasn't a prison psychologist. It was hard enough getting the convicts to work. Serra was a loner. There was no getting through to him. Whatever his problem was, it appeared that Serra was coming to grips with it. Deardorff was pleased. He told Serra to start working and returned to his office.

Serra walked off. He talked to no one, though several inmates greeted him as he passed. He looked straight ahead. He looked afraid.

About two minutes past ten, the prison guard heard something strange above the roar of the machinery. It sounded like scuffling. He walked towards the noise, which was over almost immediately.

On the grimy concrete floor between a metal desk and a loading dolly was Tony Serra. He was dead. Stabbed. The autopsy revealed eighteen separate wounds, from at least two weapons. There were also numerous bruises. It appeared as if he had been kicked and beaten as well.

Prison officials questioned the other inmate workers. Nobody saw anything. A shakedown by guards produced a zip gun and three homemade knives, apparently made that morning.

"This thing was not spontaneous," prison warden Harold Cardwell told reporters that afternoon. "This was a planned killing." Cardwell conceded that he had heard frequent rumors about threats against Serra. "But that's all they were, just rumors. We need facts, not rumors. There was nothing we could have done to prevent this."

In Phoenix, Dick Frost was furious. "You believe me now?" he sarcastically asked IRE reporters that night. "I told you. I warned you. But no one would listen. He's dead now and there goes another witness against Warren."

The news of Serra's death had shocked the team. George Weisz and Ross Becker were the first to find out about it. They were in the city room of the *Republic* when the story came in over the wire services late in the afternoon. They rushed back to the Adams and told the rest of the team.

"You're kidding," said Greene, looking up from his memo-reading. Rawlinson, Winters, and Wendland gathered around.

"God damn," said Rawlinson. "We should have believed Frost."

"No. We did right. We did what we could. We asked questions, we found out what was provable." Greene could see the anger and guilt rising in the reporters. "Now listen to me. There was no proof. We just had Frost's words. We made sure the police were aware."

"Greene's right," said Wendland. "There wasn't anything we could have done to stop it."

Serra was number nineteen in a bizarre series of violent murders and questionable deaths linked to organized crime or land fraud in Arizona.

And Dick Frost was worried that he would be number twenty. "Jesus, look at the track record," he said to Wendland one night. "Everyone connected to land fraud who was in a position to testify against the bigwigs has been hit."

Wendland tried to calm him down. "Look, Dick, you helped convict Warren on that extortion case up in Washington in 1975 and here you are. Just relax."

"Yeah, but I'm also the guy who Serra promised to talk with. Shit, maybe they think I already talked to him. And besides, look what happened to me as soon as I testified against Warren. Boom, just like that, I get indicted on land fraud charges myself."

Two nights later, Frost was back in the office with a letter. "You're next," was all it said. It was delivered to him by a Phoenix radio station employee, who said it was received anonymously in the mail.

"I went to the cops, asking for protection," said Frost. "They told me they couldn't provide it." Then he patted the waistband of his trousers. "I'm carrying a gun from now on. I'll protect myself."

Frost, who was staying at the downtown Phoenix YMCA while awaiting his land fraud trial, wasn't seen by reporters for a couple of days. When he next came by, he was even more frightened.

"Listen, I'm going to be laying low for awhile. If you need me, don't try the Y. I've moved." He gave reporters his new address in a second-rate motel across town.

"They tried to get me the other night," he said. "I had gone to the washroom, getting ready for bed. I had left my gun back in the room. I was tired, not really paying much attention when the door opened. All of a sudden, I feel somebody trying to grab my arms, to pin me back. I wheel around and I see these four black guys. I don't know how I did it, but I was able to get around them, to run out of the washroom and down the hall to my room. I got my gun and opened the door. As soon as they saw the gun, they split. But they were after me. They were going to kill me. One of the other tenants told me he had seen these guys staring at my room earlier. I called the cops and they picked them up. They were carrying knives. But the cops couldn't do anything because the four black guys hadn't really done anything except scare hell out of me. Can you imagine that? I mean, if they killed me, the cops could have held them. But since they didn't hurt me, all they could do was take down their names and warn them. Anyway, that's close enough for me. I'll be on my guard from now on."

Serra's prison murder came just as IRE's investigation into land fraud huckster Ned Warren, Sr., was winding up. And his death had a chilling effect on the reporters, who, among other things, had learned that the charmed life led by the so-called godfather of land fraud stemmed from widespread payoffs and "loans" given influential state officials charged with regulating the state's real estate industry.

Actually, it was the dead convict who had provided the major break. In January 1971, the dapper Serra, then president of a land company known as World Development Corporation, told Detective Lonzo McCracken that Warren was making payoffs to real estate officials through James Cornwall, president of the Great Southwest Land and Cattle Company. Before starting his own company, Serra had worked as Cornwall's sales manager. That initial conversation gave authorities the first tip that Warren was behind Great Southwest, then one of the state's biggest and most crooked land development firms. McCracken began investigating. By April of 1972, he had firmly established Warren's secret financial interest in the company. But before he could question Cornwall, the company had suddenly gone belly up and Cornwall had fled to Europe. And when McCracken tried to get at the books of the firm, he found they had suddenly been seized by James Keiffer, chief investigator for Arizona State Real Estate Commissioner J. Fred Talley. Neither Keiffer nor Talley would allow McCracken access to the books of the Warren company. It took a court search warrant for police to finally get hold of them.

McCracken kept digging. A few weeks later he discovered why he had had trouble obtaining cooperation from the real estate commission. Not long before Great Southwest went under, Keiffer had recieved a personal "loan" of $2,660 from Warren. Under questioning, Keiffer admitted receiving the money. But he claimed the "loan" had been repaid. When police asked to see proof, Keiffer said he had forgotten to get back the promissory note he had given Warren.

On July 25, 1973, McCracken finally located Cornwall in Salem, Oregon, and returned him to Phoenix to stand trial for the $5 million Great Southwest swindle. In exchange for probation, Cornwall agreed to plead guilty to thirty-three counts of securities fraud and to testify for the prosecution.

Cornwall said that while he was president of Great Southwest—through Ned Warren, Sr.,—he made monthly bribes of up to $300 per month to Commissioner Talley, as well as an annual Christmas "gift" of $500. In September 1974, Commissioner Talley, by then aware of the investigation, suddenly resigned his office. Two months later, at the age of seventy, he died of a heart attack.

But McCracken would not give up. Three months later, he had another major police witness. This one was Edward Lazar, Warren's chief accountant. And Lazar backed up all of Cornwall's accusations, confirming the widespread payoffs to state officials.

"It's like life insurance should we ever have any trouble with the real estate commission," Lazar secretly testified before a grand jury.

It was enough to bring bribery charges against Ned Warren, Sr. But the day after Lazar made those allegations, he was gunned down on a stairwell leading to his office parking garage. He was shot with a .22 caliber gun, four times in the chest and once in the head. Without Lazar's corroborating courtroom testimony, Cornwall's allegations were not enough.

Two days after Lazar's murder, something incredible happened. Moise Berger, the Maricopa County prosecuting attorney, who would later confess to police in a secretly tape-recorded interview that there was a "power coalition" in Phoenix trying to stifle major organized crime prosecutions, suddenly summoned Cornwall to his office.

Berger, claiming that he wanted to "test" Detective McCracken's loyalty, ordered Cornwall to go to McCracken and say that he was frightened by Lazar's murder and had changed his mind about testifying against Warren. Berger's excuse was lame. He told Cornwall that the point of the "test" was to see if McCracken would then relay this information back to Berger. If Cornwall would help him out, Berger promised to dismiss charges against him.

Cornwall went to McCracken and did as Berger had instructed. But under questioning by the detective, he admitted that he had been put up to it by the prosecuting attorney. Furious, McCracken went to his superiors. A lie detector test was arranged. Cornwall passed it. He was telling the truth. Berger, meanwhile, admitted arranging the "test," though he denied promising to free Cornwall in exchange for his help.

Less than a month later, on March 4, 1975, Maricopa County dismissed the bribery indictment against Warren. Berger had deliberately leaked information to the news media about the grand jury investigations. "I find this conduct by the county attorney deplorable," said the court.

Detective McCracken developed an ulcer. But he refused to give up. New bribery charges were filed against Warren, and by April 1975, the godfather was in court, facing a preliminary examination. Berger had assigned one of his deputy prosecutors, Lawrence Cantor, to present the government's case. Then another problem arose.

Cantor, according to police, reeked of alcohol each morning during the hearing. At one point, a police report obtained by IRE reporters noted, Cantor apparently became bored with the proceedings, "so he decided to take a nap right in the middle of the cross-examining."

There was also a chilling security breach. During a hearing recess, Cantor walked over to one of Warren's attorneys and loudly proclaimed that Cornwall would be flying to Oregon that night to visit his mother, who had become seriously ill. Police escorted Cornwall to Sky Harbor Airport that night. Curiously, Warren was on the plane Cornwall was planning to take to Portland. Cornwall was quickly hustled off. Warren's presence was more than a coincidence.

Warren was bound over to face trial. Despite the prosecutorial blunders, the detailed police work had come up with more than enough evidence.

But not for long.

On August 15, 1975, citing minor inconsistencies in Cornwall's testimony, Berger suddenly announced that he was abandoning plans to prosecute Warren. At issue was Cornwall's testimony that he had cashed a check on March 5, 1971, and given the money to Warren for transmission to Talley. Actually, bank records revealed that the check had been cashed four days later. Police were incredulous. Cornwall had been testifying from memory. He had done an amazing job. It was inevitable that there would be minor inconsistencies. But Berger, as prosecuting attorney, had used it as an excuse to dump the case.

Warren was freed. And Cornwall, who had originally been promised probation, was sentenced to serve ten to twenty years in the Arizona State Prison.

He arrived there in September 1975, joining another Warren associate, Tony Serra, who had provided the first clue to the real estate payoffs more than four years before. Serra had been behind bars for a year, after being convicted of eleven counts of land fraud.

From August 1976 through January 1977, IRE land fraud source Dick Frost had been in contact with Serra. Serra had claimed to know the whereabouts of other incriminating evidence against Warren. He had also voiced fear for his life. And on January 3, 1977, before that evidence could be checked out, Serra was murdered.

Ned Warren, Sr., had certainly lived a charmed life, the IRE reporters concluded.

Born Nathan Waxman, Warren was always the master con man, charming and witty. Among his many scams were selling advertising time on radio stations with which he had no connection; buying sheets of rolled steel on credit during World War II and then selling them the same day without ever repaying the original loan; and collecting $39,000 from well-heeled investors for a musical comedy he claimed to be producing for Broadway that, of course, never opened.

It was the latter con that first ran him afoul of the law. He spent nearly two years in Sing Sing, where prison psychologists found him to be "very superior" in intelligence, with an IQ of 133, but hampered by an "inferior moral and social capability."

He came to Arizona in 1961, with three cars, his wife, his mistress, three kids, two dogs, a cat, and just $800 in his pocket. At the time, he was on probation for another conviction, this one for concealing assets in the bankruptcy of one of his many shell companies.

In Arizona, he saw great opportunity. Though his prison record prevented him from getting the necessary real estate sales license, he went right ahead anyway, plunging into the buying and selling of mostly worthless desert land. IRE reporters had uncovered documents and letters which proved that real estate commissioner Talley knew that Warren was operating illegally but refused to do anything about it.

Exactly when Warren cemented his ties to Talley was unclear. But the reporters learned that in 1965 Talley had contacted Lee Ackerman, a Warren business partner and once an unsuccessful candidate for the Arizona governorship. According to a number of sources developed by the team, Talley explained to the Warren pal that his son was in financial difficulties and needed to borrow some money. Ackerman complied, giving the son of the real estate commissioner $7,000. Seven weeks later, J. Fred Talley, Jr., showed up as the new sales manager for Diamond Valley, one of Ackerman and Warren's land companies. It was shortly after he hired Talley's son that Warren got his real estate license. It had been personally approved by the commissioner himself.

The real estate commissioner wasn't Warren's only friend. Reporters learned that George Brooks, an investigator for the Maricopa County prosecutor's office, received $2,000 from the Warren-financed Great Southwest Land and Cattle Company. Brooks, who claimed the money was a loan, used it as the down payment on a mountain cabin. A jury believed him. He was acquitted of a bribery charge. With connections like that, the reporters had little doubt as to why Warren operated with such impunity.

Since Warren had first contacted the team in early November as the self-professed middleman for John Harvey Adamson, the Don Bolles murder suspect, reporters had kept the lines of communication open with him. Warren knew that he was the subject of intensive investigation by the team. Indeed, he almost seemed to enjoy it.

In mid-January, their research complete, the team was ready to talk with him. An interview was arranged for the evening of January 23, 1977. Warren, who had never conducted a major, on-the-record meeting with the press, amiably agreed to it.

For three days before, Drehsler and Greene, assisted by Dick Cady, the Indianapolis reporter acting as assistant team leader, labored on the bulging Warren files, preparing a twenty-three-page interview outline which would be used to guide them during the Warren questioning.

Drehsler and Greene left the IRE office shortly after five that afternoon. They expected to be back by nine or, at the latest, ten. Instead, the interview would last until one o'clock.

Cady, who remained behind at the Adams, thought the confrontation between Greene and Warren was historic. He dubbed it: "The Godfather meets God."

Warren lived in a spacious and incredibly plush house, worth a quarter of a million dollars, built into the side of Camelback Mountain, just east of Phoenix. As the reporters arrived, Warren's wife, Barbara, an attractive blonde in her early fifties, greeted them with a young Doberman pinscher she was training in the front yard. The pup was the replacement for the one that had died the previous fall, the one Warren had broken down and cried over the day he met Drehsler to discuss the Adamson deal.

Warren himself, dressed in an open-necked sports shirt, soon came out and warmly shook hands. As his wife and the frisky pup walked away, he cautioned the reporters not to talk about the dead animal in front of his wife. "It still makes her cry," he said as he escorted the visitors inside the house.

He led them into a large, expensively furnished family room, one wall of which was the actual side of the mountain. He was the perfect host, pouring drinks for the reporters from a well-equipped bar as his wife brought out a tray of hors d'oeuvres.

"I respect him," she said to Drehsler, nodding towards Greene, who was chatting with her husband. "He must have a lot of money behind him to do so much research. He's well prepared. I can't help it, but I like him."

A few minutes later, she again turned to Drehsler. "You know, if anything ever happens to Ned or me, I can guarantee that the lid will blow off this state.''

She would not be more specific, despite the young reporter's gentle prodding, and, in a few minutes, politely excused herself ''so you men can talk.''

Warren himself, meanwhile, was friendly, though Drehsler detected a bit of tightness in his voice and a nervous habit of continuously tapping his fingers together. He had one condition to the interview.

''I'd prefer it if you didn't tape-record this or take notes,'' he grinned. ''It distracts me and makes me nervous.''

The reporters reluctantly agreed. It would be difficult to remember everything, but, if that was the only way Warren would talk, they had little choice. Fortunately, there were two of them. What one forgot or was vague on would, they hoped, be remembered by the other when it came time to prepare a memo on the evening.

Warren wanted the reporters to know that he sympathized with them on the murder of Bolles. ''That was a stupid and needless act,'' he said. ''Look what happened. You kill a reporter and immediately there's fifty other reporters all over the place.'' Warren said Bolles had done only one major series on him, mostly based on his criminal record. ''I didn't like it, but there wasn't much I could do.''

He also realized that in the eyes of the media and of many in law enforcement, he was a leading suspect in the Serra and Lazar murders. ''I can only tell you that I had nothing to do with them. I will say that I talked to Ed Lazar before he went to the grand jury and that he assured me that he wasn't going to cooperate, that he was going to take the Fifth. And I was shocked and surprised to find out that he was, indeed, talking. But I'm not a murderer. That's not my style.''

The reporters wanted to know whether Warren really had been paying off real estate commissioner Talley.

He grinned. ''Let me say this. Talley did take. He once told me personally that he got an average of $10,000 a month from the various land companies.''

''But did you yourself directly pay him?'' asked Greene.

Again, Warren smiled and hedged. ''I never ordered anyone to pay Talley.''

When Greene and Drehsler told Warren that they had a number of sources (Cornwall's statements and the secret transcript of Lazar's grand jury testimony) all agreeing that the various Warren companies had paid the commissioner a minimum of $200 monthly, Warren didn't argue. His reluctance to incriminate himself in front of the reporters was understandable, obviously based on the fact that the statute of limitations on such crimes had yet to expire.

"What about Talley's son?" asked Drehsler.

"What about him? I gave him a job," said Warren, who confirmed that he did so at the request of the father and that the son was paid $200 a week for "doing nothing."

Warren conceded that he got his real estate license without paying a state fee or, as required by law, taking an examination. After it was issued, Warren told the reporters in carefully chosen words, he was "present" in Talley's office and witnessed a $200 cash payment to the commissioner. Warren himself did not make the payment. Instead, it came from another man, who just happened to be one of Warren's business pals.

"Like I said, I never ordered anyone to pay."

He also admitted that he or his employees and business pals had made "loans" to both James Keiffer, Talley's chief investigator, and George Brooks, the Maricopa County prosecuting attorney's investigator. Asked why, he would only say that the benevolence gave him "a piece of leverage" with governmental agencies which regulated his business or were in a position to do him "prosecutorial harm."

There were other friends of influence whom Warren spoke about, friends like Harry Rosenzweig, the powerful state GOP boss and confidant of'the Goldwater brothers.

"Harry and I developed a cordial relationship," said Warren. "We've met over the years a number of times, usually for lunch." He said that he had never received any political favors from Rosenzweig. In fact, Warren claimed, it was the other way around. "Harry would solicit me for political donations." Warren said he usually complied, contributing to the state Republican committee and to the campaigns of various GOP candidates, though never more than $100 at a time.

The interview lasted for nearly seven hours, with Greene and Drehsler going over dozens of the complicated deals and land companies Warren had started and, just before they went broke, unloaded to unsuspecting buyers. About 10:00 P.M., Warren drove the reporters to a nearby restaurant, where the conversation continued. They returned to his house shortly after midnight. Their arrival was watched by Wendland and Becker, who, alarmed when Greene and Drehsler failed to return to the Adams, had driven out to Camelback Mountain to stake out Warren's house and watch over their co-workers.

"Look, I admit it. I was a thief. And I was a good thief, too,"
Warren told Greene at one point. "It's not that I had to be. My family
had money, and I didn't have to steal for sociological or economic
reasons. I stole because I enjoyed the challenge and the thrill of it, the
matching of wits."

This had been a recurring theme all night. Warren made it perfectly
clear that he loved living by his cunning, and had made millions from
it. "You know," he said, shortly before the interview ended, "one
way to guarantee a cleanup of the real estate industry in Arizona
would be to make me the real estate commissioner. I know every
trick, every way to steal. I could clean this state up in six months."

The reporters believed that Warren was serious. It would be the
ultimate challenge for him, straightening out the gigantic mess he had
made.

As they shook hands and were about to leave, Greene looked for
the interview outline he had brought along. Since Warren had not
allowed the taking of notes, the twenty-three-page memo had been
placed on a foyer table shortly after they had arrived. It was not there
now.

Warren made an elaborate search of the house, claiming that he had
even awakened his wife to ask her if she had seen it. It was nowhere to
be found, he apologized with a shrug.

It made no difference, Greene said. They had covered most of the
points anyway. They bid farewell. Back at the hotel, Greene chuckled. "Mark my words, by ten o'clock tomorrow morning, we'll get a
call from Warren. The outline will have suddenly reappeared."

Greene was off by an hour. At nine o'clock, Warren telephoned.
He'd have the memo sent right over to the hotel. His wife had
mistakenly believed it to be some of her husband's own notes and had
placed it on his desk, he explained.

"Come on, Ned," Greene said. "Who's kidding who? But tell
me, what did you think of it?"

There was a slight pause, then a chuckle. "Not bad, not bad at all.
I'm glad you guys are reporters instead of cops. You did your
homework."

The Warren interview was one of the best, most of the reporters
felt. Warren himself seemed to epitomize much of what was wrong
with Arizona. He had seen opportunity and seized it. No matter that
he had broken the law, that people had died, that the life savings of the
land swindler's victims had been stolen. It was all some sort of

marvelous game, a game without rules, to be won by the player with the most nerve. That Warren felt no guilt and, incredibly, was borne no animosity by his neighbors in Arizona was evident by his plush, Camelback Mountain home. Back East, one so notorious as Warren would be careful to keep a low profile. Not so in Arizona. Out front of his sprawling house, in bold, foot-high letters, the name ''N. J. Warren'' was proudly posted next to his winding blacktop driveway. It was if he was showing off the fruits of his criminality. And none of his neighbors seemed to mind.

13 | Office Politics and Some Loose Ends

John Winters walked into the morning staff meeting the Monday after the Warren interview to find a gregarious Bob Greene almost boasting about the land fraud godfather's first official meeting with reporters. It was a dynamite interview, Greene was telling the troops, one that everyone should read.

"Warren came in and bought a state and despite a trail of murder and unbelievable heartache, he's still walking the streets. The memo spells it all out. Read it."

Winters was puzzled. "What's he talking about?" he asked Rawlinson.

"Warren—he and Alex got a seven-hour interview with Warren the other night."

It hit Winters like a kick in the groin. "That son of a bitch. That was a real chicken-shit thing he did to me." Winters turned and walked out of the office.

Rawlinson then realized what Winters was so angry about. Since October 4, the quiet, bearded reporter from the *Republic* had worked on scarcely anything else but Ned Warren, Sr. For three months, Winters had pored over literally thousands of pages of records, researched every one of the more than thirty land companies Warren had been involved in, and talked to dozens of Warren associates. He had spent days debriefing Dick Frost, perhaps the most difficult, nonstop talker any reporter could ever come across. More than to anyone on the team, Warren belonged to John Winters. The six-inch-thick files on Warren had been prepared almost exclusively by him.

Yet Greene did not even choose to tell him that the interview was going down. Winters could understand Drehsler's presence. Alex knew Warren from previous stories, and Warren was comfortable talking to him. And Winters had no quarrel with Greene's being there either. Warren was a key interview, one which Greene, as team leader, would understandably want to be a part of. But, if out of nothing more than courtesy, Winters should have been asked to go along.

Until joining the team, John Winters had never worked land fraud.

He had never wanted to, either. His specialty at the *Republic* was the mob. It was Winters to whom Don Bolles had turned over his organized crime files when the slain reporter had left the investigative beat. Winters had explained that to Greene in October, offering to make those files and his local expertise available to the team. Instead, Greene had assigned him to work Ned Warren, Sr., and land fraud, a task Winters had thrown himself into with enthusiasm, because, he confided to Koziol after getting over the initial rush of anger, "I really believe in what we're doing with this project." Winters was not the only reporter upset by Greene's often arbitrary ways.

Dick Lyneis, the *Riverside Press* reporter from California, sarcastically referred to the team effort as "The Greene Project." Lyneis was a member of the board of directors for IRE. As such, he was instrumental in the formation of the project in the first place. Even before the reporting began, he had journeyed to Phoenix to help arrange hotel accommodations and the dozens of minor details needed to set up an operating office. And now, working as a reporter on the team, Lyneis had some doubts.

"It's not that I don't think we've got some damn good stuff," he groused one night in Koziol's room over a drink. "It's Greene. Sometimes he scares the shit out of me. I think he's making decisions and doing things that we all ought to be consulted about."

"What do you mean?"

"I think he's trying to engineer reaction to the stories."

Over the past several weeks, several reporters, including Lyneis, had noticed strangers in the IRE office late at night. The strangers were all met by Bob Greene, who then gave them entire files to read. Several of them had made notes. George Weisz saw Greene give files to two Phoenix police officers. Koziol noticed a couple of FBI agents come up one Thursday night and stay in the IRE suite until past 2:00 A.M., poring over the reporters' files. Wendland spotted two state legislators over a two-night period in mid-January reading the narcotics files. When he asked Greene about it, Greene became extremely defensive. Greene's gruff explanation was that both legislators had been carefully "screened and checked" and had been given the files so that they could familiarize themselves with the extent of the state's narcotics problem. When the IRE stories were written, the two would "push for special legislation and cite our reporting with praise." On another occasion, when Lyneis tried to voice a complaint that some reporters and IRE members had serious reservations about indiscriminately sharing the files with law enforcement people, Greene became angry, shouted "Fuck it," and stormed out of the room.

"What I think he's doing is trying to set up story reaction," Lyneis said. "And I don't think that's right. Our job is to report, not to pass legislation."

And there was a major controversy within the ranks of IRE itself. Though IRE was sponsoring the Arizona investigation, the reporters working on the project were not working for IRE. Instead, they were working for their newspapers or, in the case of the few whose employers refused to pay their expenses, on their own time. Many of the Phoenix reporters were not even members of IRE.

And IRE, many felt, had become stagestruck. In November, during the very middle of the investigation, the IRE directors, meeting back East, decided they had a valuable property. So in a special board meeting they voted to hire a high-powered New York literary agent, who would negotiate the sale of "exclusive rights" to the IRE story.

Most of the working reporters in Phoenix were never officially told of the planned deal. Instead, they learned of it secondhand in January, when the IRE board and administration began calling Phoenix each day to talk to Greene, Myrta Pulliam, or Koziol—the only IRE officers in Arizona.

"It's perfect," said Pulliam one day in early January to Koziol. "This way, we have complete control of everything that's written about us. If we don't like the author the agent gets to do the book, or if we don't like what's written, then we have veto rights. Plus, we get half the profits."

Pulliam was one of three IRE board members from Indianapolis. Harley Bierce, who had been an $18,000-a-year reporter on the *Star*, which was owned by Myrta's father, was appointed executive director of IRE at $24,000 a year. Ed DeLaney, an Indianapolis attorney whose law firm represented the *Star*, was secretary of the group, even though he was not a journalist. To the members of the reporting team in Phoenix trying to finish the project, the three became known as "The Indianapolis Triumvirate." Although DeLaney and Bierce remained back in Indiana for the most part, the constant series of phone calls between them and Pulliam began to grate on the working reporters' nerves. There was too much IRE talk of a "deal" when the success of the project should have been paramount. Ron Koziol, who as IRE president had approved the hiring of a literary agent in November, had serious doubts in January.

"It was ridiculous," he confided to Wendland. "We never should have done it, especially not in the middle of the project. We're supposed to be a group of reporters, not Hollywood hustlers. This story doesn't belong exclusively to IRE or anyone else." But what disturbed Koziol the most was the Indianapolis faction's insistence on having editorial control. "We're supposed to be dedicated to the First Amendment. And now the board wants to decide just what can and cannot be written about us. What they really want to do is censor the story."

Jack Taylor, a respected investigative reporter from the *Daily Oklahoman* in Oklahoma City and a member of the IRE board, shared Koziol's concern. After failing to stop the board at a hastily called meeting from okaying exclusive filming of the team in operation by a Hollywood producer who promised to pay IRE $25,000—a project that never came off despite Bierce's success in ramrodding it through for board approval—Taylor bitterly resigned from the group. The working reporters in Phoenix did their best to ignore the political machinations of Indianapolis. But the dreams of IRE glory pushed by Bierce and Pulliam disgusted many of them. There were better things to do—like going to the dog races to investigate football players.

Early on in the project, the reporters had come across a prosperous Phoenix businessman who, besides being a top booster of the Arizona State University football team, was also an extremely close friend of the ASU coach, Frank Kush. Reporters eventually found nothing improper about the way the businessman, Anthony Nicoli, maintained his relationship with Kush and the football team. But they had come across indications that ASU football recruiting was overly aggressive. So, when IRE team member George Weisz learned in mid-January that a number of high school athletes had been brought in by Kush from all over the country for a firsthand look at ASU, the IRE reporters decided to tag along and secretly observe the way the athletes were wined and dined.

Actually, it was *Riverside Press* reporter Dick Lyneis and *Idaho Statesman* staffer Ken Matthews who first came across the ASU recruiting information. They had talked to Steve Chambers, a junior offensive tackle for ASU. Chambers said that the year before Coach Kush had made arrangements to take a number of high school recruits to Phoenix's Greyhound Park, where they were given money and betting tips.

"They'd say, 'Why don't you go and bet on those two dogs?' " said the young college player. "The high school kids were doing pretty good, too. They won on about nine out of every ten bets. It was getting pretty wild.''

A number of other past and present ASU players were interviewed. The dog track outing seemed to be a standard part of Kush's recruiting program. Several other players confirmed that money exchanged hands between the coaches and the recruits. But there was only one way to find out for sure.

On January 16, IRE assembled a six-member surveillance crew. They arrived at the Greyhound Park dog track shortly before seven-thirty and split up into several groups. On the way into the two-tiered clubhouse, Weisz found out from the track reservations girl that there was an ASU dinner reservation for forty-five, seated in the lower right section of the clubhouse. Reporters had no problem identifying the young high school recruits, most of whom were dressed in brightly colored letterman jackets or sweaters. Several ASU varsity players acted as guides.

Head coach Frank Kush, dressed in a dark blue leisure suit, was the center of attention. Several assistant coaches were also present. IRE reporters, posing as tourists and track regulars, witnessed a number of the high school recruits placing bets and winning surprisingly often. Weisz, who had graduated from college only the summer before, decided to find out more. Casually dressed and looking like he belonged in the group, he began talking with the high school players as they stood in line waiting to place bets.

On three occasions, Weisz chatted with a husky young Florida youth, whose white football shirt proclaimed him to be ''Bo.'' Although the youth had complaints about ''lame'' girls provided the recruits during their three-day visit to ASU and wanted to know if Weisz could send a couple of ''fun chicks'' up to his room in the Holiday Inn, Bo was basically having a pretty good time. He told Weisz that each recruit had been given ten dollars by the coaching staff at the start of the night, but when that sum was gone, he himself had been handed another twenty dollars to bet with. Bo's roommate on the recruiting trip was another Florida high-schooler, a safety.

''Hey, man, you know where we can score with a couple of chicks?'' the safety asked Weisz, apparently thinking the IRE member was one of the ASU player-hosts.

Weisz just grinned. It must be all that Florida orange juice, he thought.

But the roommate also admitted that the betting money had come from the ASU coaching staff. ''Whenever we run out, all we got to do

is just go up to the coaches,'' he said, sounding rather impressed with
the arrangement. He was only about fourteen dollars ahead for the
night, he told Weisz, though ''one guy at our table is really cleaning
up. He's won sixty bucks already.''

During the third race Weisz was standing next to Jerry Uhrhammer, the Oregon reporter. Uhrhammer, accompanied by IRE researcher Kay Nash, who posed as his wife, was trying to look like a
picture-happy tourist taking photographs of the track. Actually he
was snapping pictures of the recruits making bets. Weisz tugged
Uhrhammer's sleeve, indicating that they should keep quiet. For not
two feet away was ASU head coach Kush, who had briefly left the
main group of recruits for a private conversation with one of the
assistant coaches. Little did Kush know that much of what the two
said was overheard by Weisz.

''Look, there's about fifty reporters in town, asking about gambling and the track,'' Kush wanted the assistant coach to know.

''Do you think it's going to hurt us?''

''No. They're just asking a lot of questions. They talked to Steve.''
Steve Chambers, the offensive tackle who had first tipped the reporters to the dog track outings, had obviously so informed his coach.

''Maybe we'd better be careful,'' the assistant worried.

''Naw,'' said Kush. ''They're just asking some questions.''

For a moment, the two coaches lowered their voices. The roar of
the crowd watching the last stretch of the third race drowned the
conversation out.

By the time the crowd settled down, the coaches were returning to
their seats. As they left, Weisz heard the assistant note that ''I had to
get money for these guys,'' indicating the happy high-schoolers.

''Yeah, I know,'' said Kush, walking out of the reporters' earshot.

Later, just as the players and coaches were leaving, Weisz found
the kid the safety had said was the big winner. He was a husky Texas
boy.

''Hey, buddy, how'd you do?'' George asked.

The kid beamed. ''I won sixty dollars,'' he said. ''That's pretty
good, huh? They only gave me twenty to start with.''

''Who gave you twenty?'' Weisz grinned back, hoping the kid
wouldn't be spooked by the question.

''The coach. Pretty nice, huh? This is one hell of a school.''

Three days later, Dick Lyneis contacted Frank Kush for an official
reaction.

''Believe me, our recruiting program is all aboveboard,'' Kush insisted. "I'm on the board of trustees of the Football Coaches Association. I see the kinds of things that go on. And I run my recruiting the right way."

Lyneis asked Kush whether the dog track was the proper place to take young high school recruits.

"What else is there to do on Sunday nights?" shrugged the coach. "Everything else is closed, even the university's food service. Well, the track is only a mile and a half away, and there aren't that many people there on Sunday nights. So it's a good place to take the kids."

"Do the kids bet on the dogs?" asked Lyneis.

"No, there's very little of that. Maybe once in a while."

"We have learned that some of the recruits really bet quite a lot," said Lyneis. "Some of them win pretty heavily."

"Absolutely not," said Kush, looking shocked at the question. "Oh, maybe once in a while two or three of the kids will get two bucks together and bet on a dog. But that's all."

"We're also told that you or your coaches give them money to bet with."

"That's absolutely untrue."

Kush really could not have said otherwise, not if he didn't want major problems from the National Collegiate Athletic Association, which had been conducting major investigations into college football recruiting programs in recent years.

But the reporters' night at the dog track was not destined to be part of the series of stories produced by the team. While it was one of a number of interesting things the team stumbled across during the five months in Arizona, it did not relate to organized crime and political corruption. So it simply went in the files.

By the last two weeks of January, most of the reporting was complete. Suddenly, there was an end in sight. The months of around-the-clock digging had taken their toll among the full-time reporters. They were dog tired. Tom Renner was perhaps the most fatigued. With the exception of a Christmas break, he had been away from home since September. An old ulcer was acting up again. It looked like he would have to go into the hospital for a few weeks. "I'll tell you this, though," he said. "Even though I'm more proud of this story than anything else I've worked on, I'll never, ever, get involved with a project like this again."

Even Greene, the tireless bulldog, conceded that he was drained. "No more," he said. "This is my swan song. It's back to Long Island when this is over and from then on, the only out-of-town traveling I want to do is with my wife, on vacation."

John Rawlinson, who with Drehsler had come up from the *Arizona Daily Star* and remained full-time on the project, was similarly exhausted. But Rawlinson had another problem. In late January, his wife filed for divorce. Rawlinson didn't particularly want to talk about it. But his long absence from home obviously didn't help. Fortunately, they had no children. They had been married less than a year.

Some of the loose ends to be straightened out included interviews with Arizona's hoodlums. The months of work had clearly shown a major expansion of the Joe Bonanno family. Thus, Rawlinson, who had briefly interviewed the aging mobster a couple of years before, telephoned him on January 22 to set up an appointment.

Bonanno remembered Rawlinson. "Yes, you were a nice, quiet man. Polite. But what good if you come down, question me?" said Bonanno. "Any kind of question would not be good for me."

Rawlinson explained the information the team had developed on Bonanno and his activities. "We'd like your side."

"I don't care what anybody says about me because I am at peace with myself and my God," he said. "There is nothing to be arranged. I have nothing to say."

But the mob boss did have an opinion on the Bolles murder. "In fairness to good people, the people behind that bomb should be punished," he said. "What happened to Mr. Bolles was bad. I believe in the law. If you do something bad, you should be punished. I make a lot of mistakes in my life, no question. But I try to learn from these mistakes. I am at peace."

For the record, Rawlinson had to run at least one question past Bonanno. "Is it true, as law enforcement officials charge, that you are one of the country's major organized crime figures?"

"Thank you for calling," was the reply. "Goodbye now." Bonanno hung up.

But there were a number of other, more accessible, though lower level, hoods to contact. The IRE investigators had come up with 102 persons in Phoenix alone who were either members or close associates of the mob, running a prosperous but highly disjointed network of various organized crime scams. About three-quarters of the hoodlums identified by the team were from Chicago, the rest from New York. For the most part, they were bottom-drawer characters, many of them the brothers or distant relatives of big-time hoods unable to make it back home in the more structured, competitive East Coast cities, where mob businesses were run with sophisticated, long-established efficiency. The Chicago faction was the largest but the most unorganized in the Phoenix crime family. They were rivaled by a considerably smaller New York group. So far, few overt hostilities had surfaced between the two factions, though the former New Yorkers were much sharper. They also were loyal to Joe Bonanno and thus benefited from his organizational strengths, while the Chicago hoodlums were having trouble consolidating their various operations. Most of the action in Phoenix concerned the three traditional mob endeavors: prostitution, gambling, and loan-sharking.

The Chicago interests were believed by police to be under the basic control of Joseph "Papa Joe" Tocco, the brother of Albert Tocco, one of the Cosa Nostra's ranking Chicago bosses. A police listening device planted in a Phoenix warehouse in 1972 picked up a discussion in which Tocco outlined a $12-million bootleg-tape scam which would pirate the music recordings of major-label artists. Tocco was not pleased when IRE reporters tried to talk with him at his Phoenix restaurant.

"If you guys are reporters, you better get the fuck out of here before I get mad," he shouted one afternoon in late January when Dave Overton came to call. For emphasis, Tocco picked up a screwdriver and waved it menacingly in the reporter's face.

So much for that interview.

On the New York side, and considerably more talkative, was Bonanno pal Edward "Acey" Duci, a short, beer-bellied man with slicked-back hair and the tattoo of a black panther on his right arm. Duci, who had left New York in the mid-sixties, ran a go-go bar in West Phoenix; he was an old-time bookie, though he swore to reporters that he was now "one-hundred-percent legit."

"I don't care much for these Chicago guys," he told Koziol one night. "They're nothing but punks. They come here to Phoenix to make waves. I think they're nothing but rejects from the Chicago mob."

Duci liked to carry around in his wallet old newspaper clippings about his East Coast ties to organized crime. He spent most of January 15 with IRE reporters. In the afternoon, he was with Rawlinson and Becker, who stopped by his bar for a lengthy chat over a half-dozen beers. That night, Koziol and Drehsler dropped in.

It became obvious to the reporters, and was later confirmed by police, that Duci was into a lot of things, particularly prostitution, which flourished in a string of at least sixty-two massage parlors that ringed the city. How Phoenix, with 800,000 residents, could support so many different whorehouses was beyond the imagination of IRE reporters. Later, they learned that the massage parlors did most of their business in the summer, when daily temperatures often climb well over a hundred degrees. When Phoenix housewives take the children to cooler mountain climes, many husbands apparently find solace in the sleazy storefront parlors.

"Hey, you know who you guys ought to talk to?" Duci told reporters late that night. "You guys ought to meet my partner, Fat Louie."

"Who?" asked Koziol.

"Fat Louie."

The reporters knew well of whom Duci spoke. But rather than apprise him that Fat Louie was a prime subject on their hoodlum interview list, Koziol decided to play along. Fat Louie was really Robert Louis Amuso, another Eastern transplant, whose many specialties included shaking down the area's massage parlors once a week.

"Yeah, Fat Louie will give you guys some great quotes about being in the Mafia."

A meeting was arranged a few days later for the Caravan Inn Bar in downtown Phoenix.

Koziol showed up a few minutes late. As promised, there was Duci, sitting at a table with a huge hulk of a man.

"This is my partner, Mr. Amuso," beamed Duci as the Chicago reporter joined them.

Koziol's mouth dropped. Amuso was dressed like something out of an old George Raft movie, wearing a black, three-piece suit, a black shirt, white tie, and sunglasses.

"Ah, tell me, Fat Louie," said a surprised Koziol as he sat down, "do you always dress like that?"

"Naw," said Amuso. "I thought I'd just dress this way for you. You know, to kind of fit the mold."

Amuso said his main business was running five massage parlors. "They aren't really that much work," he said. "I spend most of my time sitting at home, watching soap operas on the television. I can tell you the plots backwards and forwards. They're pretty true to life, you know."

Koziol and the two characters chatted amiably for a half-hour or so. At one point, Koziol mentioned the Chicago mob's action in the bootleg tape racket in Phoenix.

"Shit," offered Duci. "That ain't nothing." He turned to his partner. "Tell him about those tapes you were selling that didn't have any music on them."

Amuso snickered. "Yeah, that's right. But that was strictly legit. See, there's nothing bootleg about a tape with no music on it."

That led Duci to inform Koziol of another Amuso scam. "My partner here is also in the television business."

"What do you mean?"

Again, Amuso, clearly enjoying the interview, was only too happy to answer. "Sure, I sold TV's," he said as Duci began giggling. "Yeah, I sell 'em real cheap. They're color TV sets. I deliver them sealed right in their factory box."

"Only thing is," interrupted Duci, anxious to get to the punch line, "those TV sets don't have any insides. Just the chassis."

"Look, Louie," said Koziol a few minutes later, trying to get the interview on track again, "let's get back to the massage parlors for a minute. I understand you've been known to shake a few of them down."

"No, not me. Do I look like I belong to the Mafia or something?"

"You ask me that, dressed the way you are?"

That reminded Duci of still another story. "One time, my partner here, he goes into this massage parlor, see? He says he wants his payoff. And to demonstrate he means business, he pulls out an automatic and begins twirling it around his finger as the madame stares real big-eyed and scared. Well, he's twirling the piece and all of a sudden, the magazine drops out on the floor. All the girls started laughing and yelling. They kicked his ass right out of there."

Both Amuso and Duci denied any involvement with crime other than the tape scam and scoffed at any suggestion of an organized crime syndicate in the city. "Look, we may be no angels, but this is a pretty nice town," said Duci.

Both men, though, had opinions about the murder of newspaperman Don Bolles.

"It was stupid that they killed Bolles," said Amuso. "If he had written something bad about me, I'd have just slapped him around a little."

"Yeah, that bombing was a pretty stupid thing," agreed Duci. "I mean if you're going to kill a man, you forget all that movie stuff. The only way to do such a thing is to take a thirty-eight and blow his brains out. Simple."

Perhaps what amazed the reporters most was the pure gall of the hustlers and con men they had encountered in Phoenix.

Another Phoenix man of interest to IRE was Herb Lieb, 56, a former Chicagoan and the owner of a dress shop and a ritzy, members-only nightspot called the Jockey Club. He was identified in numerous police reports as a contact man for major mob figures. People like James "Jimmy the Weasel" Fratianno, a mob enforcer from the West Coast, were seen in Lieb's company when visiting Phoenix. Lieb was also a boyhood pal of Allen Dorfman, a convicted swindler and the main money-mover for the corrupt Central States Pension Fund of the mob-infiltrated Teamsters Union. And, in Phoenix, Lieb was a close personal friend and business associate of Harry Rosenzweig.

"I'm as close to Harry as any man living today," said Lieb, a slim, slightly balding man, the afternoon he was visited by Wendland and Koziol. "And Harry never did anything wrong in his life." Lieb admitted that he had other friends who had raised police eyebrows. "Sure I know a lot of guys that might be called hoodlums. Hey, I'm from Chicago. I grew up on the West Side. A lot of my friends got into the rackets. Others became judges. I know them all, they know me. But I've never had any business dealings with those guys. I'm a legitimate businessman. Sure, I know some guys. But I'm away from that kind of shit. I could have had their money anytime I wanted to if I wanted to. But I'm not that kind of guy." Before the interview ended, Lieb wrote out temporary guest passes for his private club for the reporters. "When you guys get a chance, drop by. I'll show you a good time."

Back in the IRE office, Greene thought it was an invitation his reporters could not refuse. "I don't know what he wants you guys for, but there has to be a reason."

About nine o'clock that night, with Drehsler and Weisz covering both the front and rear entrances of the club, Wendland and Koziol walked inside. It was an ornate, plushly decorated disco, designed by

Dave Stevens, the same architect who had remodeled the infamous Herb Applegate party house the reporters had had such difficulty locating two months before. A sunken dance floor dominated the interior; there was a small game room for backgammon players and a leather-padded bar. Two large, stained-glass windows over the dance floor gave the place an atmosphere of refined but modern elegance. It didn't take long for Lieb to spot the reporters, who were sipping drinks at the bar and watching the club fill up with well-dressed young Phoenicians.

"Hey, you know, right after you guys left this afternoon, I talked to Harry Rosenzweig," Lieb said. "And Harry's real upset about the kinds of questions you guys are asking." He paused to let the message sink in.

"Look, Herb, we really didn't come by to talk shop," lied Wendland. "We just wanted a nice, quiet place to unwind. Let's not get bogged down in business."

"Sure, sure," said Lieb. "I imagine you guys have really been working your tail ends off. No problem. Have you enjoyed Phoenix?"

The reporters wanted to leave an impression with Lieb that they were tired and depressed, that they had had it with reporting. "It's okay."

"What do you mean, okay? This is a great town. Great people."

"You see, Herb, it's just that we're kind of tired of going around and sticking our noses in other people's business," said Koziol.

"Right," Wendland agreed. "Like this afternoon. You know, we really hated asking you those questions. I mean, you're a nice guy, Herb. So's Harry, I suppose. I mean, we really don't like upsetting people."

"Yeah," said Koziol. "This place is more our style."

Lieb chatted with the reporters a few minutes, sizing them up. He offered to buy them dinner, which they politely refused. About ten, he excused himself. "I'll be right back. I got a couple things to attend to."

"What do think?" Koziol asked after Lieb had moved off.

Wendland shrugged. "We'll know soon enough." They had just an hour remaining. Before departing the hotel, they had agreed to leave the club by eleven. If Wendland and Koziol weren't out by then, Drehsler and Weisz were to come inside looking for them.

Lieb came back in about forty-five minutes. "Still enjoying yourselves?"

"Hey, we sure are," said Koziol. Several women had approached the reporters, offering dark-eyed greetings as if they were regulars. "Look, one thing, Herb. We aren't supposed to be in here, you know? This Bob Greene guy we work for is a real stickler about the reporters socializing with people they're investigating. So if anyone ever asks, we weren't here, okay?"

Lieb was swallowing the bait. "No problem, I understand. He must be a real ass to have you guys out snooping around about Harry. Say, how would you guys like to meet Harry? He said he'd be glad to talk to you. I could set it up for Tuesday."

"No. I don't think we should," said Koziol. "Maybe later. But that sort of thing should be handled formally, you know?"

"Sure, sure. It's just that Harry and I are really upset by the things you guys have been hearing. Those stories are really wild. I'd really like to know who's spreading that kind of shit around about me. It would be worth money to me. I'd pay your expenses. I'll pay you to get to the bottom of this."

Koziol glanced at Wendland to see if it had sunk in. It had. Lieb was offering them what sounded like a bribe to reveal their news sources.

It was eleven o'clock. And Lieb, before continuing the conversation or setting a price, had been pulled away by a young woman patron and taken to a nearby table, promising to be right back.

"We got a problem," said Koziol, glancing at his watch.

"I know. You'd better get out there. Let the other guys know everything's cool."

Koziol got up and went outside.

"Hey, where'd your pal go?" Lieb was back.

"He ran out of cigars," said Wendland. "He'll be right back. Had to go out to the car."

Lieb nodded. A few minutes later, with Koziol back at the bar, Lieb said he had a friend he wanted to introduce the reporters to. It was Joe Martori, the young lawyer whose family had been friends and business partners of Bob Goldwater and Harry Rosenzweig.

Martori, a short, well-dressed man, seemed hostile. "I read a magazine article where the leader of your group, a guy named Greene, said you guys were here to assassinate Phoenix," he said.

Wendland and Koziol begged off. This was no time or place to get into an argument. Instead, they smiled and repeated the same line they had given Lieb about sneaking away from the hotel. "We don't talk shop on off hours," Wendland said.

Martori turned friendly. He talked about Phoenix, how he used to write sports for the Notre Dame college paper, and the pride he had in his family, which numbered twenty-nine, including uncles, brothers, and cousins.

They were interrupted by a telephone page for Ron Koziol. Great, thought Wendland, here we've told these people that no one knows we're here and now Koziol gets a telephone call. It was eleven-thirty.

Koziol took the call from a phone near the main door. It was Greene.

"You guys were supposed to be out of there by eleven," he said. "Let's go."

Koziol had explained the situation to Drehsler when he had slipped out of the club a half-hour before. He thought Greene would have gotten the message. "Things here aren't moving on schedule," Koziol whispered into the phone. "Everything's fine. We need a little more time."

Koziol hung up and, making sure he wasn't noticed, sneaked outside again to explain the situation to the backup reporters before returning to the group. Martori was still there, as were a couple of his law partners. But time was running out. The reporters wanted to be alone with Lieb again, to have him amplify on his remarks about paying for their news sources. Bribing a reporter isn't illegal, though such an offer certainly indicated impropriety. And that could be reported in print. But they needed more. So far, no price had been mentioned, no specific duties. Lieb looked like he had more to say. But he certainly wouldn't go further with Martori there. And Martori, who turned out to be quite amiable, showed no intention of leaving.

A second phone call from Greene prevented any further discussions.

"Goddamn it, I told you to leave. I meant *leave*," he shouted over the phone to Koziol. "It's almost midnight. Now get your asses out of there and get them out now." He slammed the receiver down without waiting for a reply.

There wasn't much else to do but leave. Hastily, the reporters made excuses about having to meet a friend and took off. Outside, after pulling away from the Jockey Club, they drove into the parking lot of a nearby shopping center, followed by Drehsler and Weisz.

"Damn it, what did you do that for?" shouted Wendland. "Why did you guys have us pulled out of there? We weren't ready to leave.

Things were just getting to the point where we'd know exactly what the guy meant.''

Drehsler and Weisz were just as puzzled as Wendland and Koziol. They had understood the situation inside the club, that everything was okay except for a difficulty in getting alone with Lieb. "It's Greene, then," said Koziol. "He made the decision on his own?"

Drehsler and Weisz nodded. "Look, we understand. You guys could have stayed in there all night as far as we were concerned," said Weisz. "We were there just to make sure nobody carried you guys out.''

It took the reporters several minutes to notice because of their heated conversation, but directly overhead and shining its bright lights on the parking lot was a police helicopter. Moments later, a squad car screamed into the lot, quickly followed by a second. The first stopped behind the IRE cars, while the second went to a far end of the shopping center.

Ironically, moments before the reporters had pulled in, somebody had smashed the window of a jewelry store in the shopping center. Police, responding to the silent alarm, found only a broken window and four hollering newspaper reporters. After viewing the reporters' ID's, the police left, shaking their heads.

Later, after calming down, the reporters would realize how lucky they were not to have had a trigger-happy cop respond to the alarm and mistake them for jewel thieves. It became one of the team's funniest stories—four of the country's allegedly top reporters so deep in a discussion that they didn't even know they were surrounded by a tense squad of armed police officers.

At the hotel, a similar shouting match with Greene ensued.

From Koziol and Wendland's point of view, Greene had been trying to second-guess them from a position of ignorance. He wasn't inside the club and thus had no way of knowing what the situation was. They were. And in their judgment, they hadn't gotten everything possible from their news source.

Greene didn't buy any of it. The issue as he saw it was clear. They had all agreed beforehand to leave by eleven. Eleven came and went and the inside team was still inside. They had not stuck to the plan. It made no difference to Greene that the outside team was completely aware of what was going on in the club. A plan was a plan and it hadn't been followed.

At 1:00 A.M., they all got tired of shouting at each other and went to bed. In the morning, it was as if the argument had never occurred.

Fat Louie, "Acey" Duci, Herb Lieb, "Papa Joe," high school kids being touted on dogs at a betting track, Harry Rosenzweig. The names and incidents seemed to blur into a carnival of the macabre. Phoenix was a world unto itself—a place where money was God and the hustler and con man were the priests. It was a city in need of help.

14 | A Twenty-Year Deal

Saturday, January 15, began as a fairly quiet morning in the IRE suite. The reporters had begun work promptly at eight-thirty. A fairly standard routine had developed. After breakfast and before starting the staff meeting, someone would read aloud "Today's Chuckle," a normally humorless and stale one-liner that appeared every day on the front page of the morning *Republic* with "Today's Prayer." The chuckles never came, but the IRE reporters kept reading them anyway, mostly out of amazement that a modern metropolitan newspaper would continue to waste space in such a trite fashion. Then, just before getting down to work, the daily low temperature from Chicago, Detroit, New York, and Indianapolis during one of the century's coldest winters would be read off the weather page. All winter in Phoenix the weather had been monotonously but beautifully the same: cloudless skies and temperatures in the low seventies. It was one of the few fringe benefits of being away from home so long.

One recent news story, however, had been of major interest to the reporters. The John Adamson murder trial had started in Tucson a few weeks before. Jury selection was still going on. Several dozen prospective jurors had been quizzed, but, because of extensive knowledge about the case, most had been rejected. That morning's *Republic* reported that Superior Court Judge Ben Birdsall had scheduled a rare Saturday session to speed up the process.

Shortly before noon, as IRE reporters were reading their files and working on the final stages of their various investigations, the telephone rang. It was Chuck Kelly, the *Republic* staffer who had been covering the trial and a friend of most of the IRE reporters.

"Adamson's confessed," he told Bob Greene. "He's admitted the whole thing. And he's named everyone else he was involved with."

The first indication that there was a break in the case had come about nine that morning when the jury selection process was to be resumed. But instead of getting down to the long, tedious questioning, Judge Birdsall had apologized to the jury panel, noting that there would be a delay.

At 11:00 A.M., Adamson, dressed in the same prescription

239

sunglasses, print sport shirt, brown trousers, and white shoes he had worn each day for the past three weeks, entered the courtroom with sheriff's deputies and his attorney. He appeared neither overly serious nor nonchalant.

Judge Birdsall came in a moment later and, in an emotionless monotone, announced to a hushed courtroom that a plea arrangement had been made between Adamson and the prosecution, that Adamson, originally charged with first-degree murder, wished to change his previous plea of not guilty, to guilty of a reduced charge of murder in the second degree.

"Is this a voluntary plea?" asked Birdsall.

"It is, Your Honor," said Adamson.

"Now, I want you to tell this court just what you did in connection with the death of Don Bolles."

Adamson's voice was firm. "On June 2, 1976, in the parking lot of the Clarendon Hotel, I placed a bomb containing dynamite under the car of Don Bolles to be detonated at a later time for the express purpose of killing him."

"Did you bring the bomb yourself to the automobile?"

"I did."

"And, as I understand it, you placed it under the car?" continued the judge, studying a number of typewritten documents in front of him.

"That's correct, Your Honor."

"Did you do anything with reference to getting Mr. Bolles to the Clarendon Hotel on that date?"

"I did, sir."

"And what, if anything, did you have to do with reference to instructing anyone concerning the discharge of the bomb?"

"I made a phone call to an individual and told him where Mr. Bolles would be at a specific time and to, where, where it was to be arranged that the bomb was to be detonated," said Adamson.

"You said this to me, but I want to make sure that I understand you correctly," the judge continued, carefully choosing his words. "You procured the bomb. You took it to the car. You put it under the car. And you made arrangements to have it detonated, all with the specific intent to kill Mr. Bolles. Is that right?"

"Yes, sir."

Birdsall then went over all eighteen terms of the proposed plea agreement submitted for his approval. Basically, it guaranteed that

Adamson would be freed from prison after serving twenty years. His sentence would be served in an out-of-state jail and would not be handed down officially until he testified fully and completely against all others who were involved in the murder. If Adamson should lie, or appeal his sentence, or try to be paroled from jail before the twenty years were up, the agreement would be null and void, and he could then be retried on a first-degree murder charge or resentenced to an even longer prison term.

For forty minutes, Birdsall questioned Adamson, making certain that the agreement was voluntary and that the defendant fully understood the ramifications. But instead of approving it, the judge explained that he needed more information about Adamson himself. He scheduled a hearing for the following Wednesday, by which time he expected that the county probation department would have prepared a background report. To make sure, he ordered the report on his desk by Tuesday afternoon.

Adamson was led off to jail and the jury was excused. There was no mention made of Adamson's coconspirators in the court proceeding. However, by midmorning, developments in Phoenix 180 miles to the north answered all of the reporters' questions. An affidavit given police by Adamson was officially filed in Maricopa County Superior Court to support the arrests of two other men—Max Dunlap and James Robison.

It was Dunlap, said Adamson in the signed affidavit, who hired him to kill Bolles. And it was Robison, a short, fat plumber and longtime Adamson pal, who, he said, assisted him in blowing up the reporter's car. Adamson's sworn statement said that Dunlap told him that millionaire rancher Kemper Marley wanted Bolles dead because the reporter had given Marley "a bad time" when Marley was appointed to the Arizona Racing Commission the previous spring. The aging Marley had to resign the job because of a controversy created by news stories which detailed his questionable performances in past state political posts, stories which were written by Don Bolles. But Bolles was not the only man Adamson said he was asked to kill. There were three others. Two of them were relatively minor figures.

Al "King Alfonso" Lizanetz, a former Marley public relations man who adopted the colorful nickname after claiming to have had a vision from God, had been sending out wild, rambling letters to reporters and politicians detailing alleged wrongdoings by his former employer. Lizanetz's name came as no surprise. Police had been tipped months before that Adamson was also going after "The King." "He's been writing a lot of bullshit about Marley," Adamson was known to have said to his drinking cronies shortly after the Bolles bombing.

Another man on Dunlap's death list was Doug Damon, who had supposedly conned Marley out of $15,000 in a deal involving the purchase of stolen silver. Adamson said he never carried out the contract because Damon had skipped town with Marley's money.

However, the fourth man Adamson was asked to kill, according to the affidavit, was very much a part of the current Phoenix scene. Adamson said Dunlap wanted him to murder state Attorney General Bruce Babbitt. The reason: "He [Dunlap] said the attorney general was investigating the liquor industry and if he could not be persuaded politically to halt it, then Kemper Marley wanted to get him killed."

Kemper Marley's wealth stemmed from many areas. Land, cattle, oil, and water helped to make him a millionaire. But his main business was liquor. And his wholesale liquor, beer, and wine company, United Liquor Company, was a virtual monopoly in Arizona.

It was also a part of an antitrust suit filed by Babbitt in 1975 that accused the Arizona Licensed Beverage Association of price fixing. Babbitt had named Marley's firm as a coconspirator. The case was still pending at the time Adamson said he was asked to kill Babbitt, and the attorney general showed no signs of abandoning it.

Kemper Marley was so big that he allegedly ordered murder contracts in package deals. The total price for the killings negotiated through Dunlap was $50,000, Adamson said.

By early afternoon, less than two hours after Adamson had admitted his role in the Bolles killing and promised to testify against the others who were involved in the plot, Dunlap and Robison were in the Maricopa County jail, held without bail on charges of first-degree murder. Police refused to comment on whether Marley was also an official suspect. "The investigation is continuing," said Bruce Babbitt.

At the IRE office, the news of Adamson's sudden confession soon became the only activity of the half-dozen newsmen. The various IRE investigations were temporarily shelved as the reporters frantically pounded out Sunday stories on the dramatic turnabout for their own papers. For several of them, it was the first real story filed in weeks. The work they had been doing in Phoenix was all prepared in memorandum form, strictly for the files. Working under deadline again reminded them what the business was all about. Even Greene knocked out a piece for *Newsday*. "It feels good to be a reporter again," he beamed that night. "But come the morn, it's back to being a slave driver."

Meanwhile there were still a few legal preliminaries to settle in Tucson before the Adamson confession could be legally accepted.

James Muth, a Maricopa County deputy probation officer, was assigned by Birdsall to prepare a probation report on the defendant, a standard procedure ordered by judges as a guide in passing sentence. On Wednesday, January 19, Muth submitted his report, complaining to the judge that he was hampered by a lack of time and information and that he was not allowed to discuss the Bolles murder with the killer because of the terms of the plea agreement. The probation officer seemed upset that Adamson was getting off too easily: "Based on the defendant's admission of guilt in the present offense, and based on the apparent nature and sophistication of this offense—that it does not appear to be a crime of passion but one motivated by profit, that others with similar motivations are allegedly involved; that the elements of a good deal of time and effort and deception on the part of the defendant all appear to be present; and that the crime itself was indeed violent—the defendant appears to be a person possessing very little respect for the rights and dignity and life of others, and he is viewed by this writer to be a significant and serious threat to the community and to society in general."

Adamson, who sat silent with his attorneys as Judge Birdsall read excerpts from the report, briefly turned around to study the courtroom spectators. Finding Muth, he stared at him for a few seconds. There was no expression on his face, just a sort of detached curiosity.

Muth's report noted that Adamson's past history "suggests a pattern of sophisticated criminal activity that has become progressively more involved and violent, and hence one not easily changed because of its increasingly sophisticated nature." Adamson drank heavily, to the point where he suffered from an enlarged liver and possible cirrhosis, said the probation officer. He smoked marijuana and snorted cocaine. He had been divorced three times, twice from his first wife, and during 1976 had mostly lived off food stamps and his wife's earnings as a nurse.

Muth also quoted Phoenix police detective Jon Sellers, the chief investigator of the Bolles murder, as saying that the plea bargaining agreement, while "a necessary and practical one," also disturbed him. For Adamson, Sellers said, was "a coldblooded killer," one he personally hoped "will never walk the streets again."

Besides Muth's sketchy probation report, there was one other document, dated Monday, January 17. It was a letter to Judge Birdsall from Bolles's widow, Rosalie.

All the pent-up emotions of long months of trying to rebuild a life for our family without a husband and father have come to the surface in the past two days. Sorting them out has been difficult but I have tried to face them honestly, without apology, and accept them for what they are.

When Bruce Babbitt brought me the news of the plea arrangement with John Adamson, I'm sure you can understand the conflicting feelings which battered my thoughts. On the one hand, there was a sense of relief that, finally, progress may be made toward bringing to justice all those responsible for Don's death. But it was naturally tempered by the knowledge Adamson would not be punished to the full extent of the law.

Don hated the necessity for plea bargaining, but he accepted it as a fact of judicial life. I take my guidance from him. In the last analysis, that bargain is a small price to pay for bringing to justice those whose callous calculation makes their own culpability even more awful than Adamson's. For without them, the children and I would still have Don.

John Adamson is an adult, responsible for his own actions, and he has no pity from me. Perhaps someday my heart will find room for forgiveness, but right now, the scars are still too deep. I am grateful to Mr. Babbitt and his staff for their extraordinary job of ensuring he [Adamson] will pay a heavy penalty for his part in this tragedy, while at the same time offering a tangible hope that everyone involved will be brought to the bar of justice.

But a full measure of vengeance against one man is far less important to us, and ultimately, to the entire community, than the assurance that these vicious people will never again be free to inflict on someone else the terrible loss which the children and I have known.

Don's integrity and devotion to truth must be worth at least that.

Judge Birdsall, clearly moved by Mrs. Bolles's letter, signed the plea bargain agreement.

Officially, Adamson would be sentenced to forty-eight to forty-nine years in prison, with a guarantee that he would be released on parole after twenty years and two months, dating from his arrest the previous June. The sentence would be served in an out-of-state prison, at the express wish of Adamson, who felt he would be murdered if jailed in Arizona.

A few days later at the preliminary hearing for Dunlap and Robison, Adamson kept his word. The court proceeding was held in the Maricopa County Courthouse before Superior Judge Edward C. Rapp.

"Tell me, Mr. Adamson," asked William Schafer III, the assistant attorney general who was trying the case, "what motive was there expressed for the killing by Mr. Dunlap?"

Adamson's voice never wavered. He still wore the prescription sunglasses which hid his eyes and made it difficult to see who he was looking at. "That Don Bolles had given Kemper Marley a bad time in the past, particularly over the appointment to the racing commission, and that Marley wanted Bolles killed. He wanted him to be the first to die."

Schaffer guided Adamson into the financial arrangements, how the $50,000 contract for the murders of Bolles, Lizanetz, and Babbitt was negotiated after Dunlap originally rejected Adamson's request for $15,000 to kill the reporter as "pretty high."

"So we negotiated a package price for all three," said Adamson.

"Where was this money to come from?"

"Max indicated that he had a key to the vault with Marley and that the money would absolutely be no problem."

The questioning moved into how Adamson enlisted the aid of Robison and how they shopped around together in various hobby shops in the Valley looking for remote control transmitters which could be employed to detonate the bomb. In late April, Adamson said, he traveled to San Diego with a girl friend and purchased a used device as instructed by Robison. For several weeks, the two experimented with the transmitter, testing it out at various locations with mock bombs. During this time period—from mid to late May—Adamson said he met frequently with Dunlap, who was impatient that Bolles be killed as soon as possible.

"We've got to get this done—he's going to start on something in two weeks," Adamson quoted Dunlap as saying.

It was Dunlap's idea that Adamson call Bolles under the pretense of having information about political figures and land fraud, Adamson said. A few nights later, Adamson said, he was in the Ivanhoe bar drinking when he heard Dick Ryan, a court stenographer, mention the reporter's name. At Adamson's urging, Ryan called Bolles and told him that he had a man who had information on land fraud and crooked politicians. Shortly afterwards, Adamson testified, he himself called and then met Bolles, using a fictional story about having an informant from San Diego who could link the state's political leaders to land swindles. The only reason for the meeting, said Adamson, was so that he would know what Bolles looked like.

On June 1, Adamson said, he called Bolles and set up the phony meeting at the Clarendon. That same day, Adamson continued, Robison delivered a bomb they had prepared several weeks before.

On the morning of the bombing, Adamson testified, he left home carrying a pair of overalls, a camouflage hat, and the dynamite. To set up an alibi, Adamson said he stopped by attorney Neal Roberts's office about 9:00 A.M. After a forty-five-minute meeting, Adamson left. On the way out, however, he said he unexpectedly ran into Max Dunlap, who also saw the attorney that morning. The two went outside to talk privately.

"I told him to tell Mr. Smith to go to the bank, that Don Bolles would be at the Clarendon House at eleven-thirty and it would be over then," said Adamson.

"Good," he quoted Dunlap as saying.

Adamson said that "Mr. Smith" was a pseudonym they used for Kemper Marley.

From Roberts's office, Adamson said, he went to the Ivanhoe and drank cranberry juice until five minutes before eleven. He then drove the half-dozen blocks to the Clarendon parking lot where, after changing into the overalls, he met Robison.

"I wonder if he will be here?" Adamson said Robison asked him.

Adamson said he told his partner that he was sure the reporter would arrive. He said Robison then asked him if he had an alibi.

"Yes, I'll be at the Ivanhoe," Adamson answered.

While the two were talking, Bolles himself drove up, parking his Datsun in a space not more than a hundred and fifty feet away. Adamson said they watched the tall, fair-haired reporter walk into the hotel.

Adamson then went over and attached the bomb to the reporter's car, he said, while Robison drove his pickup truck to a spot across the parking lot, towards the rear of the Mahoney Building. Robison, armed with a pair of high-powered binoculars, would detonate the bomb with the model airplane transmitter as soon as the reporter got back in it, said Adamson.

After getting out of his overalls, which he bundled up in a sheet and tossed near a trash barrel, he drove back to the Ivanhoe and called the hotel, having Bolles paged by the desk clerk.

"I told him the individual from San Diego was hesitant, and didn't want to be exposed," Adamson testified. "I said I didn't have any more time to spend on it and I'm sure he didn't either."

Bolles replied that if he should receive more information, he should bring it to Bolles's office in the state capitol, said Adamson.

Between 11:35 and 11:40, Adamson said, the phone in the Ivanhoe rang. He said it was for him, from Robison.

"Tell Mr. Smith to go to the bank," Adamson said he was told.

"Is it done?" he asked.

"Eyeball to eyeball," Adamson said Robison answered.

About 2:00 in the afternoon, Adamson said, Dunlap came to see him in the Ivanhoe. Dunlap told him that it was best that they meet at that time because Bolles was still alive. Undoubtedly, the reporter had by then told police that Adamson was the man who lured him to the hotel. Adamson was sure to be under police surveillance by the end of the day. Dunlap didn't want to be linked with him, testified Adamson, so future face-to-face meetings would be difficult.

"He did mention that the people in San Diego would be glad to hear that Don Bolles was not coming over there because he was supposed to go over there to investigate a bank," Adamson said. But Bolles's coworkers at the *Republic* knew of no such plans.

At the afternoon meeting at the Ivanhoe, Adamson said, he and Dunlap worked out a plan whereby money for Adamson would be left at the office of Phoenix attorney Tom Foster, an Adamson friend.

That night, on a charter flight arranged for him by Neal Roberts, who by then knew of Adamson's involvement in the Bolles bombing, Adamson said he and his wife left Phoenix. They went to Lake Havasu City, only to return the next morning after it became apparent that his name was already being circulated as the main suspect.

On Friday, June 4, two days after the bombing, Adamson testified he telephoned Dunlap at home. Adamson called from the phone at the Ivanhoe. He was worried. Upon his return from Lake Havasu, police had immediately arrested him on an outstanding warrant for defrauding an innkeeper. A half-dozen newspaper reporters were following him. Bolles was still alive. Adamson said Dunlap urged him to stay calm, assuring him that, if Adamson wanted to, he could be spirited out of the country aboard a twin-engine airplane.

"He said that Kemper and the governor had a thing down there in Mexico and they could get me out of the country immediately if I wanted to go," testified Adamson.

Dunlap told Adamson not to worry, that even if he was convicted of the attack on Bolles, he would only serve five years, said Adamson. During the time he was in jail, all he had to do was to keep quiet. Dunlap would send his wife $400 a month, Adamson said he was promised.

Adamson's mention of "the governor" set the press gallery afire. They scrambled out of the courtroom during a break in the proceedings to update the stories. Arizona Governor Raul Castro was a friend of Kemper Marley's. Marley had been the largest single contributor to Castro's campaign, kicking in more than twenty thousand dollars. And Castro was the man who had appointed Marley to the State Racing Commission the previous spring, the appointment which Don Bolles wrote about in dissecting Marley's background.

But Adamson was vague. He admitted that he could not say for certain just who "the governor" was. It could have been Castro or it could have been simply a figure of speech or a nickname for just about anybody. And even if it was Castro to whom Dunlap allegedly referred, owning an airplane with Marley did not constitute a criminal case.

Neither local reporters nor the IRE team had come up with any firm business dealings between Castro and the wealthy Marley. Meanwhile, the governor was outraged that his name had been brought into this seedy case. "I want to categorically deny any interest in anything in Mexico, the United States, or anyplace else with Kemper Marley," bristled Castro after the hearing had recessed for the day. "I have never owned, nor do I now own, any plane or have any interest in any plane with any person whatsoever. . . . I . . . categorically deny that I have ever had or presently have any business dealings with Kemper Marley."

There was one more meeting between Adamson and Dunlap, the

star witness testified the next day when the hearing resumed. About a week after the bombing, with Bolles still clinging to life, Adamson said he went to Foster's office for a secret meeting with Dunlap. "Max gave me a package, an envelope containing money. He said there was just under six thousand dollars there." Two thousand of the money, Adamson said, was to fulfill the murder contract on Lizanetz. As Dunlap left, Adamson said he again assured him that his wife would be financially supported if Adamson had to serve jail time.

Adamson had been a good witness. Despite intense and often tricky cross-examination by famed Texas criminal lawyer Percy Foreman, brought in as Dunlap's counsel for the cross-examination, Adamson stuck to his story.

Max Dunlap and James Robison were bound over to stand trial for first-degree murder. But Kemper Marley remained free. Despite Adamson's damning testimony, it was not enough to enable authorities to issue a warrant. Adamson had received all of his information from Dunlap. While his testimony could be used to corroborate allegations of Marley's involvement in the Bolles murder conspiracy, there was only one person who could finger Marley enough to make it stick in court: Max Dunlap.

And Dunlap, who had been raised as a son by the millionaire rancher, gave no indication that he was ready to talk.

The Adamson confession came as a surprise to the IRE reporters, a pleasant surprise. Somehow, seeing the wheels of justice start to move, wheels which seemingly had been rusted in place since the state was admitted into the Union sixty-five years before, lifted the IRE team's spirit.

It was also a fitting end to their reporting. For the project was nearly complete. The man whose death had brought them all to Arizona was being avenged, properly, through the courts. That, at least, was a beginning.

Their slain colleague was also being eulogized. On Saturday, January 22, Don Bolles was posthumously given the John Peter Zenger Journalism Award by the three-hundred member Arizona Newspapers Association for "distinguished service in behalf of freedom of the press and the people's right to know."

In an acceptance speech on behalf of Bolles's widow, J. Edward

Murray, the former *Republic* managing editor who had hired Bolles fourteen years ago, summed up the feelings of the IRE team as it finished the project.

"We all wish that Don Bolles were alive today to make this speech," said Murray. "But in fourteen years of trying, he was not able to make a sufficient dent on the Arizona criminal scene to prevent his own murder." Murray paused for a moment. Then he began asking the big questions.

"Why was Don Bolles, one of the best investigative reporters in the nation, able to make so little progress against the criminal element here? Or against the sleazy, soft-on-criminals attitude? And why did he have to die before Arizona woke up to what he had been exposing for a dozen years? The answers, it seems to me, lie in the flawed and rotten political fabric of this state."

Murray was speaking in Tucson. There were no IRE reporters there. But up in Phoenix, reading his speech in the *Republic* the next Sunday, the reporters who had worked so long and hard in tribute to the slain reporter clipped the Murray speech story from the paper. Many of them would take it home.

Bolles's reporting was "all but ignored by the general public, politicians, and law enforcement," said Murray.

"That lack of reaction created the sick public conduct which invited the conspiratorial murder. That is why Bolles's murder is an indictment of governors, legislators and the courts for a prolonged permissiveness which amounted to an open invitation to criminal elements to come to Arizona. That is why Bolles's murder is an indictment of the lawyers, bankers and other businessmen whose self-aggrandizing jungle ethics allowed them to collaborate with the underworld even though they knew that their actions were undermining the entire society, which they hypocritically pretended to respect. Don Bolles did his work extremely well. But the rest of the democratic process failed."

Murray, urging that Bolles's work not be abandoned, had high praise for the IRE team up in Phoenix, which, its investigative work basically completed, was about to write its series on Arizona wrongdoing.

But then, as if he were one of them, he echoed the fears of the IRE reporters, who worried that once the state's ills had been exposed and they had returned home, the series would only be drowned in apathy.

"By far the most important single requirement, however, is that the people themselves become aroused. When and if that happens, they will find ways to make their desires known. Investigative reporting, no matter how excellent, cannot accomplish much all by itself."

At the end of January, the IRE reporting was done. All that remained was to write and rewrite the stories until they were in publishable form.

There was no wild farewell party. On the last Wednesday night in January, nineteen of the reporters gathered in the apartment rented by Drehsler, Rawlinson, and Overton. They chipped in and bought twenty dollars' worth of Kentucky Fried Chicken and a couple of cases of beer.

But by eleven, most had returned to the hotel.

They were even too tired for a party.

By February 1, most of them had returned home.

15 | Revenge on Deadline

Robert Goldwater and Kemper Marley threatened to sue for libel even before the series was published.

"We must be on the right track," said Greene in mid-February as he, Dick Cady, and *Newsday* story editor Tony Ansolia directed a small platoon of rewritemen recruited from a half-dozen papers to flesh out the file information into readable newspaper stories. "They're blasting us before they even know what we'll be writing."

The pressure took the form of sternly phrased letters sent to each of the thirty-six reporters and to their various newspaper publishers threatening libel suits if inaccurate, damaging information were printed.

"My attorneys have informed me that I have the good fortune of not being viewed as [a] 'public figure' by the laws of this country," Goldwater wrote each newspaper that participated in the project, pointing out between the lines that, unlike public officials, he is entitled to his privacy and thus can sue for things politicians can't. "I understand that our relative anonymity affords us protections under the First Amendment that might not be available to those more often found in the public limelight."

Marley's attorney, Robert Mills, also indicated his client's disapproval. "Without intending to prescribe any unreasonable restrictions upon anyone's right to responsibly exercise the privilege of freedom of speech, or to appear to sound threatening, please be advised that Mr. Marley intends to preserve and pursue all remedies provided for by law with reference to any defamatory statements broadcast or published concerning him."

These undisguised threats to sue were unnecessary since every newspaper would carefully examine each of the IRE stories for inaccuracies or libelous material. Such scrutiny was standard procedure on major investigative pieces. The recipients of Goldwater's and Marley's warnings viewed them for what they were: an attempt to scare off or intimidate libel-shy editors. But the legal letters weren't the only complications encountered by IRE.

Since the beginning, the project had been the subject of considerable debate in the journalism world. The *Washington Post*, the *New York Times*, and the *Los Angeles Times*—the jealously competitive "Big Three" of the nation's newspaper industry—had all denounced the Phoenix project as gimmicky and unworkable, claiming that it smacked of elitism and was insulting to the local Arizona media, who suddenly found themselves invaded by "outsiders." Not one of the three papers had bothered to check the makeup of the team. Drehsler, Rawlinson, Overton, Weisz, and John Winters, assisted by local student interns and a couple of other *Arizona Republic* staffers, were all Arizonans. Indeed, of the other most active team reporters, only Greene, Renner, Wendland, and Koziol were outsiders. Arizona reporters had made up over half of the fulltime reporting cadre.

But were they, unfairly, picking on Arizona, as Barry Goldwater would later suggest?

"You know," mused Koziol during one of the late-night drinking sessions in the Adams Hotel bar during the height of the project, "sometimes I wonder what would happen if we used this approach not on Arizona, but Chicago. Sure, things are rotten here. But I wonder. Are they any worse than Chicago?"

"Or Detroit?" asked Wendland. "Or New York, Washington, Congress, a dozen places? What if we were to turn a team like this loose to investigate the CIA, the FBI, or the Kennedy assassination?"

Gradually, the reporters accepted their role. Arizona happened to be the focal point of their experiment for the simple reason that Bolles was killed there. His murder was the catalyst. It affected the media emotionally, prompting the sudden formation of the IRE team. And as the reporting gathered momentum, the team members found other compelling reasons for their efforts in Arizona.

The mob takeover was a classic example of how an entire state could literally be bought. There were national lessons to be learned from Arizona. Perhaps IRE's reporting would cause an awakening among the local citizens. It was still not too late to save the state.

And finally, for journalism, the Arizona project was a first. The banding together of reporters from different geographic areas with different specialties was indeed significant. Turning them loose on a single project, bound only by professionalism and not by time or the prejudices of editors tied to regional interests, held immense possibilities. If such a project worked in Arizona, it could work anywhere.

The reporters were dog tired. Even Greene, who was first in and last to leave the office each day, was affected. He looked terrible. His jowls seemed to hang to his chest. His eyes were bloodshot. One morning in mid-February, on his way to the state capitol to interview a legislator, he made it all the way down the Adams's elevator to the parking garage before noticing that his shoes were still upstairs. He had also gained even more weight from the months of expense-account living. Once during a late January interview held outside, the lawn chair Greene was sitting in sank two inches in the ground.

But, by February 22, the work was done. The stories, written and rewritten a dozen times, were piled on a long wooden table in the IRE suite. In all, there were twenty-three main investigative articles, most with accompanying sidebars. Altogether, the series was over 80,000 words in length.

Three attorneys flew into Phoenix: Andrew Hughes, whose expenses were paid by *Newsday*; John Martin, sent by the *Kansas City Star*; and Ed DeLaney, representing the IRE board back in Indianapolis. Hughes and Martin, middle-aged and bespectacled, and the younger and modish DeLaney spent the next five days carefully reading every single word, studying and debating each phrase and the more subtle nuances of the series.

Reporters instinctively distrust lawyers, especially libel lawyers. Given the power and opportunity, a lawyer will gut a story just to be on the safe side, most reporters feel. Nevertheless, legal review is a routine and necessary part of investigative reporting. For no matter how sure a newsman is of the accuracy of his report, he better be able to prove it. It is the lawyer's job to make sure every allegation is backed up.

The IRE stories would begin appearing in newspapers across the country on March 13, a Sunday. The initial report was an overview, noting the interrelated patterns of corruption in politics, real estate, and justice. Over the next three days, the "Arizona Triumvirate" of Barry and Bob Goldwater and Harry Rosenzweig would be analyzed, detailing the relationships between the trio's rise to power and their longtime associations with criminal elements. The exploitation of illegal workers at Bob Goldwater's Arrowhead Ranch—and a separate story on the harassment suffered by IRE reporters in documenting the story—was treated in depth. So were the Hobo Joe's restaurant chain story and Herb Applegate's curious relationship to mobster Licavoli. The business side of life in Arizona was treated in two days' worth of stories that profiled the huge Del Webb company and Valley

National Bank, as well as Kemper Marley's use of political influence
and money. The way land fraud czar Ned Warren, Sr., literally
bought the state of Arizona was told over a four-day period. There
were three days of narcotics stories, including a special report which
named twelve major drug trafficking rings. The mob—in the form of
the Bonanno and Licavoli families and the lesser-known and cruder
hoodlums of Phoenix and Tucson—was exposed in the series. Other
stories examined and spotlighted Arizona's curious system of law
enforcement, justice, and politics.

All of the stories had one thing in common—names were named. It
was something that, with the exception of Don Bolles's reporting and
occasional efforts by a couple of his peers, hadn't been done in
Arizona for a long time.

The lawyers read each story. Their questions were agonizingly
simple. "How do you know this?" they would ask time and time
again as a particular phrase troubled them.

Greene, chain-smoking his Pall Malls, would holler for a file. If
the attorneys still weren't satisfied, he kept team members Drehsler,
Becker, and Weisz on hand to answer in depth.

Always, the lawyers were calm and cool. Greene, as the hours and
days of legal nit-picking continued, sometimes exploded.

"Jesus Christ, the son of a bitch fucking admitted the goddamned
thing!" he bellowed at one point when Hughes questioned a statement made by a minor Phoenix hoodlum that he took orders from the
Bonanno family.

"Yes, Bob, but how do we know he was telling your reporters the
truth?"

Greene slammed his meaty fist on the desktop. "Jesus Christ! Do
we have to take you lawyers by the hand?" Ten minutes later, after
Greene had inundated the lawyers with background reports, police
surveillance observations, and a half-dozen other pieces of information documenting the point, the attorneys accepted it. The story
stood.

On Friday, February 25, the legal review was complete. And
despite the hours of tension and heated debate, the series was basically unchanged. Only a couple of stories were killed. One listed
several dozen Phoenix hoodlum hangouts. The lawyers felt that there
simply wasn't enough documentation to call them "mob bars."
Another dealt with the associations and activities of the businessman
friend of ASU football coach Frank Kush. The attorneys did not think

the associations—in the form of complicated social and financial dealings—were significant enough to risk the possibility of multi-million-dollar lawsuits.

But what impressed the IRE reporters and the lawyers after the review was completed was how well the reporting had stood the test of legal scrutiny. The reporters had done their homework. The stories were solid. They were ready to run.

Martin, the attorney sent to Phoenix by the *Kansas City Star* to review the IRE series, commented in a letter mailed to the various news organizations whose reporters worked on the Arizona project: "The series is immense in scope. It relates to many subject matters and refers to perhaps hundreds of individuals. . . . The abundance of documentation created by the reporters and editors working on the project was very impressive. Surely no previous investigative project has been so thoroughly investigated, documented by records and sources, and cross-indexed. . . . I am not only impressed by the series, I feel comfortable in defending most litigation filed by some individuals mentioned in the articles."

The IRE series was distributed to the two dozen newspapers and broadcast outlets on Friday, March 4. It was set for release for Sunday, March 13. But because of the extraordinary length and scope of the twenty-three installments, each paper was expected to rewrite and condense many of the reports. Thus, a week was set aside for each participating paper to analyze and edit the IRE series.

On Saturday, March 5, IRE itself held a meeting of its board of directors in Indianapolis. There was much talk of the literary agent's plan to enrich the organization's coffers. Ben Bagdikian, a respected media critic, had agreed to write a book on the team. A tentative deal was being worked out. The literary agent had come up with a publisher who agreed to a $30,000 advance. It would be split in half, with IRE and Bagdikian each getting $15,000. Also, there was still a possible deal in the works with TV producer David Susskind, though the IRE board was angry that no advance monies seemed to be forthcoming.

Ron Koziol, the first president of IRE, had driven from Chicago to attend the meeting. He knew that it would be his last. IRE had turned into a power-hungry machine, he felt. Koziol himself was thinking about writing a book on his Phoenix experience. Later, he would decide against the idea and return to full-time reporting at the *Tribune*. But at the March 5 board meeting, he suddenly found himself besieged by hostile questions from his fellow board members, who demanded that he tell them of his personal plans.

"There's a lot of things I may do," Koziol answered at one point. "I just haven't made up my mind."

But the questioning continued. The IRE board members didn't want Koziol to foul up their plans for an "official," IRE-censored view of the Phoenix project. Besides, as IRE president he had agreed to hire a literary agent. The board felt it wasn't fair that Koziol, in effect, then compete against the agent he helped hire.

Koziol returned to Chicago depressed. "They're not the same people," he said a few days later. "IRE started as a fraternal organization. We were all investigative reporters and what we wanted to do was improve our profession. But what I saw at that last meeting turned my stomach. They were like a pack of jackals, ready to tear the flesh off anyone who got in the way of their prize." On Monday, March 7, Koziol sent a telegram to Indianapolis, resigning as IRE president and a member of the board.

On Tuesday, March 8, IRE retaliated.

Though Koziol had resigned, an official news release from Indianapolis was issued. It made no mention of the president's resignation telegram. Instead, it claimed that Koziol had been "expelled." It was a dirty trick. But the release contained still another lie. The IRE claimed that all participants in the Phoenix project "had promised not to seek any personal profit as a result of the Phoenix project." In other words, only the IRE-controlled "official" book would be allowed.

Koziol was telephoned by virtually all of the full-time Phoenix reporters, who voiced outrage at Indianapolis's clumsy handling of the project's aftermath. There was never an agreement, either in writing or verbal, that would prevent any IRE reporter from writing magazine articles or books about his or her experiences in Phoenix. Indeed, several of the team leaders were already at work on various free-lance stories. Dave Overton had been hired temporarily as a special reporter by ABC television to cover the Arizona team's findings. Alex Drehsler was planning a book on land fraud czar Ned Warren, Sr., and had agreed to work for the BBC as a special correspondent during a week's filming in Arizona on the IRE team reports. John Rawlinson was arranging a deal to write a lengthy free-lance article for a magazine. Dave Offer and Nina Bondarook were planning similar stories for journalism publications. Wendland was writing a book.

On Sunday, March 13, five months and nine days after IRE reporters assembled in the Adams Hotel to begin work, newspapers across the nation began carrying the finished stories. For the next twenty-two days, the Arizona reports were page one news nationally and were often featured on the nightly newscasts of the three major television networks.

Among newspapers carrying all or substantial parts of the series were the *Arizona Daily Star,* the *Denver Post*, the *Colorado Springs Sun*, *Newsday*, the *Miami Herald*, the *Indianapolis Star*, the *Detroit News*, the *Riverside* (California) *Press-Enterprise*, the *Elyria*(Ohio) *Chronicle-Telegram*, the *Eugene* (Oregon) *Register-Guard*, the *Reno* (Nevada) *Journal* and *Gazette*, the *Boston Globe*, the *Albuquerque* (New Mexico) *Journal*, the *Gulfport* (Mississippi) *Herald*, the *Kansas City Star*, the *Kansas City Times*, the *St. Louis Globe-Democrat*, the *Idaho Statesman*, the *Wenatchee* (Washington) *World*, and the *Milwaukee Journal*. Scores of other newspapers which did not participate in the project gave major play to wire service versions of the IRE reports. (The *Chicago Tribune*, obviously embarrassed over IRE's underhanded treatment of Ron Koziol, did not print the series.)

Even Johnny Carson referred to the IRE reports in his late-night television comedy skits.

"Bob Goldwater was charged with a new crime today," said Carson, "conspiracy to commit poppycock." Repeatedly, when asked by other media to comment on the IRE reports detailing his associations with organized crime, Goldwater had labeled the series as "poppycock." In another monologue, Carson said: "You all probably noticed that neither Robert Redford or Dustin Hoffman was at the Academy Awards presentation last night. That's because Jason Robards sent them on assignment to investigate Arizona."

But also on Sunday, March 13, came another lie. This time, it was from the *Arizona Republic*. In a page one "statement" it informed its readers that it would not publish the IRE series. "Some of the unpublished material contains statements and allegations for which the *Republic* . . . [has] not yet been able to obtain sufficient documentation and proof to justify publication," editorialized the same paper that Don Bolles had worked for. In the fourth paragraph of the *Republic*'s statement, the newspaper denied that it had been a participant in the project. Besides John Winters, who had spent full-time on the project from start to finish, at least two other *Republic* staffers had worked with IRE reporters. "This underlines what is terribly wrong in Phoenix and Arizona," observed Bob Greene, back in Long Island. "People are not given a right to know what is going on."

The following week morale sunk at the *Republic*. Several staffers began talking about quitting or organizing a union. It was not city editor Bob Early who had made the decision not to print, but publisher Nina Pulliam. It was, felt reporters for the *Republic* and the out-of-town papers who had worked on the Arizona project, a clear indication that the power structure in Phoenix still controlled the *Arizona Republic*. Wendland's "Henny Youngman" news source, who had repeatedly warned of a double cross by the *Republic*, had been right after all.

To fill the news gap, some five thousand extra copies of the *Arizona Daily Star* in Tucson were rushed up to Phoenix each day. Similarly, the *Denver Post,* which also printed the entire IRE series, tried to increase its presence in Phoenix. They were sold out in minutes. The result was pandemonium outside the few Phoenix newsstands that carried the out-of-town publications.

"They're mad," said Sam Bard, owner of a downtown newsstand. "There was a line of 150 people waiting at the door at seven when I opened. I sold out in less than a half-hour. If I had them, I could sell one copy for ten dollars." Other more enterprising souls were hawking xeroxed copies of the stories for fifty cents apiece on downtown street corners. Picket lines went up around the offices of the *Republic* and *Gazette* by a hastily formed group known as Citizens for Freedom. "Has Barry G. Stifled the R & G?" asked one sign. "Whose Truth Does the R & G Print?" said another.

George Weisz, the IRE team researcher who remained in Phoenix after the project ended to supervise the packing and storage of the voluminous IRE files, began writing long letters to the other team reporters to keep them abreast of the latest developments in Phoenix.

"It's an unreal feeling just walking down the street in Phoenix," he wrote on March 16. "The series is the only thing that's being talked about. I wish you all could be here to feel the atmosphere. It's incredible. It's overwhelmingly good for us. It's as if these people have waited decades for someone to 'rescue them' and publicly expose this stuff. And we've accomplished that task. People are scurrying from newsstand to newsstand, out-of-town papers are being scalped in price, the *Republic* is being picketed each day."

The other media in Phoenix were quick to fill in the void left by the *Republic*'s refusal to run the series. KTAR-TV featured the IRE

series each day. KOY-Radio, in perhaps one of broadcast journalism's most unusual and innovative efforts, read each IRE story
almost word for word. Since some of the articles were as long as five
thousand words, the on-the-air reading took upwards of an hour each
evening. The two stations did not limit their reporting to just the IRE
stories. Instead, they backed them up by going out and contacting
many of the original news sources for the team, who confirmed the
details. *New Times*, an award-winning weekly newspaper that served
Phoenix and its suburbs, devoted two entire issues to nothing but the
IRE stories. And *New West* magazine, based in Los Angeles, printed
major excerpts.

The best assessment of the IRE team's effort came from law
enforcement people, those responsible for cleaning up the mess
documented in the team's 80,000-word indictment. Without exception, Arizona's legal establishment had nothing but praise for the
series.

Arizona Attorney General Bruce Babbitt: *"We were fortunate to
have this kind of a truly professional team working on the Arizona
crime problem. Their reports were very well documented. What they
did was to go out and uncover this state's very considerable problems, to put them together as never has been done before, and then to
highlight them. I think that what they did, and did so well, was to do a
thorough, professional job, like the Senate investigating committees
under Senator John McClelland. They did their job, now it's up to us
to do ours."*

Leon Gaskell, Special Agent in Charge, the FBI, Phoenix: *"Their
reports finally drew the awareness of the people of Arizona to the fact
that there is a major crime problem here. For the FBI, the stories and
the IRE findings have helped fill in some of the grey areas. We're
looking with great interest at these articles. We have obtained some
information through these articles that we intend to follow through
on."*

Vernon Hoy, Director, Arizona Department of Public Safety:
*"What they wrote about is something the police have been screaming
about for years and no one before would listen. Finally, someone is
listening. Their excellent, factual reporting will help the entire criminal justice situation in this state."*

Lawrence Wetzel, Chief of Police, Phoenix: *"The bright light
they've shined on our organized crime problem was long overdue.
From a policeman's view, the IRE investigation was a big success."*

Michael Hawkins, U.S. Attorney, State of Arizona: *"It was excellent, first-rate reporting. From their reports, we have found new things that are now the subject of active investigation."*

Philip Jordan, Director, U.S. Drug Enforcement Administration, Arizona: *"Arizona has a tremendous drug problem, perhaps the worst in the nation. The publicity these reporters have given that problem will help us tremendously."*

William Smitherman, former U.S. Attorney and, in March, 1977, director of the Arizona legislature's joint task force on organized crime: *"The stories were a great exercise in the First Amendment. Organized crime in Arizona is finally out in the daylight."*

Politicians also voiced opinions on the IRE series.

U.S. Representative Morris K. Udall described the series as "journalism at its best," but voiced the hope that there would be no tendency to "sweep this under the rug, to pooh-pooh it, to put it down as a rehash of old charges and unsubstantiated rumors. It's not a time for recriminations, it's a time for constructive action. If we're sitting here two or three years from now and organized crime continues to grow, we'll have no one to blame but ourselves."

Udall's opinion was not shared by Arizona's senior senator, Barry Goldwater.

"I think that in the last twenty-five years, I've been in Arizona a total of six or eight months," said Goldwater, shortly after the series began. "I'm a United States Senator. I have nothing to do with the state government of Arizona. I don't know a single man out here connected with crime at any level, be it the Mafia or local. I challenge them [IRE] to bring up the name of one nationally known gangster in Arizona today. If they're there, I don't know about them."

New West magazine, in an IRE-inspired piece entitled "Da Senator from Arizona," depicted a perspiring, churlish-looking Goldwater, dressed in a bolo tie and cowboy hat, standing in the middle of the desert while a group of gangsters gathered behind him around a funeral wreath. The *Arizona Daily Star* editorialized that Goldwater's professed ignorance of his home state's organized crime problems "won't wash." The *Kansas City Star* ran an editorial cartoon that copied the front dust jacket of the best-selling novel *The Godfather* showing the puppeteer's strings connected to the words "The Goldwater." And an *Albuquerque Journal* cartoon depicted an angry Goldwater talking on the telephone at his desk, surrounded by newspaper headlines on the IRE series. The caption read: "You're filming a sequel to WHAT? No, I do NOT want to be played by Marlon Brando.''

For the IRE reporters, the end of the project was an anticlimax. While the investigation was generally hailed as a success, changing gears from the months of hectic work in Arizona to the routine of their daily jobs back home was difficult. Many kept in touch for weeks by long-distance telephone.

A few were able to get a couple of weeks of leave from their newspapers as compensation for the time away from home and families. Most, however, immediately went back to their regular reporting. Alex Drehsler applied for a job with Greene at *Newsday* and was promptly hired.

Ross Becker, who had felt so strongly about the project that he quit his job in New Mexico, landed a reporting position with a medium-sized newspaper in New Jersey.

George Weisz was briefly hired as a summer investigator for the Arizona legislature's joint task force on organized crime. He was joined there by Kay Nash, one of the volunteer researchers on the IRE investigation, who took a secretarial job.

Tom Renner, the tireless reporter for *Newsday* who spent so many weeks being "Deep 'n Dirty," had grown so enamored of Arizona's climate that he began shopping around for a winter home near Scottsdale.

Dick Levitan, the Boston radio reporter, married the Boston policewoman he had been dating. He also was able to use the three-foot-long flashlight and secret tear-gas dispenser he bought in Arizona. While he was covering a riot in mid-March, his car was attacked by a group of thugs. "It worked beautifully," he cheerfully reported.

Myrta Pulliam was appointed acting IRE president until a replacement could be found for Koziol. Later, Greene was elected permanent president.

Despite the threatened suits, only three of the hundreds of persons named in the twenty-three-day IRE series had filed suit by the end of the summer. Peter Licavoli, Jr., the twenty-nine-year-old son of the aging Detroit Mafia chieftain, claimed seventeen million dollars in damages against IRE, all of the reporters who worked on the project, and most of the newspapers which carried IRE stories listing him as a narcotics trafficker. Jerry Colangelo, general manager of the Phoenix Suns basketball team, filed a $500,000 suit against IRE, accusing the group of libeling him by implying that he associated with gamblers. Colangelo was named in the IRE series as a patron of a downtown Phoenix bagel shop frequented by gamblers. And Alfred Gay, the Alaskan bush pilot who bought the Arizona border town of Lukeville, filed a million-dollar suit against the Associated Press and several Alaskan newspapers which carried IRE-inspired stories identifying him as a suspected narcotics trafficker.

Meanwhile, there were other suits not involving IRE. Rosalie Bolles, frustrated by the government's inability to file charges against Kemper Marley, filed a five-million-dollar civil suit against the powerful rancher-politician, accusing him of conspiring to murder her husband and thus depriving her of his love and care. Marley, who remained free of any charges in the Bolles murder despite Adamson's sworn testimony, promptly filed a fifty-one-million-dollar civil suit against Mrs. Bolles, contending that her allegations defamed him.

In early June, one year after her husband's murder, Rosalie Bolles remarried. Her new husband was a middle-aged Phoenix insurance agent.

IRE and its reporters won a number of press awards. The American Society of Journalists and Authors gave the group its annual Conscience in Media gold medal. Patrick M. McGrady, chairman of the society's professional rights committee, said: "IRE's Arizona project was the finest hour of American journalism—bar none." The project also received the National Journalism Award of Ball State University and a scroll of appreciation from the Sigma Delta Chi chapter at New York University. The series was also nominated for a Pulitzer Prize, to be judged in 1978.

A group known as the Behavioral Research Center of Arizona conducted a survey of 1,000 heads of households in late April 1977 and found that eighty percent of Arizona's residents had read or heard portions of the IRE reports. The study also found that forty-one percent of Arizonans believed that organized crime in their state was more serious than elsewhere in the country.

Jack Duggan, the bearded proprietor of a Phoenix nightclub who unknowingly served as an IRE source, was convicted of running a gambling operation in early May and sentenced to three years' probation and a $1,000 fine.

Four narcotics traffickers named in the IRE series as major sources of Mexican heroin were indicted in late May by a federal grand jury. State, federal, and local authorities said a number of other investigations prompted by disclosures in the series were underway.

Harry Rosenzweig was honored as "Man of the Year" by the Phoenix Association of Christians and Jews.

The Intelligence Division of the Phoenix Police Department received a half-million-dollar-a-year budget increase after the IRE series and was renamed the Organized Crime Division.

Arizona Governor Raul Castro was under "serious consideration" by the Carter administration to become the new ambassador to Argentina.

Two IRE sources had personal setbacks.

Richard Frost, one of the team's land fraud sources, was convicted in federal court of land fraud and, shortly before the series began, was sentenced to serve one to three years in a federal penitentiary by U.S. Judge Walter Craig.

In early March, land fraud "godfather" Ned Warren, Sr., suffered a serious heart attack. A few weeks later he was interviewed by reporters from his hospital bed. Warren had read the IRE series. "I'm not happy, but it's basically accurate," he said. Warren said doctors told him he only had three to five years to live.

By the beginning of May, the Arizona project was past history for the reporters. Yet another form of afterlife began to evolve. The former teammates started contacting each other for story ideas. Wendland and Koziol, whose newspapers covered the Midwest, worked together on an investigation of mob ties between Chicago and Detroit. David Offer of the *Milwaukee Journal* joined in, offering the names of businesses in his city which had shady dealings in Illinois.

Out west, John Rawlinson of the *Arizona Daily Star* and Dick Lyneis of the *Riverside* (California) *Press* planned to jointly probe the presence of organized crime in Palm Springs.

Dick Cady of the *Indianapolis Star* got on the telephone with a half-dozen former IRE team members seeking and sharing information on a nationwide garbage-disposal firm suspected of being a front for the mob.

No longer were the reporters isolated and frustrated by a lack of manpower or money in following a story out of their paper's circulation area. Because of the Phoenix project, criminals were not the only ones who were organized.

So were the media.

Don Bolles's murder had been avenged.

Epilogue

November 6, 1977—It was a lousy Sunday, cold and rainy, and there was little traffic in downtown Phoenix. The weather drastically cut attendance on the last day of the 1977 Arizona State Fair. On the way to the Maricopa County Courthouse, George Weisz thought of the spinning and gaudy lights of the 1976 version of the fair. He remembered standing in Suite 1939 of the Adams, watching those lights with a dozen supercharged reporters during the height of the Arizona Project. It seemed impossible that an entire year had passed. But the IRE team was long gone from Phoenix. Only he and student intern Carol Jackson remained in Phoenix. And they were together on this Sunday.

Weisz and Jackson began the day with bagels and cream cheese in the pressroom of the Maricopa County Courthouse. "We can't forget tradition," said Weisz, referring to the Sunday morning bagel feast the IRE team had indulged in during the project.

Jackson, who had graduated from Arizona State University over the summer, was now working full time as a reporter for the Associated Press in Phoenix. Weisz, still between jobs after briefly working for a legislative crime commission over the summer, was in the courthouse as an unofficial observer for the team.

They were covering final jury deliberations in the Don Bolles murder trial.

What Jackson wrote that Sunday was carried under her byline by the wire service into the city rooms of the other IRE reporters across the country. Weisz wrote nothing. Instead, he went through a pocketful of coins in a phone booth in the courthouse, calling a dozen of the other former team members to tell them firsthand what had happened that day.

Armed with Jackson's wire copy and Weisz's telephone account, most of the remaining team members wrote their own stories for their own newspapers. It felt good.

A Maricopa County jury, after five-and-a-half days' deliberation, had convicted James Robison and Max Dunlap of two charges, conspiracy to commit murder and murder, for the killing of Don Bolles seventeen months before. Arizona Attorney General Bruce Babbitt, in a press conference after the verdict had been returned, said he would ask for the death penalty.

"We don't have all the conspirators yet," said Babbitt, "but we will. The investigation will continue. There will be other arrests."

The trial of the two men, which lasted four months, saw a number of allegations raised. Adamson had remained adamant that he had been hired to kill the reporter on behalf of Kemper Marley. Convicted land swindler Howard Woodall, a surprise witness for the state, testified that Robison had told him that Bolles was killed because he had uncovered evidence on some sort of loan swindle involving Marley, Harry Rosenzweig, San Diego financier C. Arnholt Smith, and Bob and Barry Goldwater.

"We've got some new information as a result of the trial that gives us more avenues of investigation leading toward more conspirators," said Jon Sellers, the Phoenix police detective who had been assigned to the Bolles case.

It was the end of one chapter, and the beginning of a new one. And the IRE reporters, who had been so much a part of the first chapter, eagerly awaited the next, though they would have no more input into its writing.

For it was up to the people of the State of Arizona now. The media had done their job. Arizona's ills had been exposed, and justice, though not yet complete, was slowly being done. It was the future that was the story now.

Index